WEALTH

Ideas. Action. Impact.
Wharton School Publishing

In the face of accelerating turbulence and change, business leaders and policy makers need new ways of thinking to sustain performance and growth.

Wharton School Publishing offers a trusted source for stimulating ideas from thought leaders who provide new mental models to address changes in strategy, management, and finance. We seek out authors from diverse disciplines with a profound understanding of change and its implications. We offer books and tools that help executives respond to the challenge of change.

Every book and management tool we publish meets quality standards set by The Wharton School of the University of Pennsylvania. Each title is reviewed by the Wharton School Publishing Editorial Board before being given Wharton's seal of approval. This ensures that Wharton publications are timely, relevant, important, conceptually sound or empirically based, and implementable.

To fit our readers' learning preferences, Wharton publications are available in multiple formats, including books, audio, and electronic.

To find out more about our books and management tools, visit us at whartonsp.com and Wharton's executive education site, exceed.wharton.upenn.edu.

WEALTH

GROW IT, PROTECT IT, SPEND IT, AND SHARE IT

Stuart E. Lucas

Ideas. Action. Impact.
Wharton School Publishing

Vice President, Editor-in-Chief: Tim Moore
Wharton Editor: Yoram (Jerry) Wind
Executive Editor: Jim Boyd
Editorial Assistant: Susan Abraham
Development Editor: Russ Hall
Associate Editor-in-Chief and Director of Marketing: Amy Neidlinger
International Marketing Manager: Tim Galligan
Cover Designer: Chuti Prasertsith
Managing Editor: Gina Kanouse
Project Editor: Kayla Dugger
Copy Editor: Elise Walter
Senior Indexer: Cheryl Lenser
Senior Compositor: Gloria Schurick
Proofreader: Water Crest Publishing, Inc.
Manufacturing Buyer: Dan Uhrig

Ideas. Action. Impact.
Wharton School
Publishing

© 2006 by Stuart E. Lucas
Publishing as Wharton School Publishing
Upper Saddle River, New Jersey 07458

**Wharton School Publishing offers excellent discounts on this book when
ordered in quantity for bulk purchases or special sales. For more information,
please contact U.S. Corporate and Government Sales, 1-800-382-3419,
corpsales@pearsontechgroup.com. For sales outside the U.S.,
please contact International Sales at international@pearsoned.com.**

Company and product names mentioned herein are the trademarks or registered
trademarks of their respective owners.

Printed in the United States of America

First Printing February, 2006

ISBN 0-13-236679-7

Pearson Education LTD.
Pearson Education Australia PTY, Limited.
Pearson Education Singapore, Pte. Ltd.
Pearson Education North Asia, Ltd.
Pearson Education Canada, Ltd.
Pearson Educación de Mexico, S.A. de C.V.
Pearson Education—Japan
Pearson Education Malaysia, Pte. Ltd.

Library of Congress Cataloging-in-Publication Data

Lucas, Stuart E.
  Wealth : grow it, protect it, spend it, and share it / Stuart E. Lucas.
    p. cm.
  ISBN 0-13-236679-7
  1. Investments. 2. Finance, Personal. 3. Portfolio management. I. Title.
  HG4521.L862 2006
  332.024'01—dc22
                                    2005025552

Ideas. Action. Impact.
Wharton School Publishing

Bernard Baumohl
THE SECRETS OF ECONOMIC INDICATORS
Hidden Clues to Future Economic Trends and Investment Opportunities

Sayan Chatterjee
FAILSAFE STRATEGIES
Profit and Grow from Risks That Others Avoid

Sunil Gupta, Donald R. Lehmann
MANAGING CUSTOMERS AS INVESTMENTS
The Strategic Value of Customers in the Long Run

Stuart L. Hart
CAPITALISM AT THE CROSSROADS
The Unlimited Business Opportunities in Solving the World's Most Difficult Problems

Lawrence G. Hrebiniak
MAKING STRATEGY WORK
Leading Effective Execution and Change

Robert Mittelstaedt
WILL YOUR NEXT MISTAKE BE FATAL?
Avoiding the Chain of Mistakes That Can Destroy Your Organization

Mukul Pandya, Robbie Shell, Susan Warner, Sandeep Junnarkar, Jeffrey Brown
NIGHTLY BUSINESS REPORT PRESENTS LASTING LEADERSHIP
What You Can Learn from the Top 25 Business People of Our Times

C. K. Prahalad
THE FORTUNE AT THE BOTTOM OF THE PYRAMID
Eradicating Poverty Through Profits

Arthur Rubinfeld
BUILT FOR GROWTH
Expanding Your Business Around the Corner or Across the Globe

Scott A. Shane
FINDING FERTILE GROUND
Identifying Extraordinary Opportunities for New Ventures

Oded Shenkar
THE CHINESE CENTURY
The Rising Chinese Economy and Its Impact on the Global Economy, the Balance of Power, and Your Job

David Sirota, Louis A. Mischkind, and Michael Irwin Meltzer
THE ENTHUSIASTIC EMPLOYEE
How Companies Profit by Giving Workers What They Want

Thomas T. Stallkamp
SCORE!
A Better Way to Do Busine$$: Moving from Conflict to Collaboration

Yoram (Jerry)Wind, Colin Crook, with Robert Gunther
THE POWER OF IMPOSSIBLE THINKING
Transform the Business of Your Life and the Life of Your Business

To Mom for being the glue,
To Dad for inspiration,
To Susan for her love,
And to our kids for the future.

CONTENTS

FOREWORD

I recently asked my wife who she would consult for advice about our financial situation if I were hit by the proverbial bus. Stuart Lucas was the first name she mentioned. I think I know why. Stuart is smart and savvy about wealth management. He engenders a high degree of trust. And he does everything in a measured, well-reasoned way. We have enjoyed getting to know Stuart and his family over the years. As you read this book, I believe you will share our appreciation.

Creating trust is essential for anyone who offers advice about wealth management. In an age where everyone seems to be selling something, how do you know who will really put your interests first? More than ever, investors want independent and unbiased sources of advice. As head of Morningstar, I realize that the trust we've built over the years is essential to our success. One of the main reasons Stuart deserves your trust is that he isn't affiliated with any financial institution and he isn't selling financial products or services. Beyond that, you'll also discover that he is a person of high integrity who is out to do his best for every reader.

As a fourth-generation heir of E.A. Stuart, the man who founded the Carnation Company back in the late 1800s, Stuart knows first hand the privileges, challenges, and responsibilities of wealth. His family's approach to wealth management is a backdrop to this book—a peek through the window that you rarely experience. This gives *Wealth* unusual credibility. The author is practicing day-to-day—with real dollars—the lessons he prescribes. That seldom happens in the world of investment advice, where recommendations tend to be offered enthusiastically by those who have little at stake in the outcome. The hands-on examples here are useful for everyone, regardless of the size of your fortune.

Stuart and I share many basic beliefs about wealth management. Most important, we both have an investor's perspective. "Investors come first" is Morningstar's mantra, and you'll see in this book that Stuart approaches investing in exactly the same way. He offers insightful and practical advice. He seeks to empower investors and to give them the knowledge and tools they need to make wise decisions.

The first of the eight principles that Stuart uses as guideposts is the need to "take charge." He explains the importance of accepting responsibility—both for setting strategy and for making sure that things stay on course. Then, and only then, can wealthy individuals delegate to the experts effectively. Stuart shows, through personal experience, how his own family learned the importance of this insight. Even with access to elite professional talent, simply delegating to the experts turned out to be a mistake.

Another piece of advice that I love is Stuart's suggestion that wealth owners send an "RFP" or "request for proposal" to wealth management firms. This can trigger a competitive bidding process, which will help you understand the services you're receiving. It also ensures that things are competitively priced. This is a simple idea and something that's rarely done. But it's grandly empowering for investors.

I also applaud Stuart's holistic approach. He articulates a comprehensive, strategic view of wealth management that integrates all the issues that individuals (and their advisors) need to think about. This requires knowledge across many disciplines—investment, asset allocation, risk assessment, taxes, philanthropy, and estate planning. Many authors focus on just one aspect of the process. Their readers must figure out how to integrate and manage everything. Because he's done all this, real-time, Stuart packages advice for his readers in an understandable, cohesive *framework*. That's highly valuable.

One of our goals at Morningstar is to bring greater transparency to the mutual fund industry. I see *Wealth* as a clarion call to do the same thing in the world of wealth management. Compared to the mutual fund industry, clients of wealth management firms have much less data available to help them make informed decisions about which firms to retain. There are no benchmarks that customers can use to gauge how well they're being served. There are, of course, superb wealth advisors in the marketplace. Many are Morningstar customers. But it's tough to compare one with another in a way that allows you to identify with confidence who has the best record. Reading *Wealth* will help you do this with greater confidence.

I expect that the top wealth management advisors will read this book and share it with their clients. Better informed investors will choose better advisors, and they'll hold advisors to a higher standard. In turn, the advisors that do the best jobs of serving their clients will see their businesses prosper. It's a win-win situation.

Stuart's life revolves around his family and so does his approach to wealth management. Most books deal with this subject from an individual's perspective. It's much more difficult when a family is involved. Stuart explores the often complicated interplay between family members and family wealth, and he stresses the importance of creating a wealth plan that reflects a family's values. He also offers solid advice about family-related topics that touch on wealth management, such as parenting, education, and careers—all the while generously sharing his own family's experience.

I find it refreshing that Stuart offers a broad definition of wealth. To him, it means far more than how much one has in a bank account or the stock market. Being wealthy is about being productive, giving to others, serving society, and creating a legacy. Perhaps, most important, though, it's about taking the risks and responsibilities necessary to manage one's assets and teach one's children to do the same. Wealth, in other words, is a tool to help people across generations live more productive and fulfilling lives, and to be good citizens. To me, that's a more exciting and fulfilling proposition than merely worrying about being able to buy your next yacht.

I believe this book will help you manage your assets more effectively. But it just might inspire you, too—and help you see the full potential that your wealth can provide. The thing I admire most about *Wealth* is that Stuart places values squarely at the center of things. That notion is sadly missing from most investment planning discussions. Without values, you don't have wealth, just money.

Enjoy!

Joe Mansueto
Founder, Chairman and CEO
Morningstar, Inc.

ACKNOWLEDGMENTS

A first book is always a bigger undertaking than a new author expects, and my naiveté was no exception. At the same time, the experience has been more rewarding than I could have imagined. Perhaps its greatest rewards come from the help, support, and encouragement I have received from so many people because they believe in the book's purpose and they trust me to do the subject matter justice. To all of you I owe a great debt of thanks.

In the early days of the project, Howard Stevenson at Harvard Business School encouraged me to use my family as a case study for the book and stimulated my thinking on a number of issues, many of which tie back to his own fine book on success and significance, *Just Enough*. Paul Sturm, an experienced journalist and Director of Morningstar, helped me to navigate the publishing world and led me to my wonderful agent Doris Michaels, and ultimately to Jim Boyd at Prentice Hall. Both Doris and Jim had strong hands in shaping the book's tone and defining its audience, and I deeply appreciate their support and encouragement of me in the book writing process. Jim has also assembled a superb team. Kayla Dugger and her production team, Dan DePascuale, Jim Schachterle, and others have worked many hours to perfect and promote the book. Plus, they have been professional and a real pleasure to work with. I can only say the same of Lisa Berkowitz, my publicist. She has been tireless in getting the word out.

Doris also introduced me to Richard Koonce. Rick and I have worked intensively together over the past eighteen months to bring my dream to life. As my editor, he has been a great partner. We bring different skills and perspectives to the table and Rick has never been shy about expressing his views clearly and professionally. It was when we didn't agree that the partnership was at its strongest. We pushed each other, sometimes hard, until we found the right solutions. Rick handled these debates with great professionalism and grace, and without ego. He's also a darn good writer.

Numerous people in the financial business have been a great help along the way. Bob Doran at Wellington Management Company showed me by example how a great investment business is managed, and I am grateful for his continuing advocacy on my behalf. Jeff Thomasson, Jon Hirtle, and Shelby Notkin personify professionalism, integrity, and best practices in everything they do. Lorraine Tsavaris, Ralph Rittenour, Andy Eberhart, Susan Johnston, Karen Harding, and other folks at U.S. Trust and CTC Consulting have been strong supporters and suppliers of data that help to reinforce my message. Mark Augenstein, my wonderful accountant, was also kind enough to read through several chapters and impart his wisdom.

Joe Mansueto, tennis maestro and the soft-spoken founder and CEO of Morningstar, is a busy guy. Yet he believes so strongly in this project that he was willing to carve out the time to read the manuscript and write a compelling foreword to this book. Thank you.

Others I want to thank include: Tim Dolan, because he always makes me think; Scott Dille, my friend and former boss at Bank One; Cynthia Wambold, for making the graphics comprehensible; and Jim Eckstein, for a real-time case study. My gratitude goes also to my friends Martin Alderson Smith, Etienne Boillot, Ted Hibben, Tracy Weisman, Brian Miner, Lyle Logan, the Rosenbergs Senior and Junior, Alex DuBuclet, and Linda Litner. All of them read drafts of various chapters, contributed ideas, and offered "praise" that helped me convince Prentice Hall to take on this project. I also want to thank the members of the Harvard Business School personal finance group in Chicago for reading an early draft of my work and providing both useful feedback and solid encouragement.

From the start, my friend and esteemed professor of finance, Steve Kaplan, encouraged me to keep refining the processes I use for setting wealth management financial strategy; he was always there to help with tactical introductions and the right answers to my technical questions.

Bob McDermott and his late wife (and legal partner) Jane have had a profound effect on my family that goes far beyond my book. Their professional and practical advice has been enormously valuable to us over the decades. I got help of a different sort from Jack Lanphar. Starting more than ten years ago Jack figured out how to make things happen that seemed impossible.

I received valuable input from still others in the writing of this book. They include: Ken and Peter Lehman, Penny Pritzker, John Manley, Jack Polsky, Lenny Gail and Robin Steans, Peter Goulds, Matt and Kay Bucksbaum, and Will Doheny. Each generously added their perspective, shared ideas, and kept me thinking broadly about the issues that wealthy individuals and families face.

Three other friends with experience in publishing and media, Christopher Ainsley, Gary Lucido, and Bob Reichblum, spent hours brainstorming with me about how to hone this book's message and create a breakthrough model for the strategic management of wealth across multiple generations. Sara Hamilton at Family Office Exchange and I have had numerous conversations about wealthy families and their needs and she has been a strong supporter of the book and my ideas.

One of my toughest critics is my mentor, friend, and fellow NPR Foundation Board member, Bill Poorvu. Bill has taught me so much about investing, managing meetings, philanthropy, and values. His wisdom about business and also about life is truly inspirational to me.

No doubt, the bravest supporters of this project have been members of my family. Two years ago a group of about 12 people—cousins, parents, and siblings—came together at my request to learn about my desire to write this book and to highlight the family's experience. Many in the group were tentative about the idea of incorporating our family's story into this book. Despite their reservations, they trusted and supported me 100%. It's my firm hope that this book does justice both to their faith in me, and to our family's heritage and values.

There are three family members to whom I owe a special debt of gratitude. Dad, my brother William, and my sister-in-law Melissa are all partners with me in our family office. Their thinking touches every aspect of this book, and I look forward to decades of continued productive work with them.

A special thank you goes to my wife Susan and to my three children. At times, this project consumed me. You have taken it all in stride and been supportive throughout. You are the very best that I could ever hope for!

ABOUT THE AUTHOR

Living with wealth, managing its complexities, using it to advance worthy causes, and perpetuating his family's legacy are all topics Stuart E. Lucas knows a great deal about. For over 20 years, he's lived a double life, both as a member of one of America's wealthy families and as a senior executive in prestigious wealth management and investment firms.

Lucas is a fourth-generation heir of E.A. Stuart, founder of the Carnation Company, best known as the maker of such all-American food products as Carnation evaporated milk, Friskies pet food, Coffee-Mate non-dairy creamer, and Contadina food products. In 1985, the Stuart family sold Carnation to Nestlé, the Swiss-based global food giant.

Today, Lucas takes an active role in managing his family's wealth. Since 1988, he has been General Partner of a family partnership that invests in alternative investment funds that have generated a 16% internal rate of return since inception. He ran his family's investment office from 1995 to 2001 and now shares that responsibility with several of his relations.

Lucas has a long-standing commitment to public service. He serves as a Director of the Stuart Foundation, which supports public education, child welfare, and youth community-building programs in California and Washington. He is also Vice Chairman of the National Public Radio Foundation in Washington, D.C., where he serves on the Foundation's Finance, Investment, and Executive Committees. He also serves on the Board of the University of Chicago Laboratory Schools and on its Development Committee. In the past, he served on the Board of Visitors of the Rockefeller Center at Dartmouth College and on the Auxiliary Board of the Art Institute of Chicago.

Lucas was formerly Senior Managing Director of the Ultra-high Net Worth Group within Private Client Services at Chicago-based Bank One. This Group served the approximately 150 private clients with assets at the bank in excess of $25 million. During the 1980s Lucas worked for Wellington Management Company, a wealth management firm, serving for three years as General Manager of the firm's European business operations and before that as Assistant Portfolio Manager of a Forbes Honor Roll mutual fund.

Lucas graduated from Dartmouth College with High Honors in History in 1981 and from Harvard Business School in 1989. He holds a Certified Financial Analyst charter and has earned NASD Series 7 and 66 licenses. He is married with three children.

INTRODUCTION

Question: *What's the best way to make a small fortune?*
Answer: Start with a big one.

This book focuses on what an individual like you and families like yours can do to protect and grow your wealth, share it with others, and build lasting personal and family legacies based on it. The lessons learned and shared here come from my many years as a wealth industry professional combined with the experience of representing my family as long-time clients of the industry. There is value in having sat on both sides of the table, and I want to share that value with you.

Whether you are building your wealth over time or acquired it suddenly, whether you have a few hundred thousand in assets or a few hundred million, whether your family situation is simple or complex, the principles discussed in this book will help you sustain, grow, and, most importantly, enjoy your wealth.

Everyone dreams of striking it rich—by selling a business, scoring a great investment, receiving an inheritance, or winning the lottery. In fact, most people generate their wealth, small or large, by patiently accumulating and nurturing their asset base. Either way, integrating all of the components of wealth management into a coherent, satisfying whole is the challenge we have before us.

I was one of the lucky ones because I was born into a wealthy family. For me, the dream began with $25,000 and the founding of what became the Carnation Company by my great-grandfather E.A. Stuart in 1899. Eighty-six years later, the company was sold to the Nestlé Corporation for $3 billion, and I am a beneficiary of that wealth. But I am even luckier because I've drawn perspective from a thoughtful family legacy and a quarter century of working in financial services.

I've used this perspective to build a flexible framework that can be customized to the unique circumstances of anyone who cares about managing their wealth. That's what this book is about. My hope is that you'll use this framework to protect and grow your own wealth, share it constructively with those you love, enjoy financial security, and build a lasting personal and family legacy.

But first, I will share a little personal and family history so you can see firsthand where I'm coming from.

Good Idea, Bad Start

The story of Carnation's founding and of E.A. Stuart's pluck and grit in revolutionizing the production of fresh, safe milk products at the turn of the 20th century is the stuff of American history. So too is the fortune he amassed in bringing these products to your grandparents, parents, and now your kitchen table.

Back in the late 19th century, E.A. Stuart had a dream of making wholesome, good-tasting milk as available to the Americans of his day as sugar and salt. So in 1899, he co-founded the Pacific Coast Condensed Milk Company and spent $25,000 to buy the rights to a process for producing evaporated milk.

The circumstances surrounding E.A. Stuart's purchase of his new milk production process were hardly auspicious. In fact, in the beginning, they had all the markings of a business disaster. At first, poorly sealed cans of evaporated milk spoiled by the wagonload after leaving Stuart's plant near modern-day Seattle, Washington. Making matters worse, local customers in those days weren't convinced they needed his product anyway, not in a region where cows dotted the lush local countryside and fresh milk flowed as plentifully from local pastures as cold, clear water did from local mountain streams.

But my great-grandfather persisted. "Pluck wins. It always wins," he used to say in those challenging and sometimes dark early days. Showing flinty resolve, he perfected his milk evaporation process and improved his canning procedures.

When Opportunity Comes Face to Face with Hard Work and Preparation

Then luck struck. Or as some might say, "Opportunity came face to face with hard work and a lot of preparation." Just as Stuart perfected his production techniques, demand for evaporated milk skyrocketed as gold prospectors swept through Seattle on their way to Alaska to join the great Klondike Gold Rush. Prospectors started buying it off the shelves as fast as my great-grandfather produced it. By 1909, Carnation had grown from one plant to seven, and sales had gone from nothing to over $4 million a year. At 10 cents a can, that meant 40 million cans of evaporated milk were being produced each year.

Stuart's production process was extraordinary because it took about 60% of the water content out of dairy milk, thus making it easy to transport and store without refrigeration. Stuart, it seems, was in the right place at the right time. His perseverance, discipline, hard work, and faith—plus a little luck—launched the Carnation Company on the path to becoming a multi-billion dollar global food company.

Three generations later, the Stuart family hit pay dirt again. In 1985, international food giant Nestlé bought Carnation for $83 a share, or about $3 billion in cash. That price was nearly double the stated value of the company just a few years earlier and, at the time, was the highest price ever paid for a food company. Our extended family, which had much of its wealth tied up in the nearly 27 percent of Carnation stock it controlled at that time, suddenly landed on the Forbes 400 list of the wealthiest families in America, with close to $1 billion in collective assets!

It was an exciting time for us. We had achieved the American dream. In one fell swoop, we became wealthy beyond our wildest hopes and expectations. But therein lay the seeds of a problem.

Since Carnation's founding in 1899, members of my family had always identified closely with the company and all it stood for. The company had five presidents, three of whom were Stuarts. And even though H. Everett Olson, Carnation's CEO and the Chairman at the time of the sale, wasn't a family member, Wall Street and the business press always described the Carnation Company as "a tight-knit family enterprise."

End of an Era

The day that company executives sold Carnation to Nestlé, all of that changed. Our family's wealth, most of which was tied up for almost a century in Carnation stock, suddenly became liquid. And the family's ties to Carnation, the company that for years prided itself on giving Americans "better milk from contented cows," were suddenly severed.

The aftermath of Carnation's sale to Nestlé offered my family a unique opportunity to decide how its members would relate to one another now that they no longer had a day-to-day business to run. But that also posed some unique challenges: challenges of identity, purpose, leadership, and family legacy. Carnation had been my family's life and work for 86 years. Now that it was gone, what would we do with ourselves? In the early 1900s, when my great-grandfather had first thought about selling Carnation, his son, E.H. Stuart, Carnation's second president, pleaded with him not to. "If you do, I won't know what to do with myself," he said. Now that reality had come to pass. And we, E.A's descendants, had to deal with it.

No Strategic Approach to Wealth Management

Carnation's sale to Nestlé precipitated a crisis for our family in three ways.

First, our family never anticipated the sale of Carnation. So, our family never adopted a coordinated approach to managing our wealth, should that eventuality arise. Thus, in early 1985, when Carnation's sale was consummated, assets of nearly $1 billion suddenly got divided up among a large number of Stuart family members. Less than a decade later, there were at least seven different Stuart family branches, each pursuing its own investment goals and strategies—with widely varied results.

Second, after the company's sale, our family no longer had a single focal point for its identity. So, our common family heritage and history began to slip away. My great-grandfather and Carnation's founder, E.A.

Stuart, died in 1940. His son, E.H. Stuart (my mother's father), passed away in the early 1970s. Within a year of the company's sale, not a single Stuart family member worked for Nestlé. The last family member who worked there quipped to me that "The Stuart family connection went from being an asset to a liability."

Third, after Carnation was sold, our family's wealth was reinvested in mixed stock/bond portfolios that yielded yearly dividends. But these new investment funds couldn't begin to match the average annual growth rate of 13% that Carnation stock had enjoyed from 1899 to 1985. In fact, income distributions to Stuart family beneficiaries started to decline in the early 1990s. Soon, some members of my family, who were dependent on investment income for their lifestyles, began to emphasize fixed income investments more than in years past—a move that was destined to further erode our wealth if we weren't careful.

All of this caused me to look at the Lucas branch of the family—my parents, my siblings, and our children—with a great deal of concern. By this time, I had spent more than 10 years in the investment and wealth management industries. After graduating from Dartmouth in 1981, I had gone to work for Wellington Management Company, an investment management firm that manages hundreds of billions of dollars in assets. Over the years, I also became deeply involved in our family's financial and investment affairs as part of the Lucas family office.

My experience at Wellington Management gave me superb on-the-job training as an investment analyst, and as I looked over the state of our investments, I didn't like what I saw. The performance of our funds under the trustee who oversaw our family's assets was mediocre at best—to the limited extent I could measure it.

Alarm Bells

Between 1987 and 1994, the U.S. stock market grew a whopping 133% while the bond market grew 92.4% in value. That meant that a portfolio of 60% stocks and 40% bonds like ours *should* have grown 117% over that same seven-year period. But to my shock, my family's portfolio had not. In fact, my research showed that during the roaring bull market from the late eighties into the mid nineties, the value of our main portfolio grew only 31%. Taking inflation into account, this meant we hadn't really increased the value of our wealth *at all*.

It's Hard to Grow Assets AND Enjoy the Fruits of Success at the Same Time!

So where was the problem? First, I discovered that there were significant "costs" associated with our wealth that were continuously dragging down the value of our assets. To maintain the existing value of our assets—after distributing roughly 4% a year to family members, paying taxes, paying our investment advisor, paying brokerage fees, and adjusting for inflation—we had to generate roughly 9.5% a year in asset value growth. But because 40% of our assets were invested in bonds, the value of our stock holdings actually had to grow at an annual rate closer to 12%; almost the same 13% average annual growth rate that Carnation stock enjoyed year after year, decade after decade!

But that wasn't all.

Over time, to enjoy the same level of investment income from family trusts that my parents enjoyed, I realized it wouldn't be enough for us just to maintain the value of our assets. We had to *increase* their value because our family was getting bigger. I have three siblings, and among us we have nine children. If we wanted to live as well as my parents, we would have to generate not 12%, but nearly 17% growth in our stock portfolio year after year for the next 50 years. That's impressive even for someone like Warren Buffett to achieve!

My fellow family members and I always assumed that there would be plenty of money to pass on to our children and grandchildren. But that assumption, I realized, wasn't accurate. Even if we maintained our family's assets in the coming years, spending what we earned net of fees, taxes, and inflation, it became clear that each of my children would have nearly 90% less wealth than my parents simply because the family was increasing in numbers. Growing up, I'd often heard the expression, "from shirtsleeves to shirtsleeves in three generations." Now, I realized what that expression really meant. And I didn't like its implications.

Clearly, none of us was about to starve or see a significant near-term change in our lifestyle. But with an eye toward the future, and on what each of us wanted to do next in our lives, my family and I realized that the fortune my great-grandfather and grandfather built, which had been lovingly preserved in family trusts, wouldn't last another 86 years. My generation would have to work just as hard and be just as entrepreneurial to build our family's assets for the future as our forebears had done in the past if we didn't want to preside over a crumbling legacy.

Our Wealth Represented More than Cash

I realized something else, too. Our family's money represented more than just cash. It represented hard work, history, love, and legacy—a tangible gift from past generations of Stuarts to my own. It was meant to last a long time and to be used in ways that would benefit not just my family and me, but also society and generations of Stuarts yet unborn.

We Needed to Get a Handle on Our Investment Portfolio

My family and I needed to get a handle on the long-term management of our wealth. Otherwise, we wouldn't have a family fortune anymore—only the memory of it. What could we do to reverse the tide of our financial fortunes? Crafting a solution demanded the use of all the financial and business training I was fortunate to get at the Harvard Business School and in the volatile business of investment management. When I understood the extent of our family's long-term asset erosion problems, I presented the facts of our situation to my family. Talk about breaking a family taboo! Can you imagine convening a meeting of your family members to discuss the family's financial health? I can and did, and by reading this book, you'll be able to do it as well.

Introducing Strategic Wealth Management

I persuaded my family that we needed to take a disciplined and coordinated approach to what I call "strategic wealth management." Strategic wealth management is a philosophy and approach to wealth building that involves a number of key components—defining values; setting investment goals; deciding on a time horizon for wealth management planning (your lifetime or multiple generations); asset, liability, and cash flow management; control of spending; wealth transfer; and, tax and risk mitigation—all coordinated in a strategic, synchronized way that results in the whole being worth more than the sum of the parts. Strategic wealth management is a comprehensive approach to managing wealth productively where synergies come from careful planning and from leveraging a family's assets in purposeful ways not just for a lifetime, but, in our case, for multiple generations.

As a group, we focused on the values that we thought should drive the future management of our wealth. We talked about our family's shared heritage—a heritage built on hard work, persistence, personal flint, and private Quaker faith. We also discussed our tolerance for entrepreneurial risk-taking, expectations for earned income, our desire for investment income, and our long-term goals for the future, both as individuals and as a family. The overriding questions in all these discussions were these: did we want to go broke—slowly and with certainty? Or did we want to take measured and educated risks with the potential benefit of growing our wealth and that of our children?

We Are Stewards, Not Owners, of Our Wealth

As we wrestled with these questions, several things happened:

We began to see ourselves not as owners of our wealth, but as stewards of it. We spoke of the drifting apart of various branches of the Stuart family after Carnation's sale and agreed we didn't want our family to fracture further. So, we decided to reverse the splintering of the Lucas family assets and, together, manage our inherited wealth so that the bulk of it is passed on to future generations.

We decided to base future wealth management decisions and strategies on core family and individual values. Why focus on values first? Values establish a framework for defining your wealth management priorities.

We decided to dramatically restructure our investments and the way we interact with our wealth advisors so that our wealth could help us meet our goals, not someone else's idea of what they should be. If successful, we'd be able to generate new wealth and pass it on to future generations while still enjoying its benefits in this generation.

We realized it was critical to foster family harmony, strong communications, and wealth management leadership. Wealth management and wealth creation are difficult tasks. They require high-order management and leadership competencies, especially when issues of diversified wealth and multigenerational wealth building and transfer are involved. We recognized that this was critical to the successful long-term management of our family's assets, and you will also.

Taking Control for the First Time

As a result of our discussions, my family and I pulled our family trusts out of the Midwestern bank that managed them for years—a rare event in the clubby world of trust fund management. In an ironic twist, however, the bank didn't try to retaliate for this move or hold a grudge against our family. Instead, the bank hired me in 2001 to manage its high-net worth business and to implement for its clients many of the strategic wealth management practices and approaches that my family and I decided to put in place.

The decision my family and I made to give up our existing trustee and to take proactive control of our family's wealth management activities had profoundly powerful effects that I want to share with you throughout the book. You will also learn how to enhance your own financial success, given your own circumstances and objectives.

Philanthropy Has Emerged as a Shared Interest Among Many Family Members

Besides strengthening our bottom-line financial results, improved family communication and financial coordination has yielded other benefits. As our extended family has reconnected in recent years, we've rediscovered much about the wonderful Stuart family legacy and have come to appreciate our common family roots.

We found that many of us share a common interest in philanthropy. E.A. Stuart first set up a foundation back in 1937, and additional foundations have been established by virtually every generation of Stuarts since then. Today, these foundations focus the attention of family members on the needs of disadvantaged children, the elderly, at-risk inner city youth, schools, and other social issues. Stuart family members quietly give millions away each year in their capacities as foundation trustees and directors. Following in E.A. Stuart's footsteps, many of us also give substantial sums to charity from our own pockets and spend countless hours working with nonprofit organizations both large and small. Some of these causes are well known and prestigious, while others are small and support some of society's neediest people. I'll have much more to say about philanthropy as a family bonding agent and component of wealth management in subsequent chapters.

Closer Family Ties

Finally, because members of my immediate family today coordinate their wealth management activities, it has brought my siblings, parents, and me closer together emotionally than in years past. You should know that growing diversified wealth is not easy. It requires cutting-edge investment knowledge, a competitive spirit, and a particular personality. It also requires a commitment to communicating openly, honestly, and respectfully with other family members—even when you don't always agree with them. In the Lucas clan today, that's not always easy to do. As our family continues to grow, we must consider the concerns and interests of *all* family members in setting wealth management goals and making other critical wealth management decisions.

The Wealth-Building Legacy of E.A. Stuart

Growing up, my siblings and I were raised on stories of E.A. Stuart's persistence in the face of repeated setbacks in starting the Carnation Company. Those lessons resonate in us to this day, and I hope that our family stories make this discussion of wealth management less academic and more tangible to you, regardless of your financial or familial situation.

There's a delivery drop box from one of E.A.'s notable business failures—a dry goods business that flopped before he founded Carnation—which we keep in the kitchen of our Cape Cod summerhouse. We keep this drop box around for an important and symbolic reason: to emphasize that wealth isn't to be taken for granted and isn't easily attained. "You may have inherited wealth, but in this family you are expected to work hard," is the message my siblings and I got from our parents growing up.

The story of how E.A. Stuart ran Carnation in its early years contains important lessons—not just for running a business, but also for managing the wealth that a business creates. Many of his ideas, in fact, form the core principles espoused in this book.

- *Consistent profits are critical to successful growth.* In its 86 years as an independent company, through two world wars and the Great Depression, Carnation only lost money in three years. The key to this remarkable track record was prudent diversification, empowerment of people, and careful measurement of results.
- *Take measured and informed risks.* The entrepreneurial risks he took and his well-honed intuition were always grounded in his deep knowledge of his business.
- *Align your interests with customers and suppliers.* E.A. Stuart was always looking to partner with people, not to gain the upper hand as an adversary.
- *Conserve your wealth.* He worked hard and was frugal. To this day, my mother takes real pride in describing her family as "understated people."
- *Be useful.* This was EA Stuart's ultimate measure of success.

How My Dad Taught Me the Value of Money

A quick story from my childhood illustrates just how large a role prudence and "financial modesty" played in my family's household when I was growing up. In 1965, when my family and I moved back to the U.S. following a three-year job stint for my father in Europe, Dad bought a brand new red Plymouth Valiant. Over the next 17 years, as he rose through job ranks at Carnation, ultimately to become President of the International Division, this car remained his preferred form of transportation for virtually all business and family activities. Even when the presidents of overseas divisions turned up in Los Angeles to meet with Dad to conduct business, they always drove to company dinners, not in some shiny Lincoln Continental or Cadillac, but in my father's red Valiant!

My father so loved this Valiant that for its 25th anniversary in 1990, we bought a vanity license plate for it that read, "65 JUNK." When 65 JUNK finally gave up the ghost, my father pulled the Mercedes that my Grandmother had bequeathed him years before out of storage and began to drive *it*. By then, it was only 20 years old. "Still has many years of useful service in it," he told us.

The lesson my father taught us by keeping that less-than-fashionable Plymouth Valiant around for so long was clear: "Image *isn't* everything. Don't squander your assets. Preserve your wealth and use it for worthwhile pursuits no matter how much of it you might have." The message he sent to his division presidents was equally clear: "Cost control is important, and I lead by example."

A Book About Strategic Wealth Management

Today, my family's value system regarding money is based both on personal prudence and on an aggressive and shrewd approach to the long-term strategic stewardship and growth of wealth. You'll read a lot about these values—and others—throughout the pages of this book.

But I don't assume that my values are your values. I've learned many lessons about wealth management, both as a member of a wealthy family and as an industry professional advising others. One of the most important things I've learned is that each individual and each family has its own values and unique circumstances relating to managing wealth. This book discusses many roads to effective wealth management, not just the ones used by my family. You can explore the options and then decide which ones are right for you.

This book deals with how you can manage *your* wealth, be it for your lifetime or for multiple generations, using proven wealth management principles to do so. What I say here is directed to anyone concerned about wealth creation, wealth management, families with wealth, retirement planning, and multi-generational estate management. The book will also be of value to wealth industry professionals who are interested in providing their clients with fresh investment insights. It will also help upwardly affluent professionals and successful entrepreneurs who are interested in adopting a strategic, focused, and disciplined approach to growing and diversifying their financial assets.

With an insider's perspective, I wrote this book to share the lessons that my family and I have learned, and hopefully to spare you from some of our mistakes. Most of these lessons apply whether you are worth a few hundred thousand dollars or a few hundred million.

As you turn to Chapter 1, "Protecting and Growing Your Wealth," remember this: Wealth management isn't just about money. It's also about people, relationships, values, doing well by doing good, and, of course, family. Enjoy this book for the tools and insights it provides you. Use it as a guide to more strategic and insightful stewardship of your personal and family wealth and to the achievement of a more fulfilling life. Wealth is a *gift* you should safeguard, nurture, and share productively with others. This book will show you how.

Stuart Lucas
July 2005

1

PROTECTING AND GROWING YOUR WEALTH

"Solve your problems. Don't let them lick you."

—*E.A. Stuart*

W hat can an individual like you and families like yours do to protect and grow your wealth, share it with others, enjoy financial security, and build lasting personal and family legacies based on it?

Over the last 25 years, I have learned that effective wealth management has little to do with how much money you have or how you accumulated it. Effective wealth management is much more about how well you manage than it is about how *much* you manage. The hard lessons that I've learned as a financial industry insider and from managing substantial wealth for my family are the focus of this book and are applicable to anyone willing to meet the challenge of managing wealth. By sharing those lessons, using illustrations from my family's actual experience, I'm certain that you can avoid many of the pitfalls inherent in managing your personal wealth.

Wealth management is about more than investing, though that is an important part. Money, family, and community are invariably bound together. People pay taxes, save, spend, support philanthropic causes, and transfer wealth to their heirs. Successful wealth management involves the integrated and effective management of all these components.

Transitions

Some people build their wealth by saving money a little bit each month and managing it with the goal of having financial security in retirement. Even after years of accumulating financial assets, working with advisors, and experiencing the volatility of financial markets, they are still uncomfortable with how their assets are managed and are looking for better ways to achieve their goals.

Others achieve financial independence in sudden and sometimes difficult and tumultuous ways. Their transitions to wealth are abrupt and often stressful. Some sell a business into which they had poured their entire savings. Some retire with a pension that they are now responsible for managing. Some receive assets as a result of divorce or loss of a spouse. One of the biggest sudden and high-stress circumstances for coming into wealth is the death of a parent. Over the next 50 years, the United States will see the greatest transfer of wealth in its history. Boston College researchers John J. Havens and Paul G. Schervish estimate that, over this period, total bequests to heirs will range from $25 trillion to $65 trillion, or an average of between $500 billion and $1.3 trillion per year.[1] In many of these circumstances, people will not be prepared to take on the responsibility of their new wealth, and the event itself will often come as a surprise.

Building wealth and conserving it takes time, and it demands considered action. The key is to not do something *prematurely* that results in a significant loss of capital. For that reason, resist the impulse to act quickly or to retain outside wealth advisors before you are ready to act. Do your homework first and plan ahead.

How the Wealth Management Industry Works

Why is it important to plan before engaging wealth management advisors to manage your assets? You need knowledge to protect your interests. Unless you are a proactive, thoughtful, and informed client, the structure of the wealth management industry today actually works against your interests in three ways:

1. The wealth management goals of clients and their financial advisors can easily diverge. When conflicts of interest arise, advisors may put their own interests ahead of their clients.

2. Advisors are unlikely to fully understand or appreciate your personal and family dynamics. These dynamics are key drivers of wealth management priorities, goals, and strategies in families, and they influence many business and investment decisions—frequently behind the scenes.

3. Very few wealth management professionals have enough breadth of skill and experience to operate across multiple disciplines or to anticipate how advice offered by one expert can potentially affect that offered by another. The advice of one advisor should, ideally, complement and reinforce the value of another advisor's input. But the siloed nature of professional fields such as estate and tax law, financial planning, investment management, and banking usually works against this desired outcome.

Wealth management firms that are waiting to make money (from *your* money) include brokers, mutual fund companies, life insurers, money managers and hedge funds, law firms, banks, independent financial planners, accounting firms, and multi-family offices. The organizational culture in most firms focuses on finding a balance between getting acceptable results for the client and achieving the firms' profit goals. As with any market-driven business, the financial rewards and recognition that wealth management practitioners enjoy are based on the amount of business they bring in the door. There's a premium placed on generating revenue. It's easy to measure and is tied directly to firm profitability. But larger revenues and bigger profits don't always mean better service.

By contrast, it's *not* easy to measure the value added that a wealth management firm or advisor actually generates for a client. Thus, clients are often left in the position of having to trust their advisors without an accurate yardstick to measure their effectiveness. This is a big reason why studies of the wealth management industry show a high level of customer dissatisfaction.

This state of affairs hasn't been in the long-term interests of either party. Fortunately, the problems are not insurmountable. That's why America's wealth management industry is in a state of dynamic transition, where old business models are competing with new ones in a struggle between service and profit. No one knows which will be the winner. There is no better system than a competitive marketplace to resolve industry problems, but the process is messy and clients can get hurt. For that reason, I say: "Buyer beware!" and "Keep reading this book!"

Classic Approach to Wealth Management

Many people rush to retain wealth management advisors in whom they desire to place their trust. Clients are busy, and most are anxious to have professional oversight in place. They either look to an existing trusted advisor who helped them before (maybe with issues unrelated to current wealth management challenges) or they respond to inquiries from enterprising advisors who identify them as new business prospects. In either case, people often choose one firm immediately or decide to have multiple firms compete for their business before they really know what they want or how to assess accurately the characteristics and quality of each firm's offering. During the course of the selection process, prospective advisors are asked to explain the strengths of their firm and their own background and to describe how they would manage the assets if the prospective client chose them. The prospective client tries to absorb this information with limited relevant experience and typically chooses the most attractive-sounding sales pitch without a thorough understanding of what they want to achieve or the likelihood of doing so.

Sidebar 1.1: Learning the Language of Wealth Management

Many people's experience with wealth management advisors is minimal at best. Making matters worse, the language of the wealth management industry is often mysterious and intimidating.

I am regularly reminded (usually by one of my children) of just how much a "language barrier" can incite feelings of misgiving and uncertainty. The latest reminder of this barrier comes in the form of Pokémon, the hugely successful Japanese trading card game based on mythical creatures pitted against one another in combat. Pokémon is a game at which my eight-year-old son excels, but at which I am at best an outmatched opponent. Pokémon consists of a complex world filled with hundreds of creatures—some that evolve into others—with myriad powers and weaknesses and all with unpronounceable names. Besides trading cards, there are also stuffed animals, television shows, "how to" books, and Pokémon T-shirts. My son is both an expert at Pokémon and a supremely

---

continues

confident Pokémon salesman. Here's a typical exchange that we might have in the course of playing a round of Pokémon:

Son: Daddy, why don't you battle this Cyndaquil against my Feraligatr? Cyndaquil is really cool; he has singe attack and an HP of 50!

Dad: What attacks does Alligator have?

Son: Not alligator, Daddy, *Fer*aligatr! He has slash attack.

Dad: Oh, okay. Well, can I use slash attack instead of singe attack with my Cindyquill?

Son: No, Dad. You have to play by the rules. You should know that...

As you can see, this conversation is already a slippery slope. After five minutes of talking with my son about the arcane details of Pokémon, my head is spinning. I don't remember what HP is, let alone whether 50 is good or bad. Singe attack doesn't mean anything more to me than slash attack. As I play the game, I never quite know when the rules change, and even if I did, my facility with the vocabulary of Pokémon is too rudimentary to argue my case. (My son knows this, of course.) In addition, I haven't read the small print at the bottom of the Cyndaquil trading card, which states that its weakness is slash attack. After my inevitable loss, I don't have to ponder very long whether my son has systematically memorized all the small print this game has to offer, with the intention of clobbering me every time we engage in battle. I know he has!

When faced with managing their wealth, many individuals find themselves in situations similar to those I face when I play Pokémon with my son. They must operate in alien territory, trying to understand the parameters of an unfamiliar game while being outmaneuvered by complex rules and a vocabulary they don't understand.

To further assist you in learning the language of wealth management, please see Appendix, "Learning the Language of Wealth Management." This is serious stuff, but it's also important to have a little fun with it.

After the new client chooses an advisor, both client and advisor are limited to solutions that the advisor can provide, whether or not they are advantageous to the client. Because most private wealth advisors don't generate revenue from a client until they have sold one or more products, and because many clients want the security of knowing their assets have been invested, there's often an unspoken urgency on both parties' parts to consummate investment arrangements and to lock the client into specific solutions, often with long-term consequences.

When they rush to action, most clients have not thought deeply about their financial, personal, or family goals, how to realistically achieve them, or their comfort with financial risk before hiring their advisors. So their advisors end up driving the agenda. Most advisors inquire about the client's financial situation and learn something about his/her goals, family situation, and personality. This classic approach leaves little incentive for advisors to explain the pros and cons of all the financial options available, especially low-cost, high-value ones. After interviewing a client, the advisor typically selects the firm's investment policy that most closely matches the expressed need. He then chooses an asset allocation from among the available options. Assets are divided by major category or asset class—stocks, bonds, cash, private equity, hedge funds, real estate—and a target allocation is assigned to each category so that the total equals 100%. Then the advisor reviews his firm's stable of available investment managers and recommends a subset that represents each asset class. The client then reviews the list, approves the recommendations, and invests the target amounts.

Within a month or two, and sometimes faster, the client's strategy is set, the assets are fully invested, and the revenues are flowing to the advisor's firm. From here on out, the advisor meets periodically with the client to review the performance of the portfolio, to offer suggestions for improvement, and to make any agreed-upon changes. This classic approach to wealth management (which, as you may already have guessed, I want you to avoid) can be broken down into five steps, as shown in Figure 1.1. This classic approach is standard across the industry, and it happens time after time.

The Classic Approach To Wealth Management

Choose Financial Advisors ⟩ Set Investment Policy ⟩ Choose Asset Allocation ⟩ Select Managers ⟩ Periodic Review

Figure 1.1 This is the standard process used by most wealth management advisors.

Strategic Wealth Management

Instead of the classically flawed approach I just described, this book focuses on a new way to structure your wealth management affairs. I call it "strategic wealth management." It's not that the classic approach is wrong. It's just incomplete. Like having a gun without a good aiming system, you're unlikely to hit your target. In contrast to the classic approach, strategic wealth management is a holistic approach to wealth management that *focuses on your interests*. It explores all of your strategic options and puts you back in the driver's seat while showing you how to employ your advisors to greatest effect. Your values, your skills and resources, and how you relate to your family are at the core of the strategic wealth management approach and are key elements of what I call the Strategic Wealth Management Framework©.

For example:

Do you want to use your wealth to reflect your deeply held values and beliefs? The Strategic Wealth Management Framework can help you design a wealth management strategy that does this.

Do you or members of your family have competitive advantages that you can leverage in the marketplace to drive increased returns on your assets? The Framework can help you do that, too.

Are there family members or others to whom you wish to pass wealth, as well as the skills to manage it well? The Framework provides guidelines for doing that.

How much risk are you comfortable taking? The Strategic Wealth Management Framework can help you determine the level of investment risk that is most in keeping with your investment skills, interests, and temperament.

Are there simple, low-cost, highly effective wealth management techniques that you can use to great effect and with little hassle? Yes. I show them to you.

In Figure 1.2, you will see yourself at the center of the Strategic Wealth Management Framework. *You* are the heart of the Framework. Early on, using this framework requires more time and effort to implement than the classic approach to wealth management. But it is a more thoughtful, systematic approach designed to help you manage your wealth according to your personal and family goals, whether for your lifetime or, in some cases, for multiple generations of your family. If you follow this framework, you will also get better performance out of your advisors, and in many ways you will be a more attractive client to them.

In Figure 1.2, projecting left and right out from the core are two arrows labeled Context and Infrastructure. In order to set a coherent strategy and then execute it, you will need to evaluate the context within which you wish to operate and build an effective infrastructure to achieve your goals, based on the reality of that context.

Strategic Wealth Management Framework©

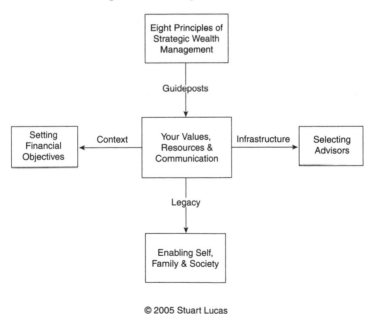

© 2005 Stuart Lucas

Figure 1.2 Use the Strategic Wealth Management Framework© to create a fully integrated plan that meets *your* objectives.

The external context in wealth management includes the financial markets and the many institutions that operate within its confines, the tax code, and for those who have a multigenerational timeframe, estate planning law. For those with philanthropic interests, the external context also includes the non-profit sector. It is critical to the success of this model that you examine the external context early in the wealth management planning process. Only by understanding the context within which you must make decisions and the specifications for an effective infrastructure can you set appropriate financial objectives and organize the right advisors to execute *your* wealth management strategy.

The dynamism of today's wealth management industry coupled with the complexity of family dynamics can make wealth management a difficult challenge. To help my family and my readers manage the process, I have devised the Eight Principles of Strategic Wealth Management to bring clarity and precision to our actions and activities within the Strategic Wealth Management Framework (see Chapter 2, "Eight Principles of Strategic Wealth Management"). I use these eight principles all the time. They are guideposts that keep me focused on the things that are most important. When decisions get complicated, the Eight Principles help me narrow my choices while maximizing the impact of those I make. They can do the same for you.

I know that the Strategic Wealth Management Framework and the Eight Principles of Strategic Wealth Management work because they have worked very well for my family and me. By using them

- You'll make sound wealth management decisions based on purposeful reflection, planning, and action.
- You'll select advisors whose skills and experience best match your financial objectives and wealth management strategy.
- You'll make sound investment decisions that are closely aligned with your investment skills, interests, and risk tolerance.

Finally, by embracing the Strategic Wealth Management Framework and the Eight Principles of Strategic Wealth Management, you'll be able to project your values and ambitions (and those of your family) outward into the external environment to achieve specific and concrete wealth management goals—*your* wealth management goals. When your strategy is a success, you create a legacy that improves your satisfaction and significance and that benefits your family and society.

The Family as a Cultural System

No two families are alike. All families, wealthy or not, are complex, dynamic organisms that are forever changing cultural systems. The culture of a family, like any other cultural system, consists of the beliefs, values, attitudes, norms, and behaviors of its members. Each family's history affects its current culture. Individual family members influence one another in countless, complex ways. Numerous external forces influence the life, identity, and culture of a family as well. Marriages bring "outsiders" into a family, while death and divorce can shatter families and shift lines of power and influence. The extended families of spouses who marry into a family exert their influence too, bringing with them new issues of culture, heritage, business success, family dysfunction, and social prominence.

Still another factor that can color the dynamics in any family is the very presence of wealth itself. Money can be tremendously empowering and can afford its owners extraordinary opportunities. At the same time, money can complicate family relationships, foster resentment, and create dependency. At the extreme, poorly managed wealth can lead to degeneracy and even corruption.

I believe that wealthy parents—like all parents—need to be intentional about instilling values of accountability and responsibility in their children when it comes to the use of money. Indeed, doing so can be critical to the family's long-term survival! Many wealthy parents indulge their children financially. In so doing, they often foster economic dependency and create a generation of children that feels entitled to the benefits of wealth, but which is ill prepared to manage the responsibilities that wealth entails. Such children often become reliant on their parents for their lifestyles and often lack the discipline to use money wisely. It's no wonder that some people believe that passing wealth from one generation to the next is doing their heirs and society a disservice.

Not surprisingly, financial dependency can affect a family in significant ways. Just how do you go about raising a generation to be empowered by its wealth, not filled with a sense of over-entitlement because of it? I don't know of a single wealthy parent who doesn't worry about this issue a great deal.

That's one more reason why wealth management is about so much more than money. It's also about fostering strong intergenerational values related to productivity, work, accountability, and personal responsibility. Doing this can ensure the health of families for multiple generations. The failure to do it can lead to family dysfunction and the rapid loss of wealth.

Taking Control of the Wealth Management Process

Using the Strategic Wealth Management Framework requires leadership—*your* leadership. Leadership is necessary to protect your financial interests and to reinforce a positive family culture. You must accept personal accountability for managing your wealth, regardless of whether you want to manage simply and conservatively or with focus and risk. It doesn't matter whether your goal is to build the next Rockefeller dynasty, launch a new start-up business, or hand over day-to-day responsibilities for wealth management to an advisor who has earned the moniker "trusted." In all cases, you, as the wealth owner, must take personal charge of your wealth management by assuming a role I refer to throughout the book as the "Wealth Strategist."

Sometimes the Wealth Strategist is an individual. Sometimes several family members work as a team to play the role. Typically, a first-generation wealth creator takes on the role him- or herself. In a multigenerational context, either model can operate successfully. However, in the multigenerational context, it is important that the Wealth Strategist serve at the pleasure of the family. Dictatorship as an American family governance structure tends to be fundamentally unstable, even when the position is earned through merit and sanctioned by the previous generation!

For those with substantial wealth and a multigenerational timeframe, a managed transition of the Wealth Strategist role from one generation to the next is a critical task. In turn, my great-grandfather, my grandfather, and then my father played the role of Wealth Strategist. Today, I share the

Wealth Strategist role with my brother William and my sister-in-law Melissa, though my father still plays an important oversight role. As a rule, our family believes in gradual generational transitions, not as a delaying tactic by the older generation to retain power, but to diligently work through the inevitable issues that arise. Time has been our ally in working out complex family and financial dynamics. It can be yours, too.

You and your family stand to benefit greatly from having a designated Wealth Strategist in place to work closely with advisors. Having been a wealth industry advisor myself, I know that the relationships I've built with designated Wealth Strategists from other families over the years make wealth management activities a lot easier and more efficient for everybody. If I'm able to work with a designated Wealth Strategist, we can optimize our working relationship in numerous ways. We use our time more efficiently, make better investment decisions during times of stress, and our decisions are based on a clearly understood set of operating principles and investment goals. As an educated client, you'll also delegate responsibility more effectively and you will confidently and accurately distinguish between good and mediocre performance.

The Nature of the Wealth Strategist's Role

The Wealth Strategist plays the critical role in developing and executing a family's wealth management strategy. He or she works closely with their family to define management plans and goals and then oversees implementation, coordinating the involvement of both family members and professional financial advisors as needs require. The key function is to integrate the advice and activities of various professional advisors and to make sure the advice is consistent with the overall wealth management strategy and goals and with the dynamics and priorities of the family.

Becoming a Wealth Strategist doesn't require detailed knowledge of investment theory, estate law, or the tax code. But, it does require the following:

- Patience and a long-term perspective
- The ability to foster good communication among family members
- Accurate assessment of your own wealth management skills and those of prospective advisors

- An informed layperson's understanding of how the wealth industry works
- Reasonable financial and managerial discipline

I'll have much more to say later in this book about the critical role of the Wealth Strategist. Suffice to say for now that the Wealth Strategist is in fact the CEO within your family, and it is the job of this individual or team to ensure effective wealth management over time.

Conclusion

This chapter introduced the Strategic Wealth Management Framework and the Eight Principles of Strategic Wealth Management and explained why it's so important for you, the wealth owner, to grasp the reins of control when it comes to implementation. Exercising strong leadership as a Wealth Strategist while following the Framework significantly enhances the productivity of your advisors, and will put you and your family on track to fully realize *your* wealth management goals.

Let's go on now to Chapter 2, where I talk in depth about the eight principles that are central to the effective management of wealth.

Chapter 1: Issues to Discuss with Your Family

1. Do you find the subject of wealth management intimidating? If so, why?

2. Are you convinced that "doing your homework" and planning ahead before hiring your wealth management advisors is a reasonable approach to take? If not, what forces compel you to act now? What are the long-term costs of acting prematurely?

3. Do you have a personal interest in closely managing your finances? If so, how much time are you willing to devote to this activity? If you do not have interest in closely managing your finances, can you structure your wealth management strategy accordingly?

4. Who is the logical Wealth Strategist for your family? Why? What if there isn't a logical choice or a consensus pick?

5. Does your family communicate well about money? How might communication be improved?

6. How would you describe the "culture" of your family? In what ways do your family's beliefs, values, attitudes, and norms shape behavior when it comes to spending and saving?

7. Has your family taken time to articulate its "culture" and how that culture should drive future wealth management planning efforts?

8. Have you ever hired someone to manage your finances? Was it a positive or negative experience? If it was negative, how can you improve things in the future?

9. Do you know how to assess the relative merits of prospective advisors? How do you know you've assembled the best alternatives to choose among instead of a middling pool of talent? (Hint: Brand alone is not the answer.) After you've hired an advisor, how and when will you know they're doing a good job?

10. What advantages do you see in using the Strategic Wealth Management Framework as a tool in wealth management planning instead of the classic approach?

Endnotes

[1] William H. Gates, Sr., and Chuck Collins, *Wealth and Our Commonwealth* (Beacon Press, 2002), pp. 9-10.

2

EIGHT PRINCIPLES OF STRATEGIC WEALTH MANAGEMENT

"Each generation that discovers something from its experience must pass that on, but it must pass that on with a delicate balance of respect and disrespect, so that the [human] race... does not inflict its errors too rigidly on its youth, but it does pass on the accumulated wisdom, plus the wisdom that it may not be wisdom."

—Richard P. Feynman
Nobel Laureate, Physics (1965)

O ver the last 25 years of managing other people's money, my personal finances, and our family's wealth, I have developed what I consider to be a useful set of principles for effective long-term wealth management. They apply equally well whether you're managing a nest egg of $1 million or $1 billion. They apply regardless of time horizon and family complexity, and they apply whether your ambitions are aggressive or conservative. For anyone concerned about managing wealth, they provide a source of stability and a critical frame of reference.

The Eight Principles of Strategic Wealth Management are at the heart of what I do every day. They are:

1. Take charge and do it early.

2. Align family and business interests around wealth-building goals and strategies.

3. Create a culture of accountability.

4. Capitalize on your family's combined resources.

5. Delegate, empower, and respect independence.

6. Diversify but focus.

7. Err on the side of simplicity where possible.

8. Develop future family leaders with strong wealth management skills.

Every decision I make, whether it involves choosing an investment manager, thinking about tax strategy, or working with my family to set goals for next year, gets filtered through these principles. Let's examine them now in detail.

Principle #1: Take Charge and Do It Early

I discussed this principle in some depth when introducing the role of Wealth Strategist in the last chapter. The Strategic Wealth Management Framework requires that you, as Wealth Strategist, articulate a set of values that will be the foundation of future wealth management planning. You must educate yourself about your family finances, existing assets, spending patterns, expected rates of return, and current estate plans. And you must decide how to structure long-term family and financial goals so they become integrated and can positively reinforce one another. Without following this first principle, you cannot go further in the wealth management process.

Managing wealth effectively requires that you take charge of the process early. Doing so even before you have many financial assets like stocks, bonds, and excess cash is highly advisable. And, if you have had financial assets for some time, there's no time like the present to start. You probably sense the costs of not engaging earlier. There are insidious forces such as taxes, fees, and inflation that can accelerate wealth erosion and eat away at your net worth even in upward moving markets. For that reason, wealthy individuals and families need to exercise disciplined leadership of the wealth building process, particularly at certain critical points in time and around key decisions that can have implications for multiple generations.

After you and other members of your family define your values, you'll have a basic template in place with which to develop a long-term strategy for your wealth. The time horizon you set for this strategy may be a single lifetime, a single generation, or multiple generations. Making a few good decisions early on can have an impact for decades, building a culture of stewardship within your family. If you simply wait for your advisors to guide you, it's likely that you will get incomplete advice, or advice that tends to fragment rather than coalesce family goals. You may wind up with good products but without an integrated strategy or the resources to implement it over time.

Principle #2: Align Family and Business Interests Around Wealth-Building Goals and Strategies

Creating strong alignment of family members around common goals is critical to ensuring successful implementation of wealth management strategies and goals—especially when they are multigenerational. Aligning interests among family members helps define a family's identity. It helps to reinforce common purposes and creates economies of scale. If a family is united around wealth management goals, for example, it has collectively more power and focus in business, philanthropy, or even politics, than would individual family members alone.

To align family members around wealth management goals, the Wealth Strategist must establish a legitimate rationale for people to want to work together. It helps if he or she is also an adept facilitator who's able to mediate conflicts, drive consensus, and ensure regular review of wealth management goals and results. The Wealth Strategist will be a lightning rod for vigorous and lively family discourse at times because family members don't always see eye to eye. The Wealth Strategist must focus constructively on surfacing and resolving contentious issues and highlighting the universal benefits of cooperation, consensus, and unanimity at other times. It's not easy.

The Wealth Strategist must be able to frame family conversations around critical objectives. He or she must ask powerful questions, recognize the psychological and financial positions from which different family members come, and be adept at focusing wealth management discussions not only on a family's history and values but also on its vision for the future. Sometimes this latter challenge is the hardest task. To shift discussions from a focus on the past (nostalgia, history, memories, heritage, and values) to the opportunities and challenges presented by the future (social and business entrepreneurship, community involvement, legacy building, and a shift from professional success to "personal/life significance") can be daunting. But families that make this shift, whether they are wealthy or not, go on to be successful for multiple generations because the family and its individual members are able to reinvent themselves.

Alignment, of course, also means structuring professional relationships with advisors so that everyone benefits or suffers proportionately from the financial decisions you make together. Wealth managers and their firms are usually smart, aggressive, and ambitious, and have their own internal measures of success that may or may not include customer service and high rates of return for clients. As you go about selecting advisors and money managers, you'll want to make "alignment of interests" a key element of the hiring process and a key filter through which you negotiate and configure working relationships. The more closely advisor interests are aligned with yours, the more likely the relationship is to succeed long term.

Principle #3: Create a Culture of Accountability

While family dynamics are always intertwined in family wealth management activities, the wealth management process itself is fundamentally a business activity. To successfully implement your strategies, you need to put accountability systems and performance metrics in place. Doing so helps to reinforce objective business goals and performance expectations. It also helps drive implementation of wealth-creation strategies and provides a reliable benchmark by which to judge the performance of the Wealth Strategist and his or her team of wealth management advisors, including accountants, lawyers, investment managers, and others.

Individuals and families should measure financial performance on the basis of overall investment return. Most financial advisors are measured by the performance of individual products and by the profits they contribute to their firms. Because these metrics are very different and sometimes in opposition, the roles and responsibilities of the Wealth Strategist and key advisors need to be clearly defined. It's also important to establish a timeline for regular review of the Wealth Strategist's and advisors' job performance as well as the financial performance of investment portfolios, trusts, and other components of the family's financial portfolio. Achieving good accountability is tough to do. Even highly sophisticated family offices that manage hundreds of millions of dollars complain about the inadequacy of the available performance measurement systems.

Creating a "culture of accountability" within the family becomes increasingly important as the number of family members involved in the wealth building process grows. Using objective performance measures can help depersonalize criticism of individuals in cases where family members are not performing. In other words, a good system of accountability makes the message, "I love you, but you are not performing," more palatable for all parties involved.

Principle #4: Capitalize on Your Family's Combined Resources

In science, one of the basic laws of thermodynamics is the Law of Entropy. It states that there is a strong tendency in our universe to move toward randomness. I sometimes think that families are subject to entropy because, so often, they seem to fly apart, much as parts of our family did decades ago. But families can overcome this tendency toward randomness.

In families of any size, resources become distributed across the membership with the passage of time. The challenge is to figure out how—and how much—to reassemble these distributed resources so they function more effectively. The tools for reversing entropy are capitalizing on the family's financial scale and the combined strength of family members' personalities, experience, skills, affiliations, and networks, all within a meritocratic culture. In order to mobilize these weapons, empathic but disciplined family leadership is key.

Sidebar 2.1: Understanding Your Family's "Nepotistic Advantages"

A key issue the Wealth Strategist must be concerned with is the family's resources—both financial and human. Taken together, these things constitute a wealthy family's "nepotistic advantages" vis à vis other families and individuals. Nepotistic advantage can be measured by the degree to which a family is able to leverage the financial assets, business skills, social prominence, and

---

personal influence of individual members to help the family *collectively* achieve its wealth management goals.

As part of clarifying a family's nepotistic advantage, here are typical questions a Wealth Strategist might ask members of his/her family:

- Do some family members possess talents or business skills that have a direct bearing on the preservation and future growth of the family's assets?

- If so, how can we leverage the entrepreneurial or professional talents of family members to maintain or improve our family's competitive advantage in the marketplace?

- How should we think about leveraging the scale of our wealth to investment advantage? What will be required of us as individuals in assuring success here?

- What are the specific areas of business or financial knowledge that family members possess? Examples include:

  Law

  Investment Planning

  Venture Capital

  Entrepreneurship

  Finance

  Economics

  International Markets

  Business Planning

  Marketing

  Technology

  Real Estate

  Other(s)

continues

- How do we want to leverage family prominence and personal influence in matters of philanthropy? What are our goals in these areas?

Putting family talents, skills, and resources to good use is every bit as important to sound wealth management as shrewd investing, strategic thinking, and the clear enunciation of values. For one thing, it fosters a sense of responsibility, ownership, commitment, and accountability among family members insofar as the wealth management process is concerned. It also helps reinforce values such as civic responsibility, community involvement, personal empowerment, and stewardship (rather than ownership) of wealth. All of these values are tremendously important to the Lucas family.

As financial assets become distributed among family members, there's a tendency to manage them separately. Sometimes legal restrictions or personal relationships make other solutions impossible. But you should recognize that there are costs associated with the distributed model. Simply put, a pool of capital with $100 million in assets has more potential investment options open to it than does a person with $10 million or $1 million because:

- Premier money managers often exclude investors who can't commit at least $5 million to that manager's current fund.
- There are legally imposed minimums to gain access to most hedge funds and private equity pools that start at $1 million per entity and go up from there. [1]
- Mutual funds, annuities, and life insurance products that impose sales charges usually charge small investors a larger percentage of assets than large ones.
- Most investment managers discount their annual management fees for large clients.
- Fewer, larger pools of capital will get more attention from both the family and from financial services providers.

- Pooling arrangements may be used to help a family member launch a successful start-up business. (A qualified investment might be risky for one individual to finance, but in the context of a whole family's assets, it might be prudent diversification.[2])

The benefits of access, fees, and focus can translate to several percentage points of additional return per year!

Nepotism Can Be a Good Thing

Americans have an ambivalent attitude about nepotism. In most families, there is tension among family members about when to work together and when to be independent. We romanticize the "rags to riches" story of the independent entrepreneur as the epitome of success, yet everyone needs help to achieve their goals. Arrangements of cooperation and assistance are neither signs of weakness nor indicators of excess benevolence. They are part of any negotiated, long-term relationship, professional or personal. Helping each other is part of any healthy family dynamic.

With the right combination of leadership, resources, and structures, families can strengthen themselves through a focus on "nepotistic advantage." The start-up company I just mentioned can benefit from the wise counsel or networking contacts of the founder's family even though only one member might be involved day-to-day. A productive family network may enable the active family member to close a key business deal, secure better credit terms, or even gain competitive intelligence that provides a fledgling business enterprise with a unique marketplace advantage.

Some investment-oriented families develop sophisticated networks of advisors, industry analysts, venture capitalists, bankers, and other kinds of information brokers that give them a boost in the area of wealth management, either before or after the family sells a primary business. You can gain added investment insight, know-how, and discipline by getting plugged into the right flow of information and analysis. Doing these things enables highly motivated individuals to spot trends, identify talent, and grasp techniques to grow and transfer their wealth with limited risk. The larger the asset base and the longer the time horizon, the more valuable an effective network will be.

The Lucas family office has benefited from these nepotistic practices for years, and we are increasingly finding ways to do the same with other Stuart family groups. In our particular situation, family members are doing this voluntarily, which makes the process of working together particularly rewarding. We work together because we want to. It's fun, and we all see benefit in doing so.

Promoting nepotistic advantage only works well as a business technique if it is coupled with a meritocratic culture. Meritocracy wards off the sclerosis that often accompanies raw nepotism. It also helps to keep non-family employees motivated.

Nepotism coupled with meritocracy can help to reinforce positive family values and equates privilege with responsibility. In the Stuart family, public service and philanthropy are important shared values. We work across family groups and within family groups to manage foundation assets and support valued organizations that are doing good works. We work from aunt to nephew, cousin to cousin, brother to sister-in-law, husband to wife, partner to partner, and parents to children. It is like weaving a web of support within our family and the broader communities in which we live.

Principle #5: Delegate, Empower, and Respect Independence

Members of a healthy family group learn how to row together *and* row separately. I have already touched on some of the advantages of working together, but it is also important to respect the individual ambitions and values of each family member and, over generations, each family unit. The challenge for the Wealth Strategist and for other family members is to balance the two and reinforce the strengths of each.

Supporting family members to identify and pursue challenges that they can call their own, away from the family's immediate influence, encourages self-reliance and risk-taking. This is an excellent way to encourage the personal growth of young adults, who, if supported by their family in their personal interests or business pursuits, learn to embrace responsibility for their life choices and to develop a sturdy sense of self-confidence. Supporting the exploration of passions by one's children (whether as young people or adults) is more than sharing in successes. Importantly, support strategies should leave room for failure: It is through failure that a person develops resilience and often learns the most. Independence, resolve, periods of trial, and ultimate success within the youngest generation can be of tremendous benefit to the family later on, especially if these individuals take on responsible positions of leadership within the family.

It is also important for family members to understand and experience the benefits of working together to reinforce the connection with the family core. The person(s) who serves as Wealth Strategist must create and make the case for encouraging other family members to willingly work together. Ideally, especially in families that manage wealth across generations, all family members can be involved to one degree or another, including in-laws. Sometimes involvement means a day-to-day commitment to the family business. But this is clearly not the correct recipe for every family member. For many, the responsibility is to remain informed, respond promptly to administrative requirements, and to participate constructively in family discussions and meetings. As the arbiter and facilitator of family discussions about wealth, the Wealth Strategist must listen, broker, offer incentives, and encourage family members to collaborate on common goals.

The principle of "Delegate, Empower, and Respect Independence" applies not only to family members, but also to members of your wealth management advisory team. After you establish clear performance expectations for your team and an accountability system that aligns their interests with your own, it's important to step back and delegate many day-to-day functions of wealth management to these competent professionals. Doing so creates highly productive client-advisor relationships because your professional team is now empowered to act on your behalf!

Principle #6: Diversify but Focus

Diversification and focus combine the best of both worlds. With diversification you achieve risk mitigation, and with focus comes the laser intensity that most people need to succeed in life. Diversifying your investments is fundamental to prudent risk control. Why, you ask? Interestingly, wealth is created most quickly and most often through success in a single business. (If you can do it, birthright, marriage, and adoption are even quicker!) However, wealth is also most quickly lost by concentrating it on only one or a few investments. So, in order to protect your wealth, it's best to diversify it. Later in this book, I describe the Lucas family office's approach to wealth management, which includes diversification in a wide range of areas, including real estate, emerging markets, oil and gas, bonds/mortgages, private equity, and other alternative investments.

The principle of diversification applies in other ways as well. Most individuals have both taxable and tax-deferred (retirement and deferred compensation plans) investment portfolios. Some have life insurance savings plans that are tax exempt to the beneficiary. A few people also control corporations. Each of these entity types receives different tax treatment. Because tax rates don't all rise and fall at the same time, it makes sense to diversify the tax treatment of your assets.

You can also think about diversification in terms of your human resources strategy. Periodically ask yourself, "What would happen if key partners on my wealth management team left unexpectedly?" Would you be able to replace their talent and specific knowledge readily? If possible, have a backup plan in place for all your key people, including yourself.

Although investment and asset diversification are prudent, my experience is that my family and I reap the most benefits—success, personal satisfaction, competitive advantage, and in business, outsized financial returns—when we struggle over specific challenges with a great deal of focused energy.

Focus and energy are also integral to the pursuit of investment management, and they "enliven the pursuit of the game." In this country, and increasingly around the world, capital markets are more and more competitive. Achieving competitive advantage[3] in the deployment of capital—a critical component to growing diversified wealth—is very difficult to achieve. Without the focus to develop investment skills that are superior to most professionals, you won't add value to your investment portfolio.

Focus and experience also improve judgment. While you should make important decisions based on fact, there are also times when you have to go with your gut (when you are adept at wealth management) and go with your values because you rarely have all the facts you need at your disposal. To this end, Wealth Strategists should always be on the lookout for ways to stimulate and pursue their own focused interests and those of their children so that they learn to trust their gut when they need to rely on it.

Principle #7: Err on the Side of Simplicity When Possible

Inevitably, advisors will present you with many fancy options for doing great things with your money. Some of these are terrific ideas, but I recommend to most people that they stick to simple wealth management strategies and products. Even if you're wealthy, it might be best for you to peg most of your investments to financial indices or to other simple, low-cost, and proven wealth management products.

Before choosing complex solutions to wealth management issues, evaluate the simple ones. Simple solutions (such as indexing) may offer you most of the benefits of more complicated plans, a higher degree of certainty, easier implementation, and greater flexibility in the face of changing personal or financial circumstances. If you evaluate the simple solutions first, at the very least you can quantify the *relative* benefit and costs associated with more complex approaches.

In my professional opinion, you should view complex wealth management strategies with a skeptical eye. These schemes, often highly remunerative for advisors at the time of sale, can subject clients to long-term risks. For example, recommendations that solve short-term problems or show lots of promise may not pan out as expected months or years in the future. Execution or assumptions may be faulty. Or solutions may work well under certain conditions, but unravel if market conditions change unexpectedly. The more complex the wealth management strategy, the more variables you have to worry about managing, and the more difficult it is to reverse course. Don't buy into complex wealth management schemes because they seem sophisticated. Instead, question why an advisor is proposing a particular course of action and why it is sufficiently better than simpler alternatives. Because many complex strategies are quite remunerative to advisors, be sure you understand how such complex strategies will also be remunerative to you!

There are occasions when a simple approach to wealth management isn't appropriate. Some families actively manage complexity to gain competitive advantage, which I will discuss in greater depth in later chapters. In such cases, a "keep-it-simple" philosophy doesn't make sense. I suggest a corollary in these instances: Err on the side of *transparency*. Because wealth management discussions are likely to be both complex and lengthy, not every family member will need or want to be involved in every conversation. However, you'll still need to communicate regularly with everyone about what is happening and gather input and ideas from people as appropriate.

Above all, avoid secrecy! Keeping secrets from responsible family members, advisors, or the government has a propensity to backfire. I've made my biggest mistakes in the last ten years by trying to keep secrets from family members. I did so in an attempt to avoid disagreements that I thought might ensue among family members. Inevitably, the secret leaked, and the problems ended up being much bigger than if I had just faced up to them in the first place. Secrecy is just one more variable you need to manage, and it flies in the face of healthy family culture!

Principle #8: Develop Future Family Leaders with Strong Wealth Management Skills

As a prerequisite to successfully building wealth over multiple generations, the Wealth Strategist must develop future family leaders. Every family has a potential reservoir of talent, energy, contacts, and business experience that can be tapped into to lay the groundwork for the future.

For example, the Wealth Strategist can nurture individuals within the family who demonstrate specific interests and aptitudes, giving them progressively more responsible positions of informal leadership for wealth building activities. The Wealth Strategist should also expose such individuals to substantive family discussions of wealth-building goals and strategies, as well as to the corrosive power (and hollow rewards) of excessive spending. Doing so helps to instill values of accountability and financial stewardship in young family members, instead of attitudes of arrogance or entitlement. Involvement in such discussions, which can begin at a relatively early age, can provide a powerful learning ground for those members of a family who will eventually bear key responsibilities for ongoing wealth stewardship. It affords them the opportunity to see the wealth management process upfront, to become comfortable and conversant with wealth management issues, and to observe how family members and wealth management professionals should interact with one another to achieve specific goals.

It's my strong personal belief that no person in the next generation should come into the family business without spending at least a decade succeeding outside the family business, and preferably in a related field. When the time comes to return to the family business, that person will have so much more to offer than if he or she hadn't had the outside experience. Of course, this approach will lead the next generation to challenge and possibly threaten existing management practices and even the authority of the senior generation. But wouldn't you rather have the family benefit from innovative leadership through the inevitable generational transitions? Also, if you are trying to send a message that you want to encourage excellence in your business, shouldn't it start at home?

In my particular case, my father encouraged me to go into the investment business rather than the food business after I graduated from college in 1981. The nearly 15 years that I spent working away from the family business taught me so much that I was later able to usefully employ on the family's behalf, thanks in no small part to my father's willingness to let me do so. My brother, William, also spent a number of years in the aerospace industry and then at an investment bank before joining the family office. He used his experience to build our investment reporting, tax, legal, and communications capabilities. It was particularly fortuitous that he married Melissa, my sister-in-law, who had many years of investment experience at a third firm, looking at different kinds of investment opportunities before sharing the investment responsibilities for the Lucas family with me. As investors, we both relish the give and take of constructive debate. Now the three of us have to find the interest and talent in the next generation.

How to Use the Eight Principles in the Strategic Wealth Management Framework

The Wealth Strategist has the responsibility of working at the center of the Strategic Wealth Management Framework (see Figure 2.1) to make the Eight Principles of Strategic Wealth Management come to life: to clarify family values, identify and marshal family resources, set financial objectives, and bring the services of professional wealth advisors to bear on achieving these stated goals. To this end, he or she must play a number of complex roles simultaneously and well.

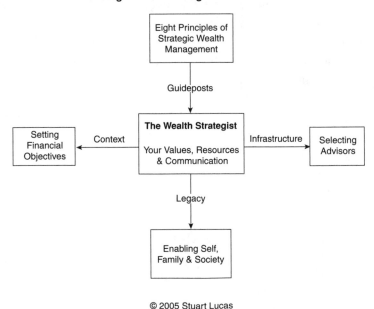

Strategic Wealth Management Framework©

© 2005 Stuart Lucas

Figure 2.1   The Wealth Strategist is at the center of the Strategic Wealth Management Framework©.

Articulate Specific Financial Goals

Along with facilitating discussion of values and family resources, the Wealth Strategist needs to lead discussions of financial objectives strategy with your family and your advisors. He or she needs to ask questions, such as the following:

- How much money can my spouse and I spend in retirement while still leaving a legacy for those we love?
- How can I help my child without spoiling him or her?
- How can my family establish shared wealth management goals across a spectrum of individual (and sometimes competing) interests?
- How can we develop a fair process for financing and monitoring the business or personal pursuits of various family members?
- How do I develop confidence that my advisors are working in my best interest, rather than the other way around? How do I prevent them from working at cross-purposes?

The Wealth Strategist is responsible for making sure that financial objectives are prudent. From a broad perspective, he or she must understand the context of investment markets, the Tax Code, and the financial services industry as components of prudent asset management. At a granular level, he or she should also be able to review suitable investment vehicles and understand the basic tradeoffs among investment risk, return potential, taxes, and spending. He or she should also look for ways to exploit the family's scale of wealth and nepotistic resources to realize greater opportunities.

Oversee Wealth Management Infrastructure and Administration

Aligning the interests of family members with the expertise of advisors requires an *integrated* approach to wealth management. To this end, one of the most critical initial tasks the Wealth Strategist must undertake is to hire a Financial Administrator, or FA. In business terms, the FA is the Chief Operating Officer, overseeing the day-to-day administration and execution of the wealth management vision that you, as

Wealth Strategist, establish. Typically, the Wealth Strategist and FA work together to manage other key advisors including lawyers, accountants, investment managers, bankers, and insurance agents. These experts may reside within a single firm or in multiple organizations. Chapter 6, "Picking Your Investment Strategy," and Chapter 7, "Making Your Most Important Hire," are devoted to a discussion of how to identify and manage your FA and other key advisors.

Mitigate Risk

Risk mitigation is another challenge of integration for the Wealth Strategist to manage. Without appropriate oversight, unintended connections and correlations can go unnoticed until they are triggered by some unexpected event that causes a wealth management strategy to collapse. For example, excessive debt, combined with lower than expected profitability and sudden illiquidity, can trigger a vicious spiral that ends in collapse. If you follow Principles 6 and 7, you are much less likely to suffer such a calamity, especially if you apply leverage conservatively if at all.

Risk mitigation also applies to operational aspects of wealth management, which need to be monitored carefully and consistently. For example, the Wealth Strategist should be constantly on the lookout for:

- Eroding personal relationships among family members
- Inadequate insurance
- Overconfidence in one's wealth management abilities
- Modestly (or badly) under-performing assets
- Overspending

All of these can contribute to missed financial goals, unexploited opportunities, and steady wealth erosion. Like the drip, drip, drip of a leaky faucet, these problems can be particularly insidious. No single problem might be significant alone, but multiple or chronic problems in one area can, over time, lead to steady and inexorable declines in asset performance and overall financial health.

Conclusion

The job of the Wealth Strategist is clearly an important one. Any challenges to the job are far outweighed by the benefits—personal, familial, financial, and societal—that can result from effective and sustained wealth management. The Eight Principles I've outlined in this chapter are important guideposts that the Wealth Strategist can use to stay focused. They can be used to weigh each substantive decision in working though the Strategic Wealth Management Framework, whether it involves a family matter, a financial matter, or an issue of integration. They keep the pressure on advisors and family members, and they encourage productivity—not only in the current generation, but potentially in future generations. Quickly, the Eight Principles will become second nature. In a complex and constantly changing environment, they are evaluative guideposts that will help maintain a steady course. They work for my family and me. I know they will also help you meet your wealth management goals and objectives.

Chapter 2: Issues to Discuss with Your Family

1. Are you the most likely person in your family to be the Wealth Strategist, or are there others, alone or with partners, who are better positioned to take on this role?

2. What are the critical *family* issues that you need to keep in mind as you develop strategic wealth management goals and plans? How will you address differences of opinion, especially when there are strongly held opposing views?

3. What are the critical *financial* issues that you need to keep in mind as you develop strategic wealth management plans and goals?

4. What are the most significant *integration* issues that you will face as you develop your strategic wealth management plans and goals?

5. Have you aligned family and professional interests around wealth building goals and strategies? If not yet, what remains to be done?

6. What accountability measures have you put in place to measure the performance of the Wealth Strategist and his/her professional advisors on a regular basis?

7. What options are open to you and your family when it comes to exploiting financial scale and nepotistic advantage? Be specific.

8. What are you doing to delegate, empower, and encourage independence among family members and advisors?

9. How effectively have you diversified your family's financial interests? What remains to be done? In what ways can you focus the family's resources to achieve your goals?

10. What are you doing to develop future family leaders who will act as future stewards of the family's wealth?

Endnotes

[1] The SEC has created two classes of private investor where financial products sold exclusively to these classes are subject to substantially less regulatory oversight than products that are sold to the general marketplace. The first qualification is "Accredited Investor"; the second is "Qualified Purchaser." Each qualification has various hurdles to meet, but if investors have at least $1 million in financial assets, they meet the first criteria and $5 million meets the second. Most hedge funds and private equity funds can only make their products available to investors who qualify for one or both classes.

[2] A common pooling structure for this purpose is a general partnership. We've used partnerships to invest in a single company and in diversified portfolios of assets. The number of partners has ranged from four to eleven but could be more or fewer.

[3] Popularized by Michael Porter, the author of *Competitive Strategy* (Free Press, 1980), this term was developed to help businesses think more clearly about how to compete effectively and to build on their structural, competitive strengths. I have found this concept to be equally valuable when applied to investing and the deployment of capital. Being smart and disciplined are necessary but insufficient characteristics of superior investors. The best are often aided by lower cost of capital, superior networks, proprietary know-how, or other lasting competitive advantages. Investors that actually have competitive advantages rarely draw attention to them, so they are tough to identify.

3

EVERYTHING BEGINS WITH VALUES

"I believe that every right implies a responsibility, every opportunity, an obligation; every possession a duty...I believe in the sacredness of a promise, that a man's word should be as good as his bond; that character—not wealth or power or position—is of supreme worth."

—John D. Rockefeller, Jr.
Excerpts from a quotation inscribed in a brass plaque in Rockefeller Center

Have you and your family taken time to discuss specific things you want to do with your lives and your wealth? Have you talked about how you want your values to shape your future and that of your loved ones? Are you even able to discuss issues of money with other members of your family?

For most of us, discussing money and wealth is difficult to do—especially in a family context. Yet having these discussions is critical for purposes of wealth management planning and choosing the appropriate investment approaches, vehicles, and timeframes to meet your needs. This chapter is intended to help you crystallize the values at the core of your Strategic Wealth Management Framework. Here are 10 questions to get started.

Question #1: What do you want to accomplish with your life and your wealth?

Some people want to use their wealth to build new companies or pursue philanthropic interests. Others want to circle the earth in a space capsule, explore the Patagonian wilderness, climb Tibetan peaks, or move to warmer climes and a simpler life. Still others (myself included) love investing and we enjoy the great challenge of trying to pass a financial legacy on to our children and grandchildren.

As I see it, there are seven major options available to you, none of which are mutually exclusive. You can do the following:

- Maximize your financial security in retirement
- Channel your assets into additional wealth-building pursuits
- Spend your money
- Create a special place to bring family together
- Become a collector

- Donate money and/or time to worthy causes
- Give money and companionship to people you care about

Maximize Your Financial Security in Retirement

Being able to retire knowing that you have enough assets to last your lifetime is a goal that often proves elusive, even for people with millions of dollars in assets. Poor investing and careless overspending can erode even significant wealth faster than you think. Also, a lot of retirees don't relish the idea of actively managing their wealth. They want to shed business and financial responsibilities, not take on new ones. So their assets suffer from chronic inattention and the insidious long-term effects of taxes, wealth management fees, and inflation.

If you fall into this camp, I have bad news and good news. The bad news is that you must take charge of managing your wealth if you want to live well throughout your lifetime and pass wealth on to future generations of your family. The good news is that there are ways to take charge of managing your financial security in retirement without taking on a huge burden.

Channel Your Assets into Additional Wealth Building Pursuits

Following a liquidity event, there are limitless options for allocating your capital in the business arena. You can do the following:

- Continue to grow your current business or career
- Start or buy a new business
- Invest in a friend's business
- Invest in the financial markets
- Explore funding a new and promising technology
- Fund proprietary research that might someday lead to a medical breakthrough
- Become an angel investor to an existing, cash-starved business that excites you or that makes a really good pitch for your financial backing

Maybe it's obvious, but I will very bluntly state two things about allocating your capital:

First, *don't*—I repeat, *don't* allocate all your capital to *one* venture. Always, *always* diversify your investments to mitigate the risk of large-scale market or business losses. If you want to invest in a business, fine. After you have done thorough due diligence on the venture, allocate 10% or 20% of your assets to that business and see if you can make it grow. If you plan to continue your career, think of it as a financial asset, too.

Second, diversify the rest of your assets across a range of investments that have little in common with your career or your speculative business venture. That way, if either the business venture or career path doesn't perform as expected, you still have a nest egg to fall back on. Better to get richer slowly than to lose it all quickly, especially if you are nearing retirement.

If you're unsure of what to do, do nothing for a while until you have time to study your situation and determine the best ways to allocate your wealth and your time. In my experience, poor capital allocation decisions are the most common and devastating destroyer of wealth—especially new wealth. I'll have much more to say about this in later chapters.

Spend Your Money

When you have a lot of money at your disposal (especially in the aftermath of a liquidity event, such as the sale of a business), the impulse to spend lavishly, and even recklessly, can be hard to resist—especially if you've worked hard for many years and deferred a lot of personal gratification to maintain your focus on wealth creation.

But every luxury has hidden costs. Spending $60,000 for a new sports car today at age 45 means foregoing $232,000 in retirement funds that would accrue by age 65 if that $60,000 were reallocated to investments returning 7% per annum.

Spending is a fun short-term fix, but I have seen far too many people regret big spending splurges only a few years later. It's hard to be a big spender and simultaneously preserve your wealth. Moreover, if you want to teach your children prudence with money, a free-spending family culture gets in the way and is hard to reverse.

Create a Special Place to Bring Family Together

Real estate can be a great investment, but for many people a vacation place is more than just a second home. It becomes an emotional homestead, a place where you go on special occasions—holidays and the summertime—to nurture family bonds, enjoy a sense of community with those you love, and create a retreat from the pressures, cares, and concerns of everyday life.

I fondly recall the summers my family and I used to spend on Cape Cod when I was a kid. There, in a home we still own beside the ocean, we always took time to swim, play games, talk, and simply hang out together. It is a place to which I still return today, along with my parents, my siblings, our spouses, and our children. In this house, and on the land that surrounds it, we find sanctuary from the hustle and bustle of our daily lives for a few brief weeks each year. And it is in this special house, with its well-worn memories, where we come each year to renew ourselves and rediscover a sense of tranquility and peace.

During our summer forays, my wife Susan and I try to slow down the pace of our lives a bit and eliminate (or reduce) some of the influences of the outside world. We have to walk up to the Inn to get the newspaper. Electronics (TV, computer, Internet) are only switched on during stormy days. But there are board games, books, jigsaw puzzles, and conversations aplenty, the kinds of activities that encourage human interaction. Just steps from our front porch there is a big yard, a pebbly beach, the cool sparkling ocean, nearby tennis courts, and miles of biking. In the evenings, dinner usually consists of fresh vegetables, fresh fish, and at least 10 to 15 people around the table representing three generations. Every evening, the sunset is more spectacular than the last.

Having a physical place to go to like this (a family summerhouse, cottage, cabin, or campground) can do wonders for *any* family—wealthy or not. It can be a place to spend time with loved ones, renew memories of the past, enjoy the company of others, and celebrate relationships.

Become a Collector

Many people of wealth enjoy amassing collections of things. There must be something deep in the psyche of human beings that drives their interest in collecting. In part, it is an intellectual challenge. Some people enjoy competing for rare objects because of the sport and social standing that goes with acquiring them.

The walls of the Art Institute of Chicago, the Metropolitan Museum in New York City, and the J. Paul Getty Museum, for example, are covered with fabulous impressionist art. When I've visited the museum's collections, it has occurred to me that this art, like so many other great public collections, was assembled by private individuals with the foresight to see and acquire what others would—only decades later—hold in high esteem.

Sometimes people are so in love with collecting that it becomes the singular focus of their lives. A few years ago, it was revealed that a couple named Herbert and Dorothy Vogel, who lived frugally in New York City on his salary as a postal clerk and hers as a librarian, had amassed a small fortune of contemporary art that they bought over a period of 35 years. They filled every nook of their small Manhattan apartment with this artwork, purchased directly from some 49 contemporary artists. In 1991, out of a sense of good citizenship and generosity of spirit, they gave their multi-million dollar collection to the National Gallery of Art in Washington, D.C., where it resides today.

Collecting art or other objects can serve many purposes. It should be fun, of course. But for some people, it can also be a way to build wealth. If you have an eye for quality, vision, and discipline, and if you conserve your collection appropriately, the investment you make can grow considerably in value over time. A few of the highest-quality private collections attract the attention of public institutions, and in those instances people may find it advantageous to bequeath their personal collections, either during their lifetimes or after they die. There are often significant tax incentives for doing so. The result is not only a generous gift to the public, but also the establishment of a family's legacy in its community.

Donate Money and/or Time to Worthy Causes

Most people who are fortunate enough to build or inherit significant wealth (and many people who aren't) regularly look for ways to "give back." By giving back, we strengthen the communities to which we are bound and make them more effective for the generations that follow us. Civic leadership is an important tradition in this country, more firmly established here than in many other parts of the world. It is one of the things that makes our country strong. The involvement of wealthy individuals and families in communities has many benefits to all parties. A devoted benefactor can serve as a catalyst to sustain the needy, promote urban renewal, or spark cultural revivals.

Effective philanthropy is often an excellent way to focus the energies and talents of wealthy individuals and their families on new goals following liquidity events. It can help reinforce family values, such as community service, education, kinship, and adherence to religious traditions. It can also provide meaningful leadership opportunities for individuals who, freed from the day-to-day obligations of making a living or running a business, can focus their time, talents, and energies on serving their communities or helping the less fortunate. Just look at what families such as the Fords, Rockefellers, Pritzkers, and Rothschilds have done with their millions over the last several generations. Their civic contributions include everything from the establishment of foundations and universities to patronage of the Arts and preservation efforts on behalf of the environment.

I'll have a lot more to say about how to incorporate philanthropy into your wealth management strategy in Chapter 10, "Making Philanthropy Part of Your Strategic Wealth Program."

Give Money and Companionship to People You Care About

Giving gifts of one's wealth and time to future generations can be enormously gratifying. Financial gifts (be they cash, property, valuable objects, or family heirlooms) mean so much more when they celebrate the special relationships between benefactors and beneficiaries that only come about through shared experience. The benefactor often gives a gift in recognition of experiences shared or milestones achieved by the parties involved.

In their wills, many people leave gifts to friends and family. These gifts often have enormous emotional meaning. They are a way of saying, "Remember me or our shared experiences." Or they may simply convey the message, "You're great. I love you, and thanks for being you." Many times, thoughtful bequests from parents to children or from friends to friends give the beneficiaries life options they might not otherwise have. Thus, such gifts can be truly empowering.

If you're contemplating the future of your wealth beyond your own death, I strongly encourage you to think about the distinctions between leaving wealth to the next generation and the more ambitious goal of managing wealth across generations. The latter implies a different set of values and operating assumptions. It involves an explicit attempt to empower future generations and imbue them with sensible values and an appropriate culture as you convey upon them the responsibility of managing wealth.

Bequeathing money across multiple generations goes far beyond normal wealth gifting. To do it well means doing it as part of a *contract* of values that you and your family establish in this generation and which future generations of your family will respect when it is their turn to be stewards of your wealth and the legacy of values and memory you've left behind. I'll have much more to say about these subjects in Chapter 9, "Promoting Entrepreneurial Stewardship," Chapter 10, "Making Philanthropy Part of Your Strategic Wealth Program," and Chapter 11, "Putting It All Together: Multigenerational Planning and Wealth Transfer."

Question #2: For how long do you want your values to shape your family's future?

All successful wealth management starts with the Wealth Strategist defining a wealth management time horizon—single-generation or multi-generation. From there, you must determine how you want your values to effect future generations of your family.

The values you emphasize during your lifetime will have an impact on your children and grandchildren even if your financial assets don't. Establishing a "family culture" based on the ideas of hard work, education, ambition, attentive parenting, and thrift can last for generations. Look at the legacies of some of our country's greatest leaders—Washington, Franklin, Jefferson, Lincoln, the Roosevelts (Theodore, Eleanor and Franklin), and Martin Luther King, Jr. The values that these individuals embody (and which they picked up from their own parents) affect millions of people in the United States to this day, while the modest wealth that they created had no long-term impact.

The values you articulate in this generation could have a similar impact on future generations of your own family—whether you pass on a great deal of wealth to future generations or not. At the other extreme, a culture of conspicuous consumption will last only as long as the money does. This is why, throughout this book, you'll see me emphasize the importance of using values and family culture to prioritize your financial goals and to shape your choice of wealth management strategies.

Question #3: When it comes to investing, would you rather "eat well" or "sleep well"?

When I ask people this question, what I'm *really* asking is how much risk are they willing to take with their wealth and how much are they willing to sacrifice to ensure that their wealth continues to grow.

A person's financial risk tolerance—as measured by the ability to cope emotionally with the volatility of their financial worth—is something that often becomes apparent only after a liquidity event, and then with the fullness of time. After a liquidity event, assets that were frozen for years in illiquid stock or controlled by someone else suddenly are converted to cash or liquid securities and become the wealth owner's responsibility. Those assets also become subject to the daily vicissitudes of the financial markets, going up and down with the markets.

For the newly wealthy person, the combination of volatility, liquidity, and changing net worth can create a rollercoaster of emotional ups and downs. A person can be euphoric one day and depressed the next, but in my experience it's the relentless assault of price *trends*, both upward and downward, that can grab hold of the psyches of even seasoned investors. I've observed amateurs and professionals alike who love risk in a bull market and hate it in a bear market.

All of this makes the challenge of finding investments with limited risk and strong potential much tougher and explains, in part, why most private investors get into markets near their tops and get out near their bottoms.

Most truly skilled investors have the opposite reaction to marketplace volatility. They know that a bear market creates the opportunity to make money. Conversely, a bull market, while desirable, doesn't last forever, so there comes a time to take profits and move on.

If you feel unnerved by seeing your newly liquid net worth bounce up and down in value, how can you remedy this situation? As a wealth advisor, I tell my clients that there are really two potential ways for them to handle market volatility:

> "You can sleep well at night by paring back your risk so that the volatility of your overall investment portfolio is reduced," I tell them, "Or, you can opt for a strategy that enables you to 'eat well,' embrace investment risk, and potentially put more 'food on your table'"—in other words, increase your net worth.

Applying the "eat well/sleep well" analogy to multigenerational wealth management becomes a little more complex. To successfully manage and grow your wealth across generations, it's not enough to opt for either the "eat well" or "sleep well" strategy. You need to follow a third path—one that combines spending restraint with aggressive investment and a willingness to live below your means. These are values that you must embrace consistently and convey to future generations of your family.

Question #4: Are there talents within your family that you can tap to further expand your family's productivity and wealth?

Capitalizing on what you're good at is always a good start for getting what you want. For that reason, when setting a wealth management strategy, consider how you and other members of your family can leverage your contacts, experience, business skills, and political and community influence not just to launch new business ventures or make new investments, but also to make your mark in other areas of society as well—for example, in politics, civic life, education, sports, entertainment, or the arts. Money is a commodity, but talent is a specialized resource!

The decision to cultivate talent within your family starts as a question of values; specifically, the values you stress and impart to your children and grandchildren. In my own family, my wife and I strive to build a culture of meritocracy. We try to stress the importance of accountability, achievement, excellence, diligence, and ambition. We believe our children need to embrace such values if they are to be successful in their own right.

Establishing meritocratic values within your family—emphasizing values of *accountability, achievement, excellence* and *ambition* to your children, in whatever they do—helps to perpetuate a family culture that seeks and nurtures competitive advantage. It is an excellent way to ensure that the next generation of wealth owners in your family grows up with a strong sense of civic responsibility and wealth stewardship, not of arrogance or entitlement. (There's much more about this in Chapter 9.)

This does not mean, of course, that everyone in a wealthy family needs or should try to be in the business of wealth creation.

I once asked one of Jacob Rothschild's advisors to tell me the secret behind the Rothschild family's success in private banking for over two centuries. To my surprise, he didn't talk about competitive advantage in banking or about the fact that Nathan Rothschild made a fortune on the London Stock Exchange in 1815 in the aftermath of England's stunning victory in the Battle of Waterloo. Instead, he told me that one of the bedrock values of the Rothschild family has always been that each family member is expected and encouraged to be the best they can be in whatever walk of life they choose—be it banking, arts and culture, education, wine making, or anything else. It just so happens that since Mayer Amschel Rothschild began the Rothschild dynasty in the late 18th century, there has been at least one terrific banker in every generation. Today, Mayer Rothschild's descendents remain overseers of several leading European private banks. In addition, they are accomplished players in numerous other fields.

There are many ways you may be able to leverage your family's competitive advantage to expand your wealth or to create new professional opportunities for yourself. For example, if your family still controls a business, that business has competitive advantages you can leverage to create new business enterprises, "spin off" ventures, or new lines of business. You might also be able to use your professional success (and social profile) in one business arena to launch an entirely new business venture or career in some other area. Merv Griffin, for example, leveraged his success as an entertainer into becoming a real estate mogul. If business is not your focus, your professional stature and business contacts can potentially position you to accomplish goals in other spheres of activity—perhaps as a political leader, community activist, or philanthropist.

Also, your spouse, siblings, children, or grandchildren may have great talents for making money, organizing people, playing music, promoting worthwhile causes, or managing businesses. Consider the talents that reside within your family and how you might want to nurture these talents for public service, to build future wealth, to improve the quality of life in your community, or to ensure your family's legacy in other ways.

As part of executing our family's wealth management strategy, for example, our investment office has found unique ways to capitalize on the varied strengths of my father, brother, sister-in-law, and me. Our office is unusual in that so many family members are involved in its operations on a day-to-day basis. This, I believe, gives us a key competitive advantage. All four of us have different personalities, but through common vision, hard work, compromise, and experience, we have built competitive advantage over a period of 20-plus years. Thanks to my brother, William, we're fortunate to have built superb management reporting and communications systems. My father, sister-in-law, and I bring other crucial skills to the mix. For example, we focus a lot of time on building and upgrading our networks with professional advisors, honing our skills in asset allocation, sharpening our market research and due diligence capabilities, and improving our system of family communication and accountability. Meanwhile, we carefully outsource most trusteeship, legal, tax, accounting, and stock picking responsibilities. Other people are simply better at these skills than we are, and we are grateful to our advisors for their skills and loyalty to us.

Question #5: Are you committed to creating a culture of accountability in your family and with your wealth advisors?

Here are five common reasons I find people don't exhibit much accountability with wealth management activities:

1. *Some people believe that because they are rich they don't have to be constrained by a budget.* For them, part of the fun of being wealthy is the freedom to be opportunistic, spontaneous, and even frivolous. Tensions can arise when a "free spending" person is asked to be accountable to a spouse, a parent, or other family members. When this happens, often the best way forward is to position a strong and diplomatic financial advisor as an impartial and prudent mediator (or disciplinarian) among the parties.

2. *Some people have good intentions but don't have the time or infrastructure to keep good personal financial records.* Simple wealth management strategies equate with simple record keeping responsibilities. Alternatively, complex strategies can fill up many storage boxes with paper pretty quickly!

3. *Many people don't know how to evaluate the performance of wealth advisors.* While most advisors you hire will provide performance data on the managers of your individual investments, many don't provide performance information on your total

portfolio, especially if your portfolio includes alternative investments like real estate and private equity. In addition, most advisors measure performance in percentage terms. While this unit of measure is important, it can be misleading because it doesn't take into account cash flows or taxes. I recommend keeping track of long-term performance not only in percentages but also in dollars, just as you see in the annual reports of public companies.

4. *People get intimidated by advisors.* Understanding the performance of a wealth advisor can be a daunting task—one that you may not feel competent to do. The wealth industry is filled with numbers and jargon that easily overwhelm even the most attentive client. It's no wonder that clients often defer to a "knowledgeable" wealth advisor for simple definitions, clear explanations, and black-and-white recommendations about investments—whether the answers are complete or not!

5. *There is no standard way to objectively measure the effectiveness of wealth advisors' decisions or recommendations, especially net of taxes.*[1] Institutional investors regularly compare their aggregate performance with one another. Medium-sized pension plans can easily learn how they rank compared to similar institutions. Large endowments all compare themselves against Harvard and Yale as well as the averages. No such comparisons are produced for private investors. You can't meaningfully compare your performance against other wealthy investors. Furthermore, very few wealth management firms produce composite performance data for their private client portfolios, so you can't measure one advisor's value added relative to another. There is a great deal of data on investment managers, but most advisors recommend you use a number of them to gain diversification. Advisors will show you lots of good-looking numbers from each manager, but when you ask them to show you the long-term aggregate performance of their actual private clients' portfolios against an appropriate unmanaged benchmark (the truest measure of an advisor's financial advice), they don't exist.

To counter all this, you will very likely need to establish performance standards by which you, other members of your family, and your wealth advisors are judged. The more complicated the wealth management strategy you apply, the more difficult it is to hold people accountable and the greater the risk that your strategy can go awry without your knowledge.

Accountability systems also serve to reinforce key family wealth management goals and priorities. They can serve as a kind of "scorecard" for assessing the performance of all parties involved in the wealth management process, including the Wealth Strategist. Accountability systems should be comprised of specific metrics developed by both you and your advisors and should be in alignment with stated investment goals and wealth management strategies.

Having a good system of accountability in place creates peace of mind when things are going well for you, early warning signs if things are not, and information that helps identify the source of problems when things are going badly. When the system of accountability gives you important feedback, it is also critical to know when, and under what circumstances, to take action—and what action to take. These are the judgments that come with skill and experience.

As generations multiply and an ever-widening circle of people owns family assets, it becomes increasingly difficult either to gain consensus on or mandate the discipline of good accountability. Under these circumstances, it is advantageous to have a culture of management and stewardship already established. A good system of accountability fosters open communication and education, especially in a multigenerational context. Where assets are owned jointly by numerous adult family members (like a family business), learning how to constructively communicate about performance and how to educate the next generation of its importance is critical to long-term success.

Question # 6: Are you bullish or bearish on the global economy, business, and investing?

Today, notwithstanding the threat of global terrorism, most U.S. investment firms are bullish on America and on the world's future economic and political health. Their analyses suggest that political instability, world war, deflation or runaway inflation, economically effective terrorism, and economic isolationism are, at most, modest threats. Further, they observe that the United States is the lone superpower and our country has not experienced a conventional war on U.S. soil since the Civil War. Democracy is taking hold in more and more countries, and with democracy comes economic vitality and a greater desire for peace. Finally, they argue, the world today is so interconnected that a massive breakdown in America's way of life is highly unlikely.

I agree with all of the foregoing—with a few caveats. First, throughout history, strong, powerful, and seemingly stable cultures have fallen victim to unseen political, economic, or military threats. It happened to the Roman Empire, the Ottoman Empire, the British Empire, and the Soviet Union.

Second, if major economies or political systems were to begin to unravel in fundamental ways, it's unlikely that your financial advisors would see the threats soon enough to avoid a large drop in your asset values. Political coups, market corrections, natural disasters, and strategic inflection points in the worlds of business, commerce, and technology are impossible to consistently forecast accurately.

Third, it's best to acknowledge that you don't know what the future will bring and to be skeptical of those who profess to know it. That's what great investors like Warren Buffett, John Neff, Peter Lynch, Howard Marks, and Seth Klarman do. Why shouldn't you? Instead, seek opportunity, hedge your bets, and diversify your assets. The strategies for doing so are outlined in the chapters ahead.

Fourth, seek to understand how your portfolio could be affected by major economic downturns, political developments, technological advances, or the emergence of new economic players or factors in the global economy. And while you ponder the nature of change in today's world, recognize that change can both be continuous (incremental) as well as *discontinuous* in nature. Examples of discontinuous events include: the Asian financial crisis of 1998, 9/11, and the downgrading of GM bonds to junk status in 2005.

The message here is to avoid extreme market optimism or pessimism. Long-term wealth management is in part a game of survival and opportunism at points of maximum stress and maximum exuberance. I try to keep a global perspective that helps me to identify inflection points, keep them in perspective, see opportunity when things look bleak, and see risk where others see only opportunity.

Question #7: To what extent are your assets under threat?

Your assets can be threatened by a variety of people and events: a divorce, a house fire, a disgruntled trust beneficiary, employees, neighbors, or the driver of an automobile with whom you happen to collide. Others who may try to take your assets include lenders, the IRS, or anyone with whom you have a contract, written or implied. And, of course, your assets can be threatened by large-scale political or economic events.

There are two basic methods for protecting your assets—acquiring insurance and safeguarding your assets from creditors. Both of these methods require different approaches after people become wealthy.

With regard to insurance, typically people carry health, property, casualty, and life insurance with the intent of helping them to maintain stable cash flow through life's disruptions and their aftermath. They insure against even small losses, like minor medical bills and fender benders that have a high probability of occurring. In fact, insurance is almost a misnomer. It's more like a subscription service. People who buy insurance are really just prepaying for things (plus a commission) that are going to happen anyway for the benefit of smoothing their ongoing cash flow.

In contrast, wealthy people should be less concerned about protecting monthly cash flow and more concerned about protecting the bigger picture—their assets. This means that if you become wealthy, you need to reorient your perspective on what insurance is meant to do. Start by opting for higher amounts on your deductibles wherever possible because you'll save lots of money, and you can afford to self-insure for small mishaps. More important, the money you save by raising your deductibles can be used instead to acquire insurance that protects you against infrequent, but catastrophic, loss. To supplement your basic insurance, invest in an umbrella liability policy to cover major losses that your basic insurance doesn't cover. Because claims against these policies are low among the total population, the cost is low and the true insurance value is great.

With regard to protecting assets from creditors, you should immediately investigate these commonly practiced options to see if any can help you:

- The creation of a limited liability company, a limited liability partnership, or a trust—all of which are common ways to limit personal liability.
- The signing of a pre-nuptial agreement (especially in the case of a second marriage) that spells out the disposition of assets in case of divorce. It's not a romantic thing to do, but it's very practical.
- Ways to protect your home. In some states, for example, you can own your home as "tenants by the entirety," which has the effect of helping to protect your home from creditors. If one owner is successfully sued, the house is protected because the courts consider the other owner to own the whole house for the purposes of establishing ability to pay a claim.

The cost of establishing and maintaining these asset protection vehicles varies widely. The ones I've mentioned can have little set up and administrative cost. Basic trusts and limited liability corporations, for example, only cost a few thousand dollars to set up. You may also want to investigate more aggressive options for protecting your assets, though I personally do not advocate such moves, given their legally tenuous status in some cases and the dislocations they can cause. These more tenuous moves include:

- Moving to another state, such as Florida, to gain an advantageous position in bankruptcy, or Nevada to eliminate state income tax.
- Setting up blind offshore trusts in such famous havens as the Cayman Islands, Bermuda, or the Bahamas.

- Becoming a tax exile and moving to another country to escape revenue agents.

Obviously, if you're contemplating any of these moves—the more common or the more exotic—get good, practical legal advice. You will incur some costs for periodic reviews of your asset protection plans, and though you may never change anything as a result of these reviews, your piece of mind will be well worth the cost for periodic reassessment of these plans by a lawyer.

Act now, in cases where you're contemplating taking extraordinary measures to protect your assets—perhaps because of a high-risk lifestyle or because you want to keep assets shielded from a potential legal dispute. Hastily arranged asset protection plans amidst pending legal proceedings will afford you little protection against adverse legal rulings. U.S. courts generally have the authority to undo protections you may have devised in anticipation of loss.

Question #8: How should my family communicate about its wealth?

I am a strong believer in early, honest, respectful, and informed communication among all family members about their wealth and how it is managed. This is something that should include (in age-appropriate ways) even the youngest members of a family. Did you know that there are comic books that are completely focused on money and wealth management issues, published by the Federal Reserve? Such comic books can be a great introduction for children into the world of wealth management without burdening them with the details of your own family's finances. That can come later.

As your family's Wealth Strategist, you should conduct your communications with family members with two objectives in mind. First, it's important within the wealth management process to nurture a spirit of kinship among family members by identifying and reinforcing common family interests and wealth management objectives. This is something that you can do on a regular basis through meetings, annual family reunions, and other means. Make the wealth management and investment execution process transparent to all family members who are likely to benefit from it. Allow everyone in that group who wants a voice in wealth management decision-making to be heard. In the long run, the combination of communication and listening does strengthen family solidarity around the pursuit of collective wealth management goals.

At the same time, as Wealth Strategist, it's important to celebrate the merits and individuality of each family member; and by so doing, look for ways to support individuals in their various personal and professional pursuits. You will have to devise parameters and expectations here—of how wealth is to be used, how and when one will have access to it, what responsibilities young owners of wealth will have (if any) in being given access to family assets, and so forth.

To this end, there is a fine line between empowerment and entitlement. The privileges of wealth come with responsibilities, so you will need to decide how to hold the next generation of family members responsible, not only for ensuring the family's memory and legacy, but also for managing the gift of wealth that is given personally to them. As Wealth Strategist, you are in a unique position to convey family values to succeeding generations of your family. In so doing, you're poised to shape the lives and characters of family members, not just in your lifetime, but in some cases, for multiple generations.

Question #9: Do you plan to build family leadership to grow your wealth over multiple generations?

This is another one of those topics that isn't considered "polite conversation" but that must take place in order to assure that wealth is transferred successfully to subsequent generations.

Families must recognize that the family members most likely to preserve or grow the family's wealth are the same individuals with the most options to build lucrative business careers outside the family. It's a healthy sign when it takes a competitive process to entice these individuals to commit themselves to the family. Managing the family's wealth can provide many professional challenges for the appropriate person or persons. The selection of the right family member(s) to be Wealth Strategist, for example, can strengthen family identity and energize the family to meet its wealth management goals.[2]

It is uncomfortable to talk about who in the family has the greatest potential and ability to preserve and grow its wealth. However, you must address this matter head on. To make this process as objective as possible, here are questions to ask within the family to assess the viability of your in-house wealth management talent, with the understanding that going outside of the family to fulfill this role is also viable:

> Who in the family has demonstrated a strong interest/competency in allocating capital and has a track record of doing so successfully?

> Who in the family is clearly in sync with the family culture and value system and is generally sensitive and able to hear the voices of others in family discussions?

> Who in the family displays the skills and temperament to be a good moderator and mediator of conflicts, if and when they arise?

> Who is willing to hold themselves accountable?

> Who in the family displays strong business instincts and acumen and has options to build a lucrative business career away from the family?

> Are there family members who exhibit entrepreneurial traits or are superb at executing the vision of others?

> Who is healthy enough to manage the physical and emotional rigors of managing the family's wealth?

Finding competent and interested family members to step up is very important in a multigenerational context. That's because professional advisors and "hired leadership" in family offices simply don't have the same stature as wealth owners. If there is family leadership, these same advisors will be much more productive in their roles.

I'm confident that, in most cases, the selection of appropriate individuals to play hands-on roles in a family's wealth management activities will emerge by family consensus, based on answering the questions I've cited here.

That said, there might be cases when you need to go outside the family for qualified leadership, although this isn't an ideal option. Choosing a wealthy family's future leaders can be designated as a responsibility of the family offices or company's Board of Directors. If you don't have a board that includes non-family members, you may want to hire the services of a leadership consultant or even an executive search firm to evaluate the position and prospective candidates.

Remember, leadership can come from within the family or from outside. By explicitly describing the required qualifications and objectively matching them with the candidate, it gives the new leader, whether a family member or not, added credibility to withstand friction within the family and to build a stable power base.

Question #10: How important is it to you to maximize tax efficiency? Will it change in future generations?

Tax efficiency is a major variable in the strategic wealth management process because it affects both the way you manage your financial assets and how you distribute them in your estate plan. For most people, taxes are either the largest or second largest controllable drain on wealth.

In an effort to maximize tax efficiency, some people manage their taxes as aggressively as they manage their investments. They work closely with lawyers and accountants to design sophisticated strategies to save every possible penny of taxes, and they are willing to be confrontational with the IRS if they are challenged. They also are prepared to manage complex administrative tasks to bolster the validity of their tax position. Some people change their city, state, even country of residency in order to reduce taxes. While in some cases this is easy enough to do, in other instances it can have a negative effect on children and family life that ultimately undercuts the wisdom of the decision.

For years, accounting and legal firms have promoted elaborate legal structures involving any number of off-shore trusts, derivative securities, complex partnerships, or life insurance to help solve client tax problems. Some schemes convert short-term gains to long-term gains.

In other cases, the value proposition has been to avoid paying taxes altogether. Sometimes people want to raise the value of an asset to give it away and take a tax deduction. Other times they want to lower an asset's value for estate or gift tax purposes. These structures can be enormously complex to set up and administer, and they can be expensive. But, they can sometimes save even more in tax payments *if they are legal*.

Many of these schemes are under attack by the IRS. With the deficits our government is piling up, the IRS is aggressively hunting for revenue raisers. When they see abusive shelters being promoted, and they have the means to turn most of them up, they evaluate the revenue-producing potential from challenging them. In the last year or two, they have moved aggressively against many promoters, including even well-reputed accounting and legal firms, as well as their clients. Because these schemes are so profitable to their promoters, it is tempting to skate very close to, and sometimes over, the legal line.

Some people take a simpler approach to tax efficiency. They like to buy and hold assets for a long time. People who manage in this way may be more interested in other things, like growing value within a company, pursuing their career, or fishing. Sometimes tax efficiency is a fortunate byproduct of having interests in other areas. In other cases, it is a conscious decision.

Many people actually feel quite proud to be able to pay their taxes. They see it as a sign of success and an opportunity to give back to their country in appreciation for that success. Where do your interests lie?

The extent to which tax efficiency is important to you can have broad implications when you are planning and executing tax strategies across generations. It can also influence family dynamics among siblings, in-laws, or children. In many wealthy families, for example, a small group of people makes decisions that affect the entire family. In this environment, the style of investing, the foresightedness of estate planning, or the decision to be adversarial in the payment of taxes can have repercussions for the whole family. On the last point in particular, the tone set by the family leaders may cause anxiety and disruption for family members who don't cope well with this approach. For these reasons, it's important that the Wealth Strategist and his or her fellow wealth managers within the family consider issues of taxes in their full family context. In many families, this causes later generations to be more conservative than the wealth creator, and rightly so.

Choosing how efficiently to manage your taxes is a personal issue. Each person must make this decision for themselves. However, if you are the Wealth Strategist, I strongly encourage you to make decisions about taxes based not only on their financial impact but also on how your tax strategy can reinforce other aspects of your Strategic Wealth Management Framework©. Remember also that there are usually simple alternatives to complex strategies that can result in modestly higher tax payments but lower costs, less stress, and greater flexibility. I have more to say about taxes and how to make them your ally in the wealth management process. See Chapter 8, "Taxes Can Be Your Ally!" for details.

Pulling the 10 Questions Together: Translating Your Values into Financial Goals

After reviewing the 10 questions in this chapter, let's pull this exploration of your values all together so that you can begin to convert them into financial goals.

It's important that your financial goals speak to and reinforce your values. You are more likely to achieve your goals—and more importantly, to gain true satisfaction—if your financial goals and values are aligned. Look at Figure 3.1 on the next page. At the top of the table, a continuum of financial goals from distribution-oriented to growth-oriented is represented by a two-headed arrow. Below "Financial Goal" is a series of issues that I discussed in this chapter and a range of possible responses, again represented by the arrows. All the issues are values-based, but some, like asset threats and tax efficiency, have an operational tone.

Go through the table, and mark where your values lie for each issue. There are no right or wrong answers here. By selecting answers to the ten questions that express your values, you can identify the financial goal that is right for you.

When you are finished, if your marks are weighted to the left, your values are more likely to align with distribution-oriented financial goals. If they are weighted to the right, your values are more likely to align with growth-oriented financial goals. This analysis is not scientific. It is meant to be an indicator, not an absolute. As you move through subsequent chapters and become more familiar with the wealth management process, you may want to revisit where you belong on this chart and why.

If you see yourself in the "Distribution-Oriented" category, it means that your financial goal is to slowly extract capital to pay for your retirement without concern for leaving your wealth to subsequent generations.

If you see yourself in the "Growth-Oriented" category, it means your goal is to enjoy the fruits of your wealth while maintaining or growing its value for future generations.

Translating Values Into Financial Goals

	Distribution-Oriented	Growth-Oriented
Financial Goal		
What You Want to Do With Your Wealth	Support for Spending	Retain and Build
Time Frame for Decisions/Control	Your Life	Multigenerational
Tolerance for Managerial Complexity	Low	High
Anxiety Tolerance	Sleep Well	Eat Well
Global View	Pessimistic	Optimistic
Asset Threats	Low	High
Competitive Advantage for Making Money	Low	High
Culture of Accountability	Low	High
Quality of Family Communication and Trust	Low	High
Leadership Development Potential	Low	High
Tax Efficiency	Low	High

Figure 3.1 For each issue listed below the line under "Financial Goal," mark where in the continuum your values lie. Are your values generally consistent with your financial goal?

As you can see from Figure 3.1, each of us approaches the management of wealth with different expectations and goals. People who want to avoid managerial complexity, and who want to spend more, will land firmly in the "Distribution-Oriented" category. Those with a long view, a culture of thrift, good family communication, a bigger appetite for risk, and who are willing to institute an aggressive accountability program are clearly in the "Growth-Oriented" category.

Many people will also be somewhere in the middle. In the next chapter, I present some detailed options under each of these two broad categories. Before finishing the book, you will be able to find the set of financial goals that correspond with your own particular values and circumstances.

Conclusion

In this chapter, I've talked about the importance of identifying what you want to do with your wealth. Building on the previous chapters, I've emphasized how important the Wealth Strategist's role is in providing leadership and searching for consensus in the expression of important family values and embracing the Eight Principles—whether over a single lifetime or multiple generations. A sound base of shared values, reinforced through trusting relationships, is the foundation on which successful financial and family strategies are built. Unfortunately, good values are not the only ones that can have lasting effect. Negative values, or intractable differences of opinion, can have an equally profound influence on families, and they can quickly lead to dysfunction and erosion of wealth. There are numerous public examples and more private ones that powerfully reinforce the point.

In the wake of a liquidity event, or at other turning points, deciding what you want to do with your wealth and building the financial and business skills to manage it will take time. Moreover, addressing the questions I've outlined in this chapter takes research, introspection, honesty on your family's part, and a willingness to have "difficult conversations" in some cases (as my own family has done). If these challenges seem daunting, consider hiring a professional facilitator to help you. We have done so, and the process can be quite illuminating. A facilitator will moderate in-depth discussions about these issues and help you and your family members articulate your views more clearly. The facilitator can also double as a scribe to record the conversations and decisions your family makes, helping everyone to be better listeners. The facilitator you hire does not necessarily need a financial background, though familiarity with business issues is helpful. However, avoid choosing someone from the financial services industry or who has other vested interests in your family's decisions. If you are worried about confidentiality, you should ask the facilitator to sign a non-disclosure agreement.

I am biased toward a multigenerational approach to wealth management. But it is not the right approach for everyone. First, not everyone has children. And not everyone has a strong enough family identity and heritage to support a multigenerational approach to wealth management planning. You may not feel inclined to give your children more than a good childhood, a good education, and the security of parental love. In a strong, stable society like ours, many people believe that it is not in the interests of their children or society to transfer family wealth from one generation to the next.

I hope you'll take away from this chapter a hint of the issues that come into play whether you decide to manage your wealth for a single lifetime or for multiple generations. As you clarify your values and family culture, they will inform how you build out your Strategic Wealth Management Framework and will factor in discussions with your wealth advisors. You'll be able to inquire more astutely into the motives and skills of prospective advisors and sense more easily whether they will be useful additions to your wealth management team.

Let's go on now to Chapter 4, "Defining Your Financial Objectives," which explores more fully how you can translate your values into financial terms that your wealth advisors can understand, act on, and be held accountable for.

Endnotes

1 Mutual funds must now provide standardized after-tax performance reports. Although these statements make it easier to compare one fund against another, the taxes payable by individuals will vary considerably from the standard information provided. In addition, no other managers are required to provide the calculation, and most do not. Aggregating after-tax performance of multiple managers is beyond the scope of most performance measurement systems in the United States today.

2 A family may be tempted to over-inflate the responsibilities and compensation of family members who are not or cannot pull their own weight within a family business. Resist the temptation to do this, because if you allow it, you'll find that the pursuit of your family's wealth management goals will suffer. So too will relationships among family members, and between family and able-bodied non-family employees. It is particularly demotivating to non-family employees, who are generally pretty good at assessing family members' performance. Ultimately, the "free rider" syndrome is counterproductive for all parties involved, so avoid it if possible.

4

DEFINING YOUR FINANCIAL OBJECTIVES

"It requires a great deal of boldness and a great deal of caution to make a great fortune."

—*Nathan Mayer Rothschild*

After you articulate the values you want to use as the basis for managing your wealth, the next task is to translate those values into financial objectives. Based on the values assessment you completed in the last chapter, your financial objectives will fall into one of two broad categories; either you will want to pursue a "distribution-driven" path to wealth management, or you will want to pursue a "growth-driven" path to wealth preservation and management.

Let's explore what's involved in following either of these paths so that you can decide which is better for you. Your lifestyle goals, spending habits, and tolerance for risk all play into which path is the right one for you.

The "Distribution-Driven" Category of Financial Management

If you opt to build a wealth management strategy based on distribution-driven financial goals...

- Your time horizon is typically 20 years or less.
- You can enjoy a relatively high level of spending because passing significant wealth to children or grandchildren, if there are any, isn't a primary goal.
- You require a lower rate of return on assets because your assets only have to last your lifetime.
- Investment, tax, and estate planning are relatively simple, and you prefer it that way.
- Philanthropic contributions are most likely current gifts directed to existing charities and non-profit causes, not endowment assets to build long-lived private or family foundations.

If you choose the "distribution-driven" category of wealth management planning, you have two sets of financial objectives from which to choose.

You can choose to *maintain your purchasing power* or to *maintain a stable income.*

Option 1: Maintain Your Purchasing Power
Guidelines:

Target after-tax spending rates:	4.0% to 5.1% of financial assets in year one, but the dollars spent increase with inflation thereafter, and the spending rate increases each year.
Maximum after-tax spending rate:	15% of financial assets per year
Required investment returns:	4.5% to 6.0% per year
Competitive advantage:	Low
Risk tolerance:	Sleep well, for about 15 years
Tax efficiency:	Low to medium

Maintaining your purchasing power is a good objective to embrace if your principal priority is to preserve a high standard of living over the next 20 years or less. The investment strategy is conservative and can be very simple to execute.

Over time, inflation increases the prices of goods and services you buy. The "Maintain Your Purchasing Power" goal makes it the top priority to keep the dollars you spend growing in lockstep with inflation. If spending does not keep pace with inflation, your standard of living declines. For example, let's say you are spending $100,000 per year today (after taxes) based on financial assets of $2.2 million. In ten years, your spending rate will need to climb to $135,000, assuming a 3% inflation rate, if you are to maintain your current standard of living. (In addition, you will have taxes and wealth management fees to pay.)

Because the investment strategy is conservative, your assets will not be very volatile, but neither will they go up in value very much. In fact, because the combination of spending, taxes, and fees you pay to your financial advisors is likely to exceed the annual rate of return on your investments, your assets will decline over time. If enjoying your retirement is a higher priority than preserving your assets, you won't be concerned about a declining asset base. In fact, many people express the desire to spend their last dollar to pay for their funeral.

As your spending grows and your assets decline, your annual spending rate will increase, and within 15 years or so could equate to 15% of your financial assets each year. Fifteen percent is not a sustainable yearly level of spending because within just a few years, you will deplete your assets. You don't want to run out of money before you die.

You might have surmised by now that the biggest challenge with this strategy is estimating how long you will live. Of course, the problem is that none of us knows how long we will live. Given that the average life expectancy continues to rise, this can be a risky approach to managing your life, even though it is a conservative way to invest your assets. Therefore, if you choose this approach when your spending rate exceeds 10% of your assets on an annualized basis, I urge you to consider cutting back immediately rather than risk hitting a brick wall of financial hardship in a few years. One way to do this is by supplementing your financial assets with earned income. Alternatively, consider whether Option 2, 3, 4, or 5 is more appropriate.

Option 2: Maintain a Stable Income
Guidelines:

Target after-tax spending rates:	2.6% to 5.8% of financial assets per year
Required investment returns:	4.5% to 8.0% per year
Competitive advantage:	Low to average
Risk tolerance:	Sleep well
Tax efficiency:	Medium to high

People who embrace this financial objective strive to provide themselves with a stable cash flow throughout their lifetimes. Their goal is to maintain a steady rate of spending while preserving the value of their assets. They recognize that inflation will eat away at their purchasing power over time, but they also anticipate that their spending needs will decline as they age. They may decide to eliminate expensive overseas vacations, buy a smaller home, or stop driving a car. If they are in their fifties or sixties, they may expect to inherit some assets from a parent or to make up any income shortfall with Social Security payments or a defined benefit pension plan.

To achieve this wealth management goal, a person typically chooses a spending rate that is tied to the value of their assets (for example, 4% per year) and holds their spending to that level. Tax payments and wealth management fees, like tax preparation and estate planning, also must be covered.

Many people fall into the "maintaining stable income" category, either through careful planning or default. The good news here is that if people manage their assets prudently and control spending carefully (no more than 4% to 4.5% of assets per year), they may be able to transfer assets at the end of their lives to others—family members, civic institutions, non-profit organizations, or other beneficiaries. They can also preserve their nominal assets and spending budget indefinitely— barring some unforeseen need to shift to the "maintain purchasing power" approach.

Shifting from Option 2 Back to Option 1

There are some major challenges for individuals who want to maintain a stable income throughout their lives. Over time, inflation will erode the purchasing power of that income to the point that it impinges on their lifestyle. In some cases, this can create real hardships for long-time retirees, many of whom are living today into their eighties and nineties.

Not only is it tough to maintain a stable income for decades following retirement, but evidence shows that elderly people also frequently experience significant medical expenses very late in life—often in the last year of life. "In fact, medical expenses are the cause of more than half of all bankruptcies filed by debtors over the age of 50," according to Senator Russ Feingold.[1]

One way to deal with spiraling expenses late in life is for an individual to switch from a *maintain stable income wealth management* goal to a *maintain purchasing power* goal. Better to deplete assets than to cause unnecessary hardship. After all, that's why you worked so hard to create and steward them in the first place.

Still, for most people, the pursuit of a *maintain stable income* approach to wealth management can, if embraced early, protect one's wealth for many years and thus create a substantial financial cushion for use if and when unexpected or even "catastrophic" expenses are incurred late in life.

The "Growth-Driven" Category of Financial Management

If you opt to build a wealth management strategy based on *growth-driven* financial goals…

- Your time horizon spans decades and is usually multigenerational.
- You need to generate above-average rates of return from your investments over time. To do this requires careful management of your assets, a willingness to tolerate volatility of investment returns, and a lower probability of achieving your desired goals.
- You must carefully control the amount of income and capital gains taxes you pay. Otherwise, you must substantially increase what are already "stretch" investment return objectives.
- You should control spending because it's the easiest wealth management factor to control—far easier, for example, than fluctuating tax rates or rates of return from investments!
- Transfer tax management, particularly in larger estates, can get quite complex and often involves a long-term philanthropic component.

If you opt for the *growth-driven* category of wealth management, there are three additional options you can choose from. You can:

1. Conserve the real value of your wealth and your purchasing power.

2. Retain real per capita wealth across generations.

3. Keep growing your wealth.

All three require that you be a disciplined investor. All three also require that you cap your spending at a maximum of 3.8% of assets per year (and preferably lower). Let's briefly discuss each of these three options.

Option 3: Conserve Real Wealth *and* Your Purchasing Power Guidelines:

Target after-tax spending rates:	0.0% to 3.8% of financial assets per year
Required investment returns:	5.2% to 10.5% per year
Competitive advantage:	Average to high
Risk tolerance:	Eat well (medium to high)
Tax efficiency:	Medium to high

When you successfully pursue this approach, you will be able to protect your income from the ravages of inflation over many decades. But you must lower your spending rate and take on more investment risk to do so. A benefit of tightening your belt and sleeping less well at night is that you will maintain the real value of your wealth.

If you take early retirement in your fifties or sixties, pursuing a strategy to *conserve real wealth and purchasing power* makes a great deal of sense, regardless of whether you want to leave a financial legacy. You (and/or your spouse) may easily live another 30 or 40 years. During this time frame, inflation will eat away more than half the purchasing power of a *maintain stable income* goal (Option 2), and following Option 1 could destroy your asset base long before you die.

The math is pretty straightforward. The more you want to spend, the more you have to make, especially if you want to conserve real wealth and purchasing power. At the top end of the "0% to 3.8% after-tax spending rate" range, you need investment returns exceeding 10% per year. The investment returns have to account for not only spending, but also inflation, taxes, and wealth management fees. To generate such returns, you will need above-average skill or above-average luck (and preferably both). But luck rarely lasts for decades. If wealth management is not your strong suit, you should keep your spending at 2.2% per year or lower to increase the odds of achieving this goal.

My great-aunt Ethel and her husband Oscar, who was president of a family-owned building products company, are a good example of a couple that embraced this wealth management approach successfully during their lifetimes. They earned modest incomes but were good savers, diligent investors, and thrifty spenders. They were also lucky.

Aunt Ethel managed a community center financed by Standard Oil Company of New Jersey. As part of her compensation, she received shares of Standard Oil stock, which later became Exxon. She never sold this stock. Instead, she used the dividends to buy other blue chip stocks, building her stock portfolio over a period of many years.

Aunt Ethel and Uncle Oscar did not have any competitive advantage when it came to investing, so they thought their investment returns would be in the lower half of the required investment return range. In order to conserve real wealth and purchasing power, they knew that their spending had to be held in check.

Over the decades, their stock portfolio in general (and Exxon in particular) grew in value. Because she never sold her oil stock, Aunt Ethel never paid any capital gains taxes on it—even though it appreciated many times in value. Over time, Exxon proved to be a terrific long-term performer in the stock market. It constituted more than half of Aunt Ethel's portfolio at the time of her death. (She outlived Uncle Oscar by more than 20 years.) Consequently, because of her steady, unwavering (relatively undiversified) investing, her financial legacy turned out stronger than she expected.

Aunt Ethel was also frugal. She had lovely taste but her own needs were simple. She had many friends and knew that friendship was much more important than material goods. She remained in generally good health into her nineties. She eventually died in bed in the house that she and Oscar were given as a wedding present. She married him at age 19.

Aunt Ethel achieved her goal to be a millionaire before she died. If times had been different or she hadn't been paid in Standard Oil stock, she might not have achieved that goal. But because of the way she lived her life, she would have had financial security in any case. That's the beauty of living below your means.

Option 4: Retain Real Per Capita Wealth Across Generations
Guidelines:

Target after-tax spending rates:	0.0% to 2.9% of financial assets per year
Required investment returns:	8.8% to 12.8% per year
Competitive advantage:	High
Risk tolerance:	Eat well (high)
Tax efficiency:	Medium to high

In some cases, families take a very long-term approach to financial planning, sometimes using a time horizon of three, four, or even five generations. Succeeding at this goal enables each family member in future generations to maintain the real income levels from financial assets (adjusted for inflation and other factors) that members of the current generation enjoy.

This is the goal that the Lucas family has set for itself. And while at first blush it doesn't look like a terribly aggressive strategy to pursue, consider this: Over time, families inevitably grow in size! My parents have nine grandchildren. This means we need to grow our assets by a factor of nine over about 70 years—about 3.1% per annum—after taking inflation into account.[2] At the same time, we need to combat the erosion of our wealth due to what I call "leakages." Leakages include spending, taxes, wealth management fees, charitable giving, inflation, losses due to successful claims made against you, and uninsured theft or casualty.

In total, leakages have cost us 8.5% per year over the last decade, and we manage pretty tightly! If you add the cost of "leakages" to the 3.1% per annum growth rate that I mentioned a moment ago, it means that we have to exceed an annual rate of return on our investments of 11.6% per year.[3] Thus, we've set the wealth management bar quite high in our family, with a series of stretch goals designed to help us reach our objectives. To reach these objectives, we have developed our investment skills in ways that give us a competitive advantage in the marketplace. I'll have more to say on our approach to investment management in future chapters.

Option 5: Keep Growing Your Wealth
Guidelines:

Target after-tax spending rates:	Less than 2% of financial assets per year
Required investment returns:	More than 8.8% per year
Competitive advantage:	High
Risk tolerance:	Eat well (high)
Tax efficiency:	Medium to high

This is still another growth-driven wealth management approach that some Wealth Strategists will want to consider. Successful entrepreneurs, for example, sometimes want to keep building their wealth by owning and managing businesses while maintaining enough liquid assets for prudent diversification in other areas. For such individuals, staying involved in a business they started or pursuing a second career after a liquidity event provides an engine for wealth preservation and further wealth creation.

A good example of a family that embraces the *Keep Growing Your Wealth* approach to wealth management is the Johnson Family, one of whose members, Samuel Curtis Johnson, founded the S.C. Johnson Company in 1886. S.C. Johnson Company is the maker of such popular household products as Johnson Wax, Saran Wrap, Glade® Air Freshener, Edge® shaving gel, Windex®, and other well-known household names.

Samuel C. Johnson, great-grandson of the company's founder who became president of the company in 1966, was a friend of my father's and a classmate of his at Harvard Business School. Sam passed away in 2004, but today a new generation of Johnson family members, Fisk Johnson, S. Curtis Johnson, Helen Johnson-Leipold, and Winnie Johnson-Marquart continue the legacy of being deeply involved in the family business. Fisk serves as Chairman and CEO. Curt has been extensively involved in the company's worldwide business development efforts and has served as Chairman of Commercial Markets. In July 2004, Helen was elected Chairman of Johnson Financial Group, the $3.2 billion dollar global financial services company founded by her father. Meanwhile, Winnie serves as president of the Johnson Family Foundation.

Clearly, by staying so closely involved in their family business, the heirs of Samuel Curtis Johnson have decided to keep growing their family wealth. Rather than simply living off the successes of past generations of Johnson family members, each has assumed a position of high executive responsibility within the company. S.C. Johnson remains one of the largest private companies in the United States today. Indeed, as the home page on the S.C. Johnson Company Web site proudly puts it, S.C. Johnson has been "A Family Company" for over 116 years.

Different Plans—Different End Results

I have just described five approaches to wealth management planning, any one of which might be appropriate for you to consider in your role as your family's Wealth Strategist. To give you a side-by-side comparison of how each of these five plans generates different financial results, please refer to Figure 4.1.

In each case, the wealth owner begins with $1 million in assets and pursues his or her financial objective successfully for 20 years. The initial annual spending rate varies for each objective, with the highest starting annual spending rate of $45,000 for the "Maintain Purchasing Power" objective (Option 1) scaling down to an annual spending rate of $20,000 for Option 5, "Keep Growing It." The bar chart shows the results for each strategy in two ways. First, the black bars show how much the original $1 million is worth after 20 years. Second, the shaded bars show the cumulative dollars spent over the 20-year period. One of the things you immediately notice is that despite the wide differences in initial annual spending rates and the huge variations in the ending assets, the cumulative dollars spent vary surprisingly little from strategy to strategy. However, if you look at the numbers at the bottom of Figure 4.1, you'll notice that the final year spending rates vary even more than the first-year spending rate. This is most pronounced in the case of the wealth owner who pursued the "Keep Growing It" objective. This individual initially had the lowest annual spending rate of all the investors but ended up spending more dollars each year than all the others. By deferring spending and effectively managing his assets, this individual ultimately wound up with much more money to spend. You can do the same thing. And if you do, you'll also have a much larger financial legacy to share with others.

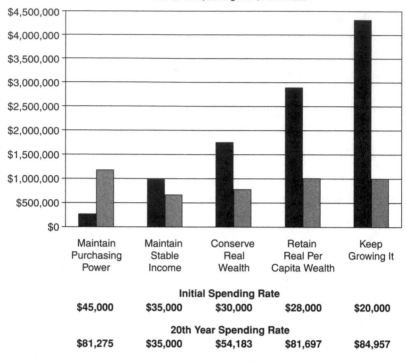

Comparison of Financial Objectives
After 20 Years, Starting With $1 Million Each

	Maintain Purchasing Power	Maintain Stable Income	Conserve Real Wealth	Retain Real Per Capita Wealth	Keep Growing It
Initial Spending Rate	$45,000	$35,000	$30,000	$28,000	$20,000
20th Year Spending Rate	$81,275	$35,000	$54,183	$81,697	$84,957

■ Assets After 20 Years
▨ Cumulative Spending

Figure 4.1   There is no free lunch. Options 3, 4, and 5 can actually maintain or grow both the real value of your wealth and your purchasing power, but they involve considerable risk and uncertainty. Options 1 and 2 involve less investment risk, but inflation degrades their viability past 15 to 20 years.

Two Market Forces that Affect Any Wealth Management Approach

While each of the five wealth management approaches has specific benefits associated with it, there are two factors—leakages and growth— that dramatically affect the outcome of any wealth management approach that you embrace, and it's critical that we talk about them.

Leakages

I've already talked briefly about leakages—things that erode your wealth—the most obvious of which is spending. Leakages also include the taxes, fees, and expenses associated with wealth management. Any net loss of assets due to litigation, fraud, theft, divorce settlements, and other successful third-party claims on your assets are leakages. (Unfortunately, these events often generate emotional losses as well.) Gifts made directly to charity are another leakage, but not to a family foundation. (Because family foundation assets are still under your control, they are not leakages until they are distributed.) In an intergenerational context, there is arguably another leakage: the division of assets among your children. Although your family's total assets may not decline, the assets available to each of your children—if you have more than one—decline by at least 50% relative to the assets you and your spouse share.

To a large extent, you have some control over all the leakages I've just outlined. One final leakage over which you have no control is inflation. Inflation slowly but powerfully depletes the value of one's wealth. Just ask any retiree who has had to live on a fixed income for a decade or more!

Growth

So what about growth? Stimulating asset growth is a function of four factors:

1. Income and capital gains you earn from a business or career.

2. Broad and efficient asset deployment that mimics the average performance of financial markets. Another term for this is passive management or Index Investing.

3. The ability to generate above-average returns in specific assets or asset classes, relative to the amount of risk incurred in doing so, through active management or what I call Active Alpha Investing.

4. Financial windfalls that occur as the result of inheritance, marriage (divorce), and adoption.

Growth Factor #1: Income and capital gains you earn from a business or career. Many wealthy people continue to work even when it's no longer necessary to maintain their desired lifestyles. Motivated by personal drive or professional ambition, they embark on second careers after liquidity events or they start new businesses—either of which enables them to continue growing their wealth for years and even decades.

Sidebar 4.1: Have You Factored the Future Financial Worth of a New Career into Wealth Management Planning?

An important factor you must weigh in the wake of your liquidity event is the value of future earnings streams generated by your career. Just like investments, career paths have differing risk characteristics and different time horizons.

In determining how to invest your financial assets following a liquidity event, you need to do two things. First, assess the risk to your wealth management strategy of relying entirely on existing assets for your lifestyle. Then, factor into these calculations the potential *new* wealth you might be able to create by embarking on a new career or livelihood.

If the circumstances that created your wealth initially are unlikely to repeat themselves, it makes sense for you to manage your wealth conservatively. Athletes, actors, and rock stars come to mind in this category. They may make lots of money for a time, but their careers tend to be fickle. Building a nest egg when the getting is good can stave off hardship when the opportunity passes.

Similarly, if the same factors that created your wealth also affect broad financial markets, it makes sense for you to invest your financial assets in places that are relatively immune to the markets. In the 1990s, for example, investment bankers and dot.com entrepreneurs should have diversified their financial assets away from the stock market, precisely at the moment the market was booming. This would have put their career and financial risk in better balance.

On the other hand, real estate tycoons *today* might find that shifting some assets into the stock market, including small technology companies, would make sense for them as a wealth diversification tactic.

Some people who have or expect to inherit substantial wealth may not be tied to an existing career. There's both good news and bad news here. With wealth comes the opportunity for individuals to take risks with their careers while still providing financial security for their families. However, developing a new career can be risky. All too often, wealthy people compound such risks by tying a significant portion of their existing wealth to the success of a new career. This action—often personified by successful business executives who try to become entrepreneurs, owners of sports teams and businesses in new fields, or angel investors—is extremely risky and often ends in disappointment.

There are usually ways you can mitigate the risks of such activities, garner valuable business experience, and reap financial rewards from your business ventures without exposing large amounts of your personal capital to such activities. This is a critical area of discussion for you to cover with your *wealth management advisor.*

Growth Factor #2: Broad and efficient asset deployment that mimics the average performance of financial markets (Index Investing). Since the Italian Renaissance, the economic, social, and political evolution of Western culture has generally followed a positive trajectory, significant disruptions notwithstanding. Furthermore, Western culture seems more stable and our economies more manageable and less volatile than they were 100 and even 50 years ago. Since World War II, many economies and countries around the world have followed similar trends. Mature countries like the United States, England, and Germany continue to grow fairly slowly and steadily, while other countries like China, India, Brazil, Chile, and Korea—often referred to as emerging markets—are today growing with both greater speed and volatility.

If you use an Index Investing strategy (see Chapter 6, "Picking Your Investment Strategy") to participate broadly in financial markets through stocks, bonds, commodities, and real estate, you're likely to benefit financially in ways that mirror the economic growth in the countries I've just mentioned. With indexing, an investor buys individual securities or index funds in an effort to match the performance of a broad-based index, such as the S&P 500, the Wilshire 5000, the Russell 2000, or others. The investor's goal is to design an asset allocation that includes a range of indices that collectively behave in a manner that is consistent with whichever of the five financial objectives were chosen. This is called strategic asset allocation. An investor then chooses financial instruments that match the indices' performance and diversifies his or her assets across them.

Growth Factor #3: The ability to generate above-average returns in specific assets or asset classes (Active Alpha Investing). Most successful people convince themselves that they have special insights that have directly led to their professional success. These feelings often carry over when they decide to invest in financial markets. These feelings of investment prowess are reinforced by many investment advisors who feel that they, too, have special insights that will enable them to make more money for their clients, with the same or less risk than the broad markets represented by the indices.

It is the desire to apply these insights that leads so many people to try to "beat the market" or "add value" to investments whether they have the true talent to do it or not. Some succeed. Others fail. (This is in marked contrast to indexing (or passive investing), where everyone is equally successful by design.) This activity is referred to as active investing, and the measure of value added is called "alpha."

What is "alpha"? Simply put, alpha is the difference in performance between an investment portfolio and a financial market index that exhibits similar risk characteristics. An investment portfolio creates positive alpha when it outperforms the financial market index and negative alpha when it underperforms the financial market.

The behavior of a financial market, as expressed in an index, is the sum of the activities of all the different investment portfolios in that market, many of which are actively managed and seeking positive alpha.

However, for every investor that actually generates positive alpha, another investor must, by definition, generate negative alpha. When you add together all the alphas, positive and negative, in theory they add up to zero. Alpha is a "zero-sum" game. In fact, because of "friction costs" that include brokerage transactions and management fees, alpha is less than a zero-sum game in the real world. This means that, on average, investors under perform their relevant indices. Because 90% of the markets' activities are driven by highly sophisticated, well-trained, institutional investors, competition for alpha is very tough. So if you are going to engage in Active Alpha Investing, you must think about how you and your advisors are going to be in the minority that is a taker of alpha rather than a giver of alpha.

Many people confuse good performance relative to an index with alpha. This usually happens when the risk of an actively managed portfolio is significantly higher than the index against which it is being compared, and the index is performing well. Most of us are familiar with a painful consequence of misattributed alpha. In the late 1990s, growth stocks went wild and value stocks were complete duds. Any manager who owned a lot of growth stocks but compared his performance against broad stock market indices like the S&P 500 had great-looking performance from 1995 to 1999, and to many investors and their advisors alike, appeared to generate lots of alpha. When the market reversed between 2000 and 2002, what appeared to be positive alpha to the undiscerning investor turned out to be volatility. The volatility that worked in the investors' favor when markets were going up obliterated their portfolios when reversals came. Yet, during the growth stock collapse, the portfolios of most true value managers actually increased in value.

Financial leverage in a portfolio, like borrowing on margin or speculating in derivative securities, also increases volatility. It helps performance when asset prices are going up and hurts performance when they are going down. But leverage does not add alpha in rising markets. It just looks that way.

Growth Factor #4: Financial windfalls through inheritance, marriage (divorce), and adoption. It never hurts to have a windfall to stimulate your asset growth, and inheritance is an increasingly common way that many people are adding to their wealth today. The wealth that this country has generated in the last 20 years alone has been colossal, and in the next few decades, trillions of dollars will be transferred to baby boomers by their elderly parents.

My own family has benefited from inheritance and adoption. My mother was adopted by E.H. Stuart, the son of Carnation's founder, who then bequeathed wealth to her and to other family members. More recently, one of my brothers adopted one of his children, which means this child will likely benefit from an eventual inheritance from him.

Wealthy families sometimes worry when a family member marries someone who "doesn't come from money." A prospective spouse is sometimes perceived as more of a gold digger than a committed partner. On the other hand, my wife's family feared that my family's wealth might somehow make her own family seem less important to her. Sometimes it is a parent who worries about their child's choice of a spouse. Sometimes it's the adult child who worries about the financial implications of a parent's remarriage. With all this said, money "issues" sometimes provide a smokescreen for avoiding discussion of other issues (real or imagined) that sometimes arise in families around marriage, divorce, adoption, and other life-altering family events.

The Interplay Between Growth and Leakages

Pay careful attention to the interplay of growth factors and potential leakages when you set your financial goals. If you only focus on one, it's like trying to clap with one hand. It doesn't work. If you make spending plans that are incongruous with your financial engine, you won't be successful. If you think diligently about how to create alpha but don't consider the impact of your strategy on your tax efficiency or expenses, you'll end up with a lot less in your pockets than you expect. The longer your time horizon, the more tightly you must manage your wealth, and the more disciplined you must be about both growth and leakages.

Specifically, if your wealth management time horizon is multigenerational, you need to "live below your means" to pass wealth on to future generations. You've already seen that if you can live below your means in the short term, it can actually net you more income and more assets in the long run.

Everybody's personal and family situations are different, and there are no right or wrong goals here. Still, it's important to understand the tradeoffs among various objectives and to match your skills with your objectives.

Putting Numbers to the Different Approaches

Effective and integrated wealth management is a complex, coordinated effort. To help you better understand the subtle interplays between growth and leakages, look at Figure 4.2. The horizontal axis of this graph represents annual after-tax spending rates, and the vertical axis represents the required annual gross rate of return to support them. Behind the scenes, the graphs account for additional leakages, including fees, taxes, and inflation. Within the graph are four lines rising from left to right that represent all five financial objectives discussed earlier in the chapter except "Keep Growing It." The fifth objective, "Keep Growing It," occurs at any point on the graph that is above and to the left of the "Retain Real Per Capita Wealth" line.

Figure 4.2 Spending more gives you less latitude to increase your investment returns and maintain your wealth.

Sidebar 4.2: Assumptions Used in These Graphs

The target rates of return I've expressed in Figure 4.2 and subsequent versions of it are derived by adding together five leakages that are both a reality of the world we live in and the financial expression of the personal goals attached to long-term, diversified wealth management. The five leakages are as follows:

1. Spending—This is an after-tax number. It includes not only spending on goods and services but also donations and gifts.

2. Income and capital gains taxes—both federal and state. Taxes are calculated on growth of assets. Net tax rates range between 20% and 30% based on the strategy, assuming a federal long-term capital gains tax rate of 15% and income tax of 35%. Portfolios with low target returns are assumed to be fairly tax efficient, but income is a larger percentage of total return. Portfolios with required gross returns above 7.5% have tax rates of 24% to 25%. Although there is less income in the portfolios, they are more actively managed and hold more hedge funds and other assets that are less tax efficient. Higher federal tax rates or residency in a high-tax state would require a higher tax rate assumption.

3. Fees, including asset oversight, legal, accounting, consulting, and administrative fees can range widely. The fees are graduated, with the most conservative portfolios charged 0.5% and the most aggressive charged 1.3%. Direct investment management fees are subtracted before calculating the gross investment return and are not included in these figures. Many wealth management-related fees have limits on tax deductibility that are not factored in.

4. Inflation, as measured by the Consumer Price Index (CPI). Over the last 50 years, inflation has averaged 4.1%. I use 3.0%.

5. A multigenerational growth factor. The typical wealthy family in America grows in numbers over time. Even if the wealth creator has only two children, these children typically marry and, on average, their spouses bring less potential for

inherited wealth to the marriage. Then each couple in the second generation has two children, who also marry. In this example, if the third generation wishes to have the same per capita wealth as the first, and the time between each generation is 30 years, then the family's wealth must quadruple over sixty years. This equates to 2.3% growth per annum. If there are three children in each generation, the figure rises to 3.7%. In this model, I use 2.5%, which assumes some combination of wealthy spouses and average growth in numbers across generations among wealthy families.

Figure 4.2 assumes that within the parameters set for each goal, the required return and the spending rate rise or fall in tandem. For example, if you want to maintain real per capita wealth, an 11% target return is compatible with a 1.5% after-tax spending rate, but not with a 2% or 3% rate. In order to achieve the goal with a 2.3% after-tax spending rate, you need to achieve a 12% gross compound rate of return. If, on the other hand, there is adequate earned income to live on without spending a portion of investable assets, the required return will decline to 8.8%.

I have not factored transfer taxes (including estate tax) into the required return calculations. But if I did, the required return in Figure 4.2 would rise for really wealthy people. There is an alphabet soup of techniques (most are referred to by acronyms like GRAT, ILET, or CRT) available today that lowers these taxes, but the larger the estate the more likely that significant taxes will become due. I have not added transfer tax to the analysis because the estate tax is so highly variable in how it is applied and is so uncertain today.

Litigation costs, uninsured theft, divorce settlements, alimony, and other non-investment leakages that we all hope are zero, but which do arise with frequency, are also not included in the analysis.

For each objective, you can see that as your desired level of annual spending increases, the required annual rate of return to meet that objective increases.

As you move from less-aggressive objectives [i.e., "Maintain Purchasing Power" (lower right)] to more aggressive goals [i.e., "Retain Real Per Capital Wealth" (upper left)] on the graph, I've lowered the maximum annual spending rate to account for the added risk of more aggressive objectives, more speculative (and volatile) investments, and the erosion to asset values that occur with spending, especially in declining markets. Conversely, you'll notice that, as wealth management objectives become less aggressive (moving upper left to lower right), the required annual gross return on investments drops, and your ability to spend more increases.

Now look at Figure 4.3. I've now eliminated the gridlines from Figure 4.2 and added two horizontal lines that represent the range of performance that many experts suggest is "reasonable to expect" for long-term returns from diversified stock and bond portfolios. The placement of these horizontal lines assumes that the long-term average annual return from equities is 8.5% and 4% for bonds. Some people believe that these figures are low, and hopefully they will be. But with current inflation ranging between 2% and 3% annually, the real, inflation-adjusted returns in this model are only slightly below the actual long-term averages, even though they are well below the returns experienced in the great bull markets of recent memory in stocks and bonds. And it is consistent with the general growth of earnings and dividends in corporate America. The 4% annual rate of return on bonds is approximately the yield on high-grade, long-term bonds at the time of writing.

The top horizontal line represents the annualized average rate of return that one can reasonably expect from a typical aggressive portfolio that is 80% stocks and 20% bonds using the rates of return presented in the last paragraph. The bottom horizontal line represents the annualized return from a typical conservative portfolio that is 80% bonds and 20% stocks. I think that having a portfolio that is more than 80% in one asset class gives you inadequate diversification. Most standard investment portfolios should fall in the zone between these two horizontal lines.

Managing wealth within this 4.9% to 7.6% zone of annualized performance is the province of most wealth management firms and is what you can reasonably expect from them if they manage your wealth efficiently over the next decade or two. But most investors and their advisors should not expect a lot more.

Figure 4.3 If you want to maintain wealth and spend above 1.5%-2.0% of it each year, solely investing in a diversified investment portfolio managed by your financial advisor is not likely to achieve the desired outcome. On the other hand, if you are conscientious, and you get prudent investment advice, you can probably achieve financial security for your lifetime.

Finding the Right Financial Objective for the Lucas Family

Now that you've learned about the different wealth management strategies, I'd like to share with you the experience of my own family in the hopes that this will bring to life the concepts that I've been describing throughout this chapter.

Take a look at Figure 4.4. In the early 1990s, members of my family were spending annually (on average) about 2% of their financial assets, after taxes, and we were invested in a 60%/40% stock/bond portfolio.

Figure 4.4   In 1993, our spending was constrained, but our wealth was still likely to erode over time.

At the time, the majority of institutionally-managed trust portfolios with stated growth objectives were managed this way. We were at the point just above the midpoint of the two horizontal lines that is marked "Lucas 1993." Figure 4.4 shows that our strategy more than maintained the nominal value of our wealth but over time would lead to a loss of real asset value and real distributable income.

In the year or so before I joined the family office full time, some members of the family expressed interest in raising their annual distributions from 2% to close to 3%. In response, our corporate trustee changed the asset mix from 60%/40% (stocks/bonds) to 50%/50%. Because bonds produce more income than stocks, this shift allowed the trustee to distribute more money to the beneficiaries. At the time, this significantly raised people's income, but in the long-term, it threatened to accelerate the decline of our real net worth. Figure 4.5 shows how our wealth management strategy shifted its focus away from a position closer to "Conserve Real Wealth" toward one of "Maintain Stable Income."

1995 Lucas Strategy

Required Gross Compound Return

14.0%
12.0%
10.0%
8.0%
6.0%
4.0%
2.0%
0.0%

Lucas 1993

Some Lucas's 1995

Expected long-term return from 20%/80% stock/bond portfolio

Expected long-term return from 80%/20% stock/bond portfolio

0.0%   2.0%   4.0%   6.0%

After-Tax Target Spending Rate

— Retain Real Per Capita Wealth — - Conserve Real Wealth
— Maintain Stable Income — - Maintain Purchasing Power

Figure 4.5 Changes in strategy threatened to accelerate wealth erosion, and we didn't realize what was happening.

Although this move increased people's income initially, over 20 years it was destined to reduce their inflation-adjusted spending power. The decision by some family members (designated as "Some Lucas's 1995") to move in this direction also fractured what had been a unified family investment strategy, splitting resources and diluting our investment focus. These were not pleasant developments!

Starting in early 1995, we held family discussions to highlight the changing situation and to discuss our future path. I encouraged the family to think carefully about the long-term asset-depleting implications of the decisions people had made. After much thought and conversation, we came to a consensus that our current course was a mistake. Instead, we agreed on three goals that could be shared by everyone going forward:

1. We would try to maintain our real per capita wealth across generations. (This would require moving to the left and up on the graph.)

2. We would constrain our spending to a rate that was consistent with long-term, growth-oriented trusts invested for total return.

3. We would take calculated investment risks (and risk a little lost sleep) in hopes of reaping far larger returns from our investments in the long run.

By agreeing on these objectives, we gambled that we actually had the skills, resources, contacts, and judgment to achieve a well above-average return on investments over an extended period of time. These goals reversed the 1995 split and pushed the whole family to the same position, which is marked "Lucas 1997" in Figure 4.6.

Our decision to pursue more aggressive goals also pushed us well above the higher of the two horizontal lines that indicate the range of performance expectations one normally has for a portfolio of stocks and bonds, even an aggressive one. Also, it meant that we began to manage our wealth very differently than we had in the previous ten years.

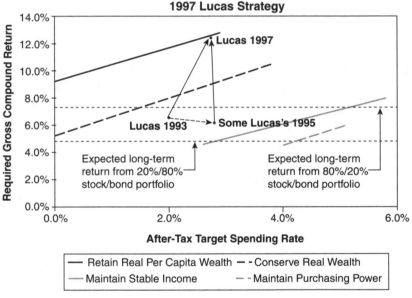

Figure 4.6 Rethinking our strategy based on the Strategic Wealth Management Framework© brought us to a sustainable strategy…if we can execute effectively.

During the lengthy process of studying and eventually understanding the strategic tradeoffs available to us, we learned two important lessons that most financial planners don't discuss openly with clients:

1. If you want to maintain or grow your wealth while spending more than 1.5% to 2.0% of it each year net of taxes, the investment strategies most financial institutions promote and execute are likely to disappoint you.

2. You are not likely to be able to spend more than 3.5% to 4.0% of your financial assets per year and have a financially secure retirement.

Benefits of a Unified Wealth Management Approach

I'm very proud that the Lucas family decided back in the mid-1990s to establish a unified strategy because it has enabled us to leverage competitive and nepotistic advantage. It is a decision that has registered multi-million dollar benefits for us. More importantly, we communicate better today than we ever have. We're able to air problems when they arise, discuss them openly, and work through them to collective resolution. This isn't to say we don't ever have issues with one another. However, we have machinery and infrastructure in place that enables us to balance collective wealth management goals with individual interests, passions, and pursuits.

Each member of our family has individual goals that are not always consistent with the collective goals of the Lucas family. For example, my sister has no children, so she has less interest in multigenerational strategies. But we have built enough flexibility into our structure to accommodate her individuality to a degree that is acceptable to all. At the same time, we have built a collective set of values and identity around managing our wealth that we all enjoy and find to be beneficial.

While developing a unified wealth management strategy has worked well for my family, not every wealthy family will want to adopt this approach. You'll need to appraise your situation honestly. The family dynamics have to be healthy and functional, and people have to be willing to compromise on their goals, communicate regularly, and work together. But if the basic ingredients are in place, the potential is there for a family's collective assets to perform considerably better than if assets are distributed and invested separately among various, independent family groups.

Adjusting for Tax-Deferred Assets

Most investors have assets in retirement plans, annuities, life insurance, or deferred compensation plans that give them some control over how the assets are invested and spent. Since the assets in these plans do not pay taxes as they grow, they will grow faster than those in your taxable accounts, all other things being equal, if you are not withdrawing any spending. However, when it comes time to withdraw assets for spending purposes, to achieve spending parity, you will probably have to withdraw more pre-tax dollars from a tax deferred account than you will from a well-managed taxable account. This is true because the tax rate on distributions from tax-deferred accounts is likely to be higher than it is on distributions from taxable accounts.

If tax-deferred assets make up a substantial portion of your net worth, it may be modestly easier to achieve your financial objectives than suggested by Figures 4-2 to 4-6, but only modestly. The ultimate outcome will be determined by a number of factors, many of which are difficult to control or predict. I will discuss retirement plans, annuities, life insurance, and other forms of deferred compensation some more in Chapter 8, "Taxes Can Be Your Ally!"

Growing Wealth While Spending It Is Hard to Do

Growing real wealth is so difficult because an investor has to achieve growth factors that outweigh periodic bear markets and the drip, drip, drip of wealth erosion caused by the various leakages I described earlier. Consider these facts about the U.S. stock market over the past century.

From 1900 to 2002:[4]

- Inflation has averaged 3% per year, thereby lowering actual yields on all investments by that percentage.
- The U.S. stock market has earned an average annual return of 9.7%, 6.7% after inflation, and under 5% after inflation and taxes. High return periods tend to come in bunches, with long dry spells in between.

- U.S. bonds have earned an average annual return of 5.5%, 2.5% after inflation, and close to zero after taxes and inflation. Of note, they have declined in value for 22 years, five years of which were in a row (from 1965-1969).
- Money market funds have averaged an annual return of 4.4%, 1.4% after inflation, and a negative real return after taxes.

In Figure 4.7, I track rolling 20-year annualized returns of the U.S. stock market from 1900 to 2002, adjusted for inflation. After adjusting for inflation, I also show in the shaded section the range of required returns you need today to reach the goal "retain real per capita wealth," as depicted in Figure 4.2. The difference between the low end of the range and the high end is accounted for primarily by the difference in annual spending rate. For the low end, I have chosen a spending rate of 1% per annum, and at the high end, it is 2.9% per annum. I've shown the average real return for the entire 102-year period using the appropriately labeled dashed line.

Required Rate of Return, Inflation-Adjusted, to Maintain Real Per Capita Wealth with Spending Between 1.0% and 2.9% Per Year

Figure 4.7 Growing wealth while spending it is tough to do.

What conclusions can you draw from this chart?

- In nearly 70% of the 20-year periods shown, stock market performance *would not* have enabled you to retain real per capita wealth—even if you kept your annual spending to just 2.8% of assets and had a portfolio of all equities.

- Even if you had lowered spending to a miserly 1% of assets/year, you *still would not have* achieved any growth-driven objectives in 25% of the 20-year periods if you invested entirely in U.S. stocks.
- The *average* real return over the century was *not* adequate to retain real per capita wealth at a 1% spending rate, even if you had been 100% invested in an equity portfolio.

In reality, growing real wealth through use of traditional stock market vehicles (i.e., mutual funds or traditional stock/bond portfolios) is even harder than Figure 4.7 suggests, for the following reasons:

- First, most people can't withstand the extremes of a highly volatile 100% equity portfolio, nor do I recommend it. To put things in perspective, the precipitous stock market crash from October 1929 through June 1932 would have left an equity investor with ten cents for each dollar invested right before the crash! Subsequent vicious bear markets, including 1973–74 and 2000–2002, while not quite as volatile, left most committed equity investors severely bloodied. In some cases, having a more diversified portfolio actually increases the odds of achieving your objectives with lower volatility.
- Second, I calculated the range of required returns to maintain per capita wealth shown in Figure 4.7 using current tax rates. Capital gains tax rates today are the lowest they've been since they were enacted in 1929, and income tax rates are at the low end of the historic range. Higher tax rates would raise that range and lower your odds of winning.
- Third, I base the data in this graph on a broad index of U.S. stock market performance, and most managers under perform the index over long periods.
- Fourth, this analysis considers *average* results but does not analyze interim circumstances. The real world is less forgiving than averages. The stock market doesn't bang out the same positive return every year; far from it. There's a high probability that during each of these 20-year periods, you will experience a bear market. You also pay taxes and fees and distribute income. In a bear market, the combined effect of all these factors can erode your wealth so much that you will never recover sufficiently to participate profitably in upward markets again.

Pulling It All Together

So, what's the bottom line here? It's this:

You have a very good chance of achieving distribution-driven goals for your wealth as long as:

- Your time horizon is less than 20 years.
- Your investment portfolio is tax and fee efficient.
- Distribution levels are kept in check.
- You diversify your assets and don't reach for excessive risk in hopes of making a little more money.

You can achieve these goals with limited risk using a simple and straightforward approach, leaving you with lots of time and energy to pursue your passions.

But if you want to achieve *growth-driven* goals while spending above 1% to 2% per year, it's a major undertaking. You must achieve at least two out of three of the following:

- Be very disciplined about managing leakages.
- Develop and maintain a competitive advantage in investing or career management that few other people have, including the large majority of wealth advisors.
- Be prepared to coordinate a complicated and sophisticated set of financial, legal, and managerial resources.

To achieve a *growth-driven* goal with long-term gross compound returns above 7.6% per annum (a reasonable return from a well managed portfolio of 80% stocks and 20% bonds), it becomes exponentially more complicated, and increasingly uncertain, to achieve each additional percentage point of return.

Managing Leakages and Growth Issues

Take a look at Figure 4.8. I list each of the five financial objectives and the associated leakages and growth factors to be managed as part of pursuing each objective. As target annual returns grow, so do the number of management challenges associated with realizing them. And, the dynamics of family values and culture have a profound influence on pursuing any of the five financial goals.

Critical Wealth Management Issues

	Maintain Purchasing Power	Maintain Stable Income	Conserve Real Wealth and Purchasing Power	Retain Real Per Capita Wealth	Keep Growing It
Leakages					
Spending	√	√	√	√	√
Taxes	√	√	√	√	√
Fees	√	√	√	√	√
Non-Investment Risk Mitigation	√	√	√	√	√
Inflation			√	√	√
Multi-Generational Factors			?	√	?
Growth Factors					
Manager Alpha			?	√	√
Tactical Asset Allocation			?	√	√
Leverage Management			?	√	√
Market Participation	√	√	√	√	√
Strategic Asset Allocation	√	√	√	√	√

Figure 4.8   As your financial objectives get more ambitious, your management challenges increase.

Many people believe that wealth management is largely a function of asset management—a growth factor. But, as you can see from this matrix, there is at least as much complexity in managing leakages. Moreover, the more aggressive your wealth management goal becomes, the greater the managerial complexity associated with each relevant leakage and growth factor. This is also true when it comes to molding and nurturing family values, identity, and human capital over extended periods of time.

The Advantages of Scale

If your goals are multigenerational, involve spending rates much above 1%, and are *growth-driven*, scale can work to your advantage. Consider the example of two wealthy individuals and their families represented in Figure 4.9. Both have assets of $15 million following a liquidity event. Client 1's assets are in a single pool of cash and publicly traded securities. Client 2's assets are divided into a variety of legal or administrative entities.

Comparative Scale Analysis

Client 1

(Assets: $15 million)

• Cash & Public Securities Portfolio ($15 million)

Client 2

(Assets: $15 million)

• Residences ($3 million)

• Cash value of a life insurance policy ($2 million)

• Retirement and profit sharing plans ($4 million)

• Assets in trust for children ($1 million)

• A family partnership ($2 million)

• Directly owned liquid assets ($3 million)

Figure 4.9   In wealth management, scale is a big advantage if you can achieve it.

Client 1 has far more investment options and better focus than Client 2. Client 1 has a greater scale of wealth (at $15 million) in one place, and he can focus all of his attention there. Client 2's largest single entity (his retirement and profit-sharing plans) is worth a much smaller $4 million, and he must divide his attention and administrative resources across six different entities. As you'll see, there are both practical and legal benefits to "scale" of wealth.

The practical benefits to scale include greater access to unique investments and reduced costs. Although it is possible for investors to access most of the thousands of mutual funds that are listed daily in *The Wall Street Journal* with no more than $10,000, some outstanding money managers around the country won't work for individual investors unless they bring at least $1 million, $5 million, and even $25 million, in some cases, to the table. Occasionally, these highly exclusive managers commingle the assets of their investors into a single pool. In other cases, they manage each client's assets as a separate account.

Here are some ways that scale of wealth can help you:

Large-scale wealth gives you easier entrée to managers who command high entry requirements. The more sought after the manager and the more specialized his/her skill set, the higher the minimums required for investment. Put another way, the greater the perceived potential of a manager to "add value" to an investment, the more capital you need to get in the door. This happens to be true for business reasons and, in many cases, regulatory reasons.

You enjoy lower management fees, in many cases, for being a deep-pocketed investor. Reduced cost is a benefit of scale for high net worth investors. Managers who oversee separate accounts of public securities usually do provide fee breaks as account sizes increase. As financial management, measurement, and tracking systems become more sophisticated, more managers are offering separate account management for amounts of $250,000 or less. However, at account sizes below several million dollars, fees for these separate accounts are significantly higher than they are for comparable mutual funds, with no indication that they improve performance.

There are also a number of fund managers who operate "institutional" mutual funds, common trust funds, limited liability partnerships, or investment trusts with minimums well above typical mutual funds but who invest primarily in public securities. These vehicles usually have lower fees than their retail equivalents.

Those investment firms that manage their clients' assets in alternative investments like hedge funds and private equity typically do not give a $10 million investor a fee break over a $5 million client, though some will afford such a benefit to a $100 million investor.

Larger investors enjoy lower sales charges. Scale influences sales charges. Many investment vehicles, including mutual funds, annuities, and life insurance have "loads" or sales charges attached to them that are triggered at time of purchase or time of sale. As a general rule, the larger the client, the smaller the percentage sales charge. Some mutual funds use another type of sales charge called a 12b-1 fee that is deducted each year you own a mutual fund, which is supposed to be allocated to funds marketing. Many mutual funds have various classes of shares with varying fee and load structures. Make sure you get the class with the lowest possible sales charges given your asset size. In some cases, you can negotiate the fund you can access based on the size of your total investment in the fund, not just at each account's level of investment. If you add to a mutual fund position, you may also be able to get lower rates for the total investment.

One way you can sidestep the issue of sales charges is simply to avoid "load" funds or funds that charge 12b-1 fees altogether. Unless you plan to hold the investment for a very long time, the cost of such funds is rarely recouped relative to other similar funds that have no loads. One of the beauties of establishing this little rule is that you eliminate a substantial percentage of all mutual funds from your universe of possible investments (making your life simpler) while arguably enhancing your return potential.

In some cases, scale DOES NOT matter. Many of the fees associated with managing each legal entity you own (i.e., a trust, partnership, or limited liability company) are the same whether the assets total a few hundred thousand dollars or ten million dollars. Each entity also has standard overhead costs associated with maintaining and managing individual tax identification numbers, tax returns, bank accounts, and governance documents that you must periodically review and revise. Do you really need all the entities and investments that you have?

Regulatory Issues with Scale

The Securities and Exchange Commission (SEC) has created several classifications of investor, based on scale, and has put in place regulatory safeguards for some but not others. Investment firms that operate unregistered hedge funds or private equity operate with less regulation than mutual funds. To protect investors, the SEC restricts investment firms from accepting investors below certain size criteria in their unregistered funds. The SEC *presumes* that investors who meet the size criteria have specialized knowledge of investments and are conversant with the risks and reward potential of these investment opportunities.

A minimum of either $1 million in net worth qualifies you to be an "accredited investor" or a minimum of $5 million in *financial* assets to be a "qualified purchaser" for individuals, though for some legal entities the figure is higher. There is also an income test that individuals can use to become an accredited investor. Some portfolio managers require investors to meet both tests, while others are content if investors meet the lower standards. The SEC is considering raising some of the size criteria.

It's hard to participate effectively in alternative investing unless you have $5 million in a single entity today. However, the financial marketplace is entrepreneurial, and a growing number of financial firms are creating investment vehicles that allow investors with fewer assets to participate in alternative investments.

Size also matters when it comes to retirement and estate planning. The larger your assets, the more planning that's required to manage wealth in retirement and to efficiently pass your wealth on to the next generation. Estate taxes get particularly complicated and potentially onerous when it comes to multi-million dollar estates. So too does managing the alternative minimum income tax and the other income tax implications of retirement plans, insurance policies, and deferred compensation plans. You'll find more about these topics in Chapter 8 and Chapter 11, "Putting It All Together: Multigenerational Planning and Wealth Transfer."

Where the Rubber Meets the Road—Making Your Financial Objectives Work for Your Family

Deciding on a specific financial objective for your family isn't easy because each family member has different views of money, is at a different stage of life, and may have plans for the future that don't align with other family members. Don't be alarmed—you are a typical American family, this is to be expected, and as Wealth Strategist, you must deal with this issue in a forthright way.

Typically, family members in or near retirement are relatively risk-averse and need to generate higher levels of income from their investments. In contrast, younger, more risk-tolerant family members in the prime of their careers don't need unearned income because they are working. In still other cases, young people may be trust beneficiaries, but not for several decades. In these instances, the trusts can grow aggressively because they don't have to make distributions in the interim.

In many wealthy families, there are individuals who are dependent on their wealth for income. These include the physically or mentally handicapped and those who have chosen careers where pay is not commensurate with their contribution to society. Preschool teachers, poets, artists, and administrators of community service organizations are just a few examples here.

What Do You Do?

How do you juggle numerous financial objectives simultaneously? And how do you optimize your total family's wealth management strategy?

If you set your gross investment return requirements (highlighted in Figure 4.3) within the 4.9% to 7.6% annual range, you can use readily available retail investment products to meet your financial goals. By keeping your investment strategy and accountability procedures simple, you should be able to keep track of various portfolios and their investment strategies without problems.

If, however, your wealth management goals are multigenerational, your gross investment return goal exceeds 7.6%, or you crave simplicity in your financial affairs, you should consider developing a unified family strategy for wealth management.

By developing a unified family strategy around asset growth and leakages, you can reinforce common bonds and values between and across generations while preserving room for the needs and interests of individual family members. Developing a unified family wealth management strategy also rewards the good intra-family communication necessary to refine and perpetuate key values over time. It can also help bring important dimensions of scale to the long-term growth and preservation of your wealth.

Conclusion

In this chapter, I've explained the two paths you can take with wealth management activities. You can opt either for a *distribution-driven* approach to wealth management, which typically has a timeframe of your lifetime. Or you can adopt a *growth-driven* approach to wealth management, the timeframe for which is often multigenerational. Indexing and the use of traditional investment vehicles, such as mutual funds, should enable you, in most cases, to achieve *distribution-driven* financial goals and some *growth-driven* goals. Pursuing *growth-driven* financial goals that incorporate significant spending from financial assets involves a far higher order of investment sophistication, market knowledge, and tolerance for risk-taking, which we will explore in more detail in later chapters.

You, as Wealth Strategist, will need to decide which of the two paths to wealth management planning makes the most sense for you, your family, and your financial circumstances. There are no right or wrong choices here. There are clearly tradeoffs associated with each approach, and understanding these is critical in order to achieve your wealth management goals.

If you opt for a *distribution-driven* approach to wealth management, you can, in many cases, enjoy a relatively high annual spending rate because your assets don't need to last beyond your lifetime. However, if you opt for a *growth-driven* wealth management approach, especially one with a time horizon of multiple generations, you must pay close attention to "leakages" and other factors that can erode your wealth. You must make a concerted effort to live below your means, especially if you want to preserve or increase real per capita wealth in subsequent generations. And you must take a proactive approach to wealth building.

To help you become an effective Wealth Strategist, this chapter has acquainted you with some fundamental dynamics of financial management as you prepare to work closely with professional wealth advisors in the areas of investing, asset allocation, estate planning, tax law, and accounting.

Before you begin working with a professional team of advisors, however, it's important that you understand more about the professional wealth industry today—how wealth advisors work, how they make their living, and what motivates them to work on your behalf. That's the focus of Chapter 5, "The Enchanted Forest, The Secret Society, and The Capital Kibbutz."

Chapter 4: Issues to Discuss with Your Family

1. What do you see as your most likely wealth management planning timeframe? Is it your lifetime or multigenerational?

2. What are your specific financial objectives? Do you want to base your financial future on a *distribution-driven* approach to wealth management or a *growth-driven* approach?

3. If you chose a distribution-driven approach to wealth management, are you more inclined to maintain purchasing power of your spending or to strive to retain nominal wealth over your lifetime even if it means reducing your purchasing power over time?

4. If you choose a growth-driven approach to wealth management, which approach most closely matches your needs?

    a) Retain real wealth

    b) Retain real per capita wealth

    c) Keep growing your wealth

5. What is your attitude toward spending? Are you by nature a big spender or are you frugal? To what extent do you see your own spending activities as either a threat to or critical component to effective wealth management?

6. How skilled are you at wealth management? What are your specific wealth management skills, if any? If you have invested well in the past, were you smart or lucky? What are your potential weaknesses as a Wealth Strategist? In what areas will you need to identify and recruit high-caliber professional wealth advisors—or family members—to balance you out?

7. Are you happy with your current rates of return on investments? If so, what do you base this assessment on? If not, what do you think you need to do differently to generate better and more consistent rates of return?

8. What are the key "leakages" that you can identify based on an examination of your own portfolio? Which of these do you see yourself able to readily control? Which are likely to be more difficult to control? Based on Figure 4.8, prioritize the top three leakages that threaten the long-term preservation and growth of your wealth.

9. What can you do, based on reading this chapter, to bring more financial discipline to your spending and your wealth management activities?

10. What systems, if any, do you have in place to measure and manage both growth factors and leakages?

11. To what extent do you enjoy "scale" of wealth? Write down on a piece of paper your key assets by entity size. Also, list and identify any liabilities.

12. Are you currently able to leverage the scale of your wealth in your financial and wealth management endeavors with advisors?

13. How happy are you with the level of service you currently are receiving from wealth advisors?

14. Are you conversant with the various factors, including the *long-term* effects of leakages and advisors fees, which currently affect the bottom line value of your assets?

15. Do different members of your family have different wealth management goals and priorities? Describe these.

16. Do you currently have in place a unified family strategy for wealth management? If so, how well is it working? Are you pleased with it, or does the plan need to be tweaked to be more administratively efficient and to more directly serve collective and individual family interests?

17. How well are you able to facilitate family conversations about wealth management goals? How frequently do you review goals with family members? How frequent are your communications with various family members regarding family wealth management matters?

Endnotes

1 Congressional Record Statement of Senator Russ Feingold on the Senior Homestead Amendment, March 1, 2005, http://www.senate.gov/~feingold/statements/05/03/2005415658.html.

2 In Figure 4.2, I present a more general model for maintaining real per capita wealth across generations. In that model, I use a factor of 2.5% instead of 3.1% because our family is somewhat more prolific than average and it is also possible for children or grandchildren to marry and then inherit assets from their spouse's family, lowering the required rate of return to maintain the objective.

3 In fact, the gross rate of return needs to be somewhat higher because we can't generate a return on the 8.5% in leakages each year.

4 Source for market and inflation data: Cambridge Associates, LLC. After inflation and tax numbers are the author's estimates.

5

THE ENCHANTED FOREST, THE SECRET SOCIETY, AND THE CAPITAL KIBBUTZ

"Those that have wealth must be watchful and wary…"

—*Thomas Haynes Bayly*

Now that we've discussed your values regarding wealth (Chapter 3, "Everything Begins with Values") and the various options you have when it comes to wealth management goals (Chapter 4, "Defining Your Financial Objectives"), it's time to talk about the wealth management industry—into whose hands you may ultimately place your wealth for investment. It's a mysterious industry that you must learn to navigate, but for which no easy-to-follow roadmap exists. Within the industry, I will introduce you to three different worlds: "The Capital Kibbutz," "The Secret Society," and "The Enchanted Forest."

Stepping into any of these worlds is like stepping off a plane in a far-away country where you don't know the language or customs. As you might expect, an eager horde of people await your arrival, jostling for position to serve as your guide to each of these strange and exotic lands. Whom should you choose?

It's essential that you learn how to navigate the wealth industry well so that you can be an effective Wealth Strategist. It's also important to understand how the wealth management industry works so you can pick appropriate investment strategies to support your overall wealth management goals.

The good news is that I've been a part of the wealth management industry for many years and have a strong granular knowledge of how the industry actually operates. The bad news is that the industry is in the throes of a complex struggle between service and profit where issues of ethics, competition, market self-regulation, and federal law can sometimes play out at an investor's expense.

As your guide to the wealth management industry, it's my hope that you'll become much more familiar with what you need to do to be a successful investor and what to do when it comes to working with industry professionals.

What precisely do you need to know about the wealth management industry today in order to navigate it well and avoid investor pitfalls? The first rule of working with wealth management firms today is "buyer beware." I say this because you must—as with any industry—steer clear of working with unscrupulous advisors. I also say this because you must be an educated consumer, even when working with ethical advisors and wealth management firms with sterling reputations. For example:

- You must understand how advisors and firms are compensated and how they measure their own success.
- You must know what your own objectives are and be able to evaluate and differentiate the value propositions of different wealth management firms and advisors.
- Finally, you must know something about the world of investing and, even more importantly, know what you don't know.

In the wealth management industry today, having a little bit of knowledge can be a dangerous thing. That's because you, as an individual investor, are really a "free agent" investor. Like free agent athletes, you're in charge of your destiny, whether you realize it or not. In most cases, you are best off assuming that there's no one there to protect your interests from others or against your own ignorance. Even though U.S. regulators do more than those in any other country to protect the interests of individual interests, education is still the best protection.

Regulation

The financial services industry is one of the most heavily regulated on the planet, in large part because the government wants people to have confidence in the markets. Still, my advice is that you should act as if the industry is not regulated.

In 1974, a landmark piece of legislation was passed by Congress that injected the financial markets with unprecedented creativity and entrepreneurialism and at the same time made them a more dangerous place for the individual investor. This legislation was called the Employee Retirement Income Security Act, or ERISA. (See Sidebar 5.1.)

Sidebar 5.1: ERISA and the Prudent Investor Rule

Before ERISA, pension plans and other kinds of institutional investments were governed by something called the "Prudent Man Rule." The Prudent Man Rule dictated that every investment that pension plan administrators made had to be of high quality and safety. If a pension plan portfolio consisted of 60 stocks and 20 bonds, for example, each security in this portfolio was *individually* analyzed to see if it was a prudent and reasonable investment. It was common practice for pension plans, endowments, and other institutional investors to hire one diversified financial service firm to manage their assets (or, at most, a few). The service provider managed all the assets in-house and did most of the administration as well. The industry was highly regulated and safe, and conservative portfolios were pretty much the norm from one firm to the next. There were relatively few competitors, and they each built long-term, stable, and relatively price-insensitive client relationships.

Under ERISA, the "Prudent Investor Rule" replaced the "Prudent Man Rule" as the guiding principle for designing investment portfolios. The Prudent Investor Rule takes into account the benefits of diversification. It recognizes that a well-constructed collection of individually risky assets may *collectively* have significantly less risk. In other words, it has "risk-defraying" characteristics.

This subtle change completely transformed how institutional portfolios are invested today. For one thing, it introduced the notion of "risk" into investment planning and selection as never before. It created legal protections for institutions so they could gain exposure to small capitalization companies, venture capital, opportunistic real estate, and many other "risky" investments. It also created the flexibility for them to hire smaller, specialized investment managers, opening the market to new and dynamic competitors. This change of thinking in how portfolios should be managed opened the door for boutique investment firms with focused expertise to take hold, adding new competition and

> creativity to the markets. It also led to institutional investors wanting to invest with the best possible investors in each asset class, regardless of the firm they worked for. Many more investment options and many more managers led institutions to develop "open architecture."

The enactment of ERISA into law proved a major boon for institutional investors. Although the legislation was directed principally at pension funds, it changed the thinking of many other institutional investors, such as endowments and foundations, and eventually the market for wealth management services. After ERISA became law, institutional investors diversified their investments out of traditional stock and bond portfolios, managed by banks and traditional investment houses, and began to invest with specialized boutique money managers and investment firms. "Open architecture" was born, and with it came the opportunity for institutional investors to take advantage of a wide range of proprietary and highly innovative products offered by organizations of widely different structures and sizes. Open architecture offered institutional investors the opportunity for much greater returns on their investments than had been possible in the pre-ERISA environment.

The Four A's

The more forward-thinking institutions realized that the opportunity for greater returns equated with greater need to analyze risk correctly. They saw that managing effectively in this new environment demanded that they develop strong in-house competencies to manage their investments. In the mid-1980s, David Swenson, Chief Investment Officer of the Yale University Endowment, and Jack Meyer, the Chief Executive Officer of Harvard University's endowment, became innovative Active Alpha investors, aggressively investing in real estate, private equity, venture capital, risk arbitrage, distressed debt, and emerging markets. As the investment portfolios got more complicated, Meyer, Swenson, and others focused on building strong in-house competencies in four key investment areas. I refer to these as "The Four A's":

- **Acumen**. Large institutional investors recognized that the most important success factor in investing was the accurate identification of investment opportunity. So, they developed strong expertise in the areas of research, professional oversight, quality administration, and sophisticated systems. These resources are expensive and are best amortized over a substantial asset base. Only large institutional investors can afford this.
- **Access**. Scale, sophistication, and long time horizons are all attributes that help investors gain access to the most attractive investment opportunities. Large institutional investors recognized this and began leveraging the scale of their assets to achieve access to the best opportunities and the finest talent in traditional and alternative investments.
- **Alignment of Interests**. Client/advisor alignment was pioneered by large institutions in order to protect their long-term investment interests. The belief was that investment managers entrusted with managing money should share appropriately in both success and failure, and conflicts of interest should be avoided or, at the very least, managed with the clients' interests put first.
- **Accountability**. Large institutional investors pioneered the use of strong administrative and accountability systems to measure fund/advisor/manager performance. Such systems are critical in giving pension plan managers, endowment directors, and other institutional decision makers the management information they need to act with confidence. Accountability in its broadest sense involves tracking fund performance, measuring/monitoring manager performance, and flagging problems if and when they arise.

Leading institutional investors attracted experienced professionals to construct and manage their portfolios. They did detailed research on portfolio construction, the behavior of asset classes, and the skills and ethics of managers. They hired staffs to assemble and aggregate, often by hand, the performance information they compiled from managers. They researched the amount of risk individual managers took to achieve particular returns. The same staff also double-checked the bookkeeping of their investment advisors in the same way that you and I might balance our checkbooks.

To assist such institutions with investment planning, a whole consulting industry blossomed in the wake of ERISA and is still a leading intellectual force in the investment world today. Institutional consultants, such as Greenwich Associates, Mercer, Cambridge Associates, Monticello, and Ennis Knupp, typically charge institutional investors anywhere from $100,000 to $1 million a year—or more—for the advice and support they provide.

The Mutual Funds Industry: Open Architecture Comes to Private Investors

With the success of open architecture in the institutional world came increasing interest in similar access and choice by private investors. Mutual fund companies were the first of the private wealth management firms to respond to this market demand. Taking a page from the marketing playbook of consumer companies like Coke, which in the 70s, 80s, and 90s pursued product differentiation with a vengeance (adding Diet Coke, Cherry Coke, Classic Coke, Vanilla Coke, Caffeine Free Coke, and so on to its product line), mutual fund companies soon began to offer a wide array of products via open architecture to retail investors. And the industry grew rapidly.

In 1970, there were 355 equity mutual funds, most of them broadly diversified. Today, 35 years later, nearly 160 times as much money is invested in mutual funds as there was in 1970. And there are roughly 4,400 mutual funds from which an investor can choose. Only about 600 of these funds are broadly diversified mutual funds while approximately 3,800 are equity mutual funds narrowly focused on specific industries, size of companies, international markets, investment styles, and so on.[1]

The product differentiation strategy that mutual fund companies have embraced over the past 35 years has proved a financial bonanza for these firms. According to Barron's magazine, the top three mutual fund families today (Vanguard, Fidelity, and Capital Guardian) have more assets under management than the next 30 combined.[2] When Jack

Bogle started Vanguard, he had only a handful of mutual funds under management. Today *The Wall Street Journal* lists 88 (162 share classes) for Vanguard. Fidelity publishes prices on 176 (234) funds each day. Franklin/Templeton, #4, but with a quarter of Vanguard's assets, has 80. Interestingly, Capital Guardian's American Funds (#3) has only 26 funds.

Mutual fund firms have discovered that giving investors a lot of fund choice is good for business. While broadly diversified mutual funds today might charge investors only modest investment management fees of 0.7% or less, specialized portfolios like a small capitalization fund or international fund can potentially charge much higher management fees—sometimes more than double the diversified mutual fund fees cited previously, or 1.5%.

So, if a mutual fund salesperson today can convince a client to transfer a percentage of their assets from lower fee diversified portfolios into higher fee specialized portfolios, that salesperson can potentially increase his/her fee income from that client a great deal—even if the client doesn't invest any more money.

Firms also discovered that if they have lots of products for sale, there are always some funds in their stable that are performing really well. The funds that do well become the focus of marketing efforts, they get good ratings from Morningstar (a leading provider of independent investment research), and they become the best vehicles for bringing in new assets. In fact, over 80% of the money that gets invested in mutual funds today goes into funds that get four or five stars (on a one-to-five point scale) from Morningstar.

Unfortunately, the link between a fund earning four stars from Morningstar for good past performance and that fund's ability to continue outperforming the market is quite weak. Morningstar publishes this concern regularly. And almost every time you receive performance information from an investment manager, it says in the fine print that "past performance is not an indicator of future results."

One-Stop Shopping for Mutual Funds—Open Architecture Widens

As mutual funds proliferated in the 80s and 90s and firms recognized the benefits of diversifying their product lines, Charles Schwab, founder and Chairman of Charles Schwab, Inc., came up with a new business model for personal investing that forever changed the mutual funds industry. In 1992, he created Schwab OneSource, which enabled individual investors to buy mutual funds from a number of different companies through a single point of contact at Schwab. This one-stop shopping format made it easier for investors to keep track of their mutual funds and made fund administration for wealth advisors using the Schwab system far easier. Schwab OneSource didn't bring open architecture to mutual funds, but it certainly accelerated its widespread adoption. It has been hugely successful. Fidelity followed Schwab's lead a year later in 1993 by offering its own version of one-stop fund shopping, *FundsNetwork*. By 2000, *FundsNetwork* was offering 3400 funds for sale. Many other mutual fund firms have followed suit.

What's ERISA Done for Individual Investors? Not Much!

While the introduction of open architecture proved beneficial to large institutional investors that could afford to develop deep in-house competencies to manage their accounts, it has not proven beneficial to individual (retail) investors.

First, open architecture left individuals on their own when it came to developing the investment skills and business acumen to manage their investments through supermarket fund shopping. And results show that individual investors (often guided by professional advisors) haven't fared well when put in charge of selecting their investment vehicles. From 1984 to 2004, for example, the stock market earned an annual rate of return of 13.0%. This is a great return, well above the average of the last 100 years. However, the average equity mutual fund earned only 9.9% over this same period, an underperformance of 3.1%.[3] This may not sound like a big difference, but consider this: Had you invested $10,000 in the stock market in 1984, you would have had $115,231 in

---

2004 (excluding taxes). Had you invested the same amount in the average mutual fund, you would have only realized $66,062!

The analysis doesn't end there. Because most people tend to buy investments that have done well in the past rather than those that might do well in the future, the average dollar invested in equity mutual funds only returned 6.6% during the period from 1984 to 2004, or $35,904 on that $10,000 initial investment.[4]

Second, ERISA deals with the tax-exempt world, but individual investors pay taxes. In Spring 1993, two researchers—Robert H. Jeffrey and Robert D. Arnott—released a groundbreaking study titled "Is Your Alpha Big Enough to Cover Your Taxes?" in the *Journal of Portfolio Management*. They took a top-down approach that studied the actual long-term performance of actively managed equity mutual funds. The study showed unequivocally that in most cases the answer to their question was a resounding "No!" Their conclusion raised a lot of controversy in the trade press among active managers, but their research and conclusions were sound. In 2000, in the same well-respected journal, Arnott and two other researchers published a re-examination of their original work, with even more data and better analysis. In response to this updated work, Robert H. Jeffrey had the following to say in an article he wrote several months later in the *Journal of Wealth Management*.[5]

> This newer, broader, and deeper study shows once again that "the vast majority of alphas are not big enough to cover their taxes." But the icing on Arnott's empirical cake is the observation that while 14% of the funds over a 20-year period outperformed the Vanguard 500 on an after-tax basis by 1.3% per year, the 86% that underperformed did so by 3.2%. My math is pretty simplistic, but I'm not thrilled with the odds of a bet on which I have a 14% chance of picking up 130 basis points of return, and an 86% chance of losing 320.

Over the years, others have tested long-term investment performance of active managers—of mutual funds and separate accounts alike—on both a pre-tax and an after-tax basis. Most of them come up with similar results. Because the majority of active managers don't outperform the index, it should come as no surprise that even fewer managers do so when measured on an after-tax basis.

Third, ERISA doesn't help individual investors from the standpoint of fees. For example, there's a cost problem that individual investors have with mutual funds, for example. Repeated studies by academics and industry practitioners confirm that mutual fund management fees, administrative fees, marketing fees, and transaction costs are all a drag on the performance of actively managed mutual funds and give them an overall lower rate of return than if you were to invest in index-linked investments. The same cost trends prove true when comparing bond mutual fund performance against the bond market itself.

Fourth, and the biggest problem of all, ERISA and open architecture have spawned an environment in which individuals sell and buy investments with greater frequency than in the past. Before open architecture, most owners of mutual funds invested for the long term. But today, people read in the newspaper about funds that are outperforming the market. Or they hear some stock market forecaster rhapsodize about a hot new stock on *The Today Show*. Or they watch as Wall Street analysts discuss their top stock market picks of the week with Geoff Colvin on *Wall Street Week with Fortune*. All this makes it hard for the average investor to resist the impulse to buy or sell stocks when he or she is hearing the message almost daily: "Act now!"

One firm, Capital Group, possibly the most respected investment management firm in the world, has gone against the trend. Its mutual fund family, "American Funds," has only 26 funds but has $655 billion under active management. Capital Group strongly discourages investors from flipping from fund to fund. I don't think it's coincidental that over the last 11 years, at least, this family of mutual funds has had the best investment performance in the country,[6] excluding the sales commissions that their funds charge.

In short, while open architecture has been great for institutional investors and the mutual funds industry, it hasn't worked out as well for private investors. Instead, private investors have become caught up in the excitement and complexity of open architecture without having the investment acumen and access to investment options that institutional investors have. Private investors also have much more difficulty aligning their interests with advisors or holding their advisors accountable for results than large-scale institutional investors.

Mutual funds are only one place where individual investors can get lost in the fog of the rapidly changing wealth management industry. There are other places as well.

Should I Use a Retail Brokerage?

It is a badge of honor and a sign of success for private clients to be advised by blue-blooded firms, such as Merrill Lynch, Goldman Sachs, or Morgan Stanley. All three are outstanding firms that have built great businesses. Major banks, such as UBS, Citibank, and JP Morgan, also have huge brokerage operations. They all possess the Four A's, and so do many others. They share their expertise with their clients, but many also use it to trade the firm's capital, often in competition with their clients.

The leading brokerage firms and their affiliated investment banking activities are at the epicenter of the financial services world today. They see trends early and have both muscle and smarts to assess and take advantage of opportunity. Their forté is trading assets and selling ideas. They make money by completing transactions, whether they are distributing mutual funds, trading blocks of IBM stock, or floating an IPO. These transactions make money for the firm, whether the deals subsequently make money for clients or not. If clients of these firms simply bought and held their investments, the brokerage business would not be very profitable. But clients don't. Encouraged by their investment advisors, clients periodically sell some funds and purchase others, always generating fees for their advisors when they do.

Brokerage firms have tremendous expertise, but because of their transaction-oriented cultures and because they often sell both internally manufactured products and third-party products, they have conflicts of interest that you, the Wealth Strategist, must manage.

Trust Bank Services

Banks have historically been major players in the private wealth business. While the Glass-Steagall Act of 1933 prevented them from engaging in the brokerage business and interstate banking restrictions limit their distribution reach, for over a century firms like Northern Trust, JP Morgan, and U.S. Trust built substantial businesses to set up and manage trusts for their private clients. Trusts have several functions. One of them is asset management. Many private clients who lack investment acumen, scale of wealth, and the infrastructure to manage their investments delegate these responsibilities to trust banks in hopes of better results and less complexity in their own lives.

Unlike mutual fund companies, trust businesses have been slower to embrace open architecture. Part of the reason is trust law, which is governed at the state level, not the federal level. Changing trust law to ensure easier use of open architecture by trust businesses is logistically more complex and takes greater time to accomplish due to the lack of uniformity of trust laws across the U.S.

For almost 20 years since ERISA became law, most state trust laws were still mired in the "Prudent Man Rule" (see Sidebar 5.1). Finally, in 1992, a national body called The American Law Institute, trying to encourage states to adopt the "Prudent Investor" concept for trusts, created a document called the Restatement (Third) of Trusts. This document updated the legal principles of trust investing to reconcile with emerging best practices in the wealth management industry.

After the Restatement (Third) was completed, states began to change their trust laws in earnest. But more than 10 years later, only two-thirds of states had adopted most of the updated principles. Until state laws are amended, there is too much legal risk for trusts in those states to embrace open architecture.

Trust companies that act as trustee have a high standard of fiduciary responsibility that they must follow. This means they have a legal duty to safeguard their clients' interests. These organizations tend to have conservative cultures and less cutting-edge investment expertise. They are more concerned about protecting their clients' assets than about helping clients maximize their returns. Employee compensation structures are often lower and less incentive-driven than in brokerages or mutual fund firms. But their interests are more closely aligned with clients than in many other financial firms.

Trust companies and their conservative approach to wealth management occupy an important niche in the wealth management industry. As trillions of dollars are passed from one generation to the next over the next fifty years, I predict that trust companies will eventually capture a significant share of these assets.

The Gap in the Individual Investment Process

With open architecture, the total shape of your investment program is even more important than the individual mutual funds, stocks, hedge funds, or other products in your portfolio. Remember that from 1984 to 2004, the average mutual fund generated a return of 9.9% but the average investor only earned 6.6%. With all the upheaval (mergers, deregulation, and re-regulation) that's taking place in the private client business, there doesn't seem to be much focus on helping individual investors acquire The Four A's of investing. Advisors get paid to sell financial products, not strategy. Private clients become enamored with products and fail to perceive the need for a strategic approach to wealth management. Institutional investors like Swenson and Meyer saw the need for a strategic approach to investment management, and they filled the gap. Attempts to address the need for a strategic approach to investing in the individual investment market have largely been unsuccessful, except for a few consultants who work with families that have assets of $100 million or more.

If your private client portfolio is simple, you don't need to build The Four A's beyond a basic level. And you can achieve that basic level on your own. However, if you want to invest the way institutions invest, in specialized products and in things like venture capital or hedge funds, you have to be just as skilled as they are to have a chance of winning. Just how tough is this?

How Can You Distinguish Among Wealth Advisors?

There are few businesses where salespeople can make more money than in wealth management. As a result, the industry attracts many bright individuals. These are the folks that most individual investors hire in hopes of achieving The Four A's needed to compete using complex strategies and products. Wealth management professionals are highly competitive, have a nose for new business, and possess great powers of persuasion. They exude success and smarts, wear designer suits, carry platinum credit cards and thick pitch books, and they are supported with billions in advertising dollars.

To the inexperienced person with newly liquid assets, salespeople from wealth management firms present two challenges. First, a prospective client can potentially sit through hours of PowerPoint presentations from different wealth management firms outlining their investment options without being able to truly differentiate one value proposition from another. Second, in these interactions, it can be even tougher to discern the track records of individual advisors in adding value to their clients, even when they work for firms with good reputations.

So, how do you measure one wealth advisor's knowledge of financial markets against that of others? How do you gauge a person's instinct for the market, his or her knowledge of emerging market trends, or the degree to which he or she is ethical in their everyday client interactions?

Believe me, it's tough. A friend of mine, an entrepreneur, recently sold his software business. Even before sale terms were finalized, my friend was inundated by phone calls from representatives of leading wealth management firms. After listening to hours of sales presentations, he complained to me that the exercise made his head spin, and in the end he couldn't differentiate one sales pitch from the next:

> I didn't learn anything I could use from all these meetings. Whenever I told one of these sales reps that I couldn't differentiate his proposal from all the others, I was told my analysis wasn't "granular" enough. So, I went back and reviewed all the proposals again, but again came to the same conclusion: I couldn't tell one from another. Eventually, I began to worry that by the time I had

gotten granular enough to distinguish the differences among the proposals, they would be inconsequential, and I wouldn't be able to see the forest for the trees in any case!

Each team of prospective advisors explained to my entrepreneur friend why its firm was the best choice to manage his money, and each brought stacks of material to back up their arguments. Each firm managed billions of dollars in investments and offered him a vast array of investment products. All the teams presented diversified investment strategies that included smatterings of hedge funds and private equity offerings. In every case, they offered up mountains of financial data along with colorful pie chart diagrams.

No team, however, tried to educate my friend about how to distinguish among wealth management proposals. And while each team espoused the virtues of its firm and the services it offered, none could demonstrate its track record of adding *long-term* value to investors' *aggregate* portfolios, other than by offering reference checks with their satisfied clients.

My friend's dilemma is typical of that faced by anyone trying to choose among financial advisors today. Not only do many firms' investment models look alike, even within the same firm there can be vast differences in the quality of investment execution among advisors, and even from client to client using the same advisor.

In the end, five different firms presented equally impressive wealth management models to my friend. But because he couldn't differentiate among their value propositions, he ended up choosing three of them and splitting his assets among them, hoping that in a few years he will have better information with which to make future investment decisions.

A year or two from now, it's my guess that one of these teams whose performance appears to be falling behind will be tempted to play catch up by recommending riskier investments to my friend. If he accepts their recommendations and the investments do well, that firm will keep his business and may get more. If the recommended investments decline in value, that firm was probably going to lose his business in any case. In this kind of head-to-head competitive arrangement with wealth management firms, the investor rarely emerges the victor. The odds are stacked in favor of the advisor in a "heads I win, tails you lose" way because the advisor makes money whether the client does or not.

Meanwhile, my friend will be very busy overseeing three teams of advisors and trying to juggle their investment advice—a tough challenge indeed. A long-standing industry manager, commenting on the manner in which some clients "manage" their investment advisors, puts the challenge this way: "Wealth advisors are much better salesmen than their clients are wealth managers."

Sidebar 5.2: What You Don't Know You Don't Know Can Hurt You!

In many cases, people are ambitious for their wealth to grow quickly, but don't have the skills and resources to make it happen. When confronted with decisions, they may get overly aggressive, make rash decisions, err by employing the wrong advisors, fund ill-considered projects, or quickly spend a fortune that may have taken generations to build. If such individuals are lucky, they stumble early on and only in a modest way. This allows them time to scale back ambitions and risk-taking to more appropriate levels. But in some cases, people with a lot of money don't learn about the perils of wealth management until it's too late.

The bull market of the 1990s made it easy for many people to overestimate their own investment skills. Almost everyone— from day traders to dot.com millionaires—was rapidly rewarded for taking risks because of the general rise in stock prices. Indeed, as people put more and more capital into the stock market, the rewards got better and better. However, instead of being emboldened by the rising stock market, wealth advisors should have prompted their clients to take money out of the market to keep their assets in balance—and clients should have listened to them when they did. But many investors and their advisors became greedy. They exercised imprudent aggressiveness and a lack of discipline during this period, and they were overly exposed to the brunt of the bear as soon as the markets cracked.

continues

Even investment superstars can get caught in the trap of mismatched ambition and skill. For example, hotshot traders at the infamous hedge fund shop, Long Term Capital Management, leveraged and concentrated their personal wealth in their own heavily leveraged fund in mid 1998. When the financial markets moved against them in ways that even these experienced financial gurus did not anticipate—19 months before the bear market began in March 2000—their personal net worth declined by hundreds of millions of dollars and their investment activity threatened the stability of the U.S. financial system, all in a matter of weeks!

Successful salespeople identify attractive prospects quickly; then they foster empathetic relationships that result in the sale of services. Beyond meeting minimum client expectations, they must effectively manage the dynamic tension between the quality of advice they offer to clients and the revenue they generate for their firm.

Today, some advisors have a strict fiduciary duty to put their clients' interests first, as defined by the Securities and Exchange Commission (SEC). Investment advisory firms and their representatives have this duty. Broker dealers and their registered representatives meanwhile operate under a different set of guidelines, defined by the National Association of Securities Dealers (NASD). Hedge fund managers and bankers do *not* have a strict fiduciary duty. Neither do many salespeople of life insurance or annuities.

Some salespeople operate under more than one set of compliance rules. At the same time, laws and regulations designed to curb abuses by wealth management practitioners, no matter how carefully crafted, contain nuances and loopholes that leave clients open to exploitation. The strict regulatory environment governing mutual funds, for example, hasn't prevented recent improper trading scandals.

As you can see, it can be very confusing (even for sophisticated clients) to determine whether a salesperson is giving quality advice.

So how does one effectively navigate the wealth management industry today? It isn't easy, but you can do it. I like to think of the industry today as being divided into three unique worlds. I describe these three worlds as "The Enchanted Forest," "The Capital Kibbutz," and "The Secret Society."

Each world is inhabited by financial professionals ready to assist visitors with asset management. Each has a distinct culture and value proposition. These worlds aren't constrained by the lines that once separated brokerage firms from mutual funds from trust banking; each world may contain all three. The only thing that you, the private investor, must do is decide which of the three "worlds" is the best destination for you. Let's look at each of them in turn.

The Enchanted Forest

I refer to the first world as "The Enchanted Forest." It is an investment land populated by ambitious clients and equally ambitious wealth advisors, both looking for the secret formula to investment success.

On its face, The Enchanted Forest is a beautiful and alluring place—its people energetic, entrepreneurial, and gregarious. The wealth advisors who live in The Enchanted Forest, for example, are compelling salespeople who regale prospective investors with stories of their investment prowess and client success. "Come with me, and I'll show you how to make money," they note to prospective investors in their face-to-face client meetings, marketing brochures, in their expensively produced TV ads, and on their breezy and interactive Web sites. They offer to act as financial guides to neophyte investors who can't understand the markets and who don't really want to understand the vagaries and complexities of investment, asset allocation, stock diversification, and wealth management goal setting. They add to the allure of their promises with slick advertising, enthusiastic market predictions, and expert commentary on the ever-changing nature of investing.

For their part, the clients you find in The Enchanted Forest are usually in search of easy keys to prosperity and financial success. In many cases, newly (or soon to be) wealthy people are open to suggestions and vulnerable to persuasion—traits that can make them easy prey for advisors who overwhelm them with financial jargon and promises of quick market success.

As a result, marriages of convenience often take place in The Enchanted Forest—between ambitious wealth industry people on the one hand and eager and impressionable investors on the other. When private clients sign on with an investment "guide," their guide entertains them, dazzles them with investment savvy, helps them choose investments, and collects his or her fees. Some of these investments do well, and when an investor scores success, his or her investment guide trumpets that news to the forest's treetops, hoping to entice other would-be investors to sign on board as well. Meanwhile, other investments languish, are quietly sold off and soon forgotten—by client and advisor alike.

Many of the investment "guides" that operate in The Enchanted Forest are hard-working professionals with winning personalities. They are usually competent and ethical, but sometimes not. In any event, investors invariably marvel at their energy, creativity, and grasp of investment principles and theory. Such adoration, mixed with insecurity, keeps clients coming back to these advisors for advice time and time again, even when there's not a real track record of success to support doing so.

As its name implies, The Enchanted Forest is occupied by many clients and advisors alike who think and act like they know what they're doing when it comes to investing, but just don't have The Four A's to compete against leading institutional investors. Remember when, in Sidebar 5.2 I said that when it comes to investing, make sure you know what you don't know? Well, there are a lot of people wandering around inside The Enchanted Forest who don't really know what they're doing. Yet the stakes they face may be high.

Conversely, some clients might simply play in The Enchanted Forest to have a good time, knowing full well there are better ways to generate alpha. For them, it doesn't really matter if they blow a little money;

they're in the game for the thrill of the chase. A good example of the kind of fun-seeking investor you often find in The Enchanted Forest is what I refer to as "The Country Club Gambler." The Country Club Gambler is drawn to The Enchanted Forest not to generate alpha, not to preserve his or her wealth, not to ensure a secure retirement, but largely to have fun. So, he or she dabbles in hedge funds, buys and sells securities or mutual funds, or invests in venture capital because doing so gives them a rush and puts them a little bit out there on the investment edge.

The Country Club Gambler is a casual investor—at least insofar as his Enchanted Forest investments are concerned. To him, investing is a high-end hobby, a kind of "brain candy" that goes hand in hand with discussions about economics, politics, and how successful companies grow. A Country Club Gambler may get into investing because he likes doing the math associated with calculating the odds of success or because he enjoys watching charts of stock prices tick up and down. Other Country Club Gamblers like the adrenaline rush of buying a stock at $10 and selling it at $20; or they are driven by greed, especially in the heat of a bull market. Still others use investing as a way to bond with their friends. They form investment groups or compare notes about their latest tips while playing poker at the club. Some of them even brag from time to time.

A common form of the Country Club Gambler is the "Angel Investor." I regularly observe people who've made some money trying their hand at providing financial support for fledgling businesses. Some are also interested in sitting on the boards of the companies they back. Angel Investing is theoretically a great way to grow your wealth on the back of other people's hard work. But it is also very risky. Angel Investing provides some really expensive education for most who are brave enough to try it. But that doesn't matter to the Angel Investor. To him or her, the heroism of embracing a compelling "vision of the future" wins out over the reality of short-term negative cash flow. At least it seems that way to me when I've heard some Angel Investors describe why they do what they do.

Sidebar 5.3: The Perils of Angel Investing

Angel Investing is not for the faint of heart. One of the reasons that being an Angel Investor is so attractive to many wealth creators is that they correctly identify that the one resource many capital-starved companies want more than anything is money. The potential to be of help to fledging cash-starved start-up companies, especially those whose mission is close to a benefactor's heart, or that are involved in exciting research or breakthrough technologies can be tough for a business entrepreneur to resist.

The problem is that many would-be Angel Investors are overconfident about their ability to invest in viable enterprises. So, their due diligence is inadequate, or their knowledge of capital structuring doesn't adequately protect their interests, or they don't have the right industry contacts. The situation can become especially perilous if the start-up venture is in a field or industry unknown to the Angel Investor. In one recent case, someone who had operated and then sold a successful business lost more than 25% of his net worth within two years of his liquidity event because of a misguided angel investment. All the while, several of his advisors pleaded with him to reconsider how he was investing his money. He was asked to consult with industry experts, to audit the numbers that were being given to him, and to stop putting good money in after bad. But all of this was to no avail. Unfortunately, this is an all-too-frequent occurrence.

Suffice it to say that Country Club Gambling is more a form of entertainment than a real investment strategy. And entertainment almost always comes with a cost. But based on the billions of consumer dollars people spend every year to go to football games, attend concerts, gamble in Las Vegas, or ski in Lake Tahoe, cost never seems to get in the way of a lot of people having fun.

While obviously you pay for football tickets or seats at a rock concert, most of the time there is no perceived out-of-pocket cost to Country Club Gambling, which makes it appear inexpensive—and all the more seductive. If you start investing with $100, you'll probably finish with at least $100 in your pocket. Your assets' growth may just not keep up with the market.

If you have fun doing it, indulge your desire to be a Country Club Gambler. But like any sport or leisure pursuit, do it in moderation, and watch out for creeping "opportunity costs" that, if unchecked, can begin to put a real crimp in your lifestyle or drag down the earnings from your "real" investments.

You may wind up being one of the few who is good enough to truly create alpha with a Country Club Gambler's strategy. But until you find other outlets for entertainment or convince yourself that you're good enough to really become a serious investor, I encourage you to allocate only a small portion of your net worth to this strategy. By doing so, you'll get all of the mental stimulation, adrenaline, and stories that go with investing, but if things go wrong, the pain you suffer isn't that severe.

Sometimes country club investments do, in fact, pay off and turn into serious alpha-generating investment strategies. This is exactly what happened to me. After nearly a decade in the investment business, I started out investing in alternative investment funds very slowly. But unlike many investors in The Enchanted Forest, I didn't sit back and wait for magic to strike. I did my homework nights and weekends. For nearly seven years, I ran a small experimental partnership before my family and I had the confidence to add alternative investments to our core strategy. Since then, we have learned a lot and been pleased with the results. We have built The Four A's, and our investment results have improved considerably, but now I am nervous all the time about what can go wrong!

The Secret Society

"The Secret Society" (not to be confused with some fraternity or elite military organization) is a domain for those who have figured out how to add value ("positive alpha") to investment assets. It is the world of hedge funds, private equity funds, concentrated actively managed mutual funds, and opportunistic real estate professionals that outperform standard investments. It is also the world of skilled business owners and people who leverage their careers to great business and financial advantage. E.A. Stuart and his son E.H. were bonafide members of The Secret Society, even though neither of them ever bought a stock. Finally, it is a world widely speculated about in the pages of business and finance magazines because most of its players like to keep low profiles and actively avoid the press.

In the domain of The Secret Society, inhabitants have learned how to consistently add value through good investment performance. Their return on investments exceeds expectations relative to an index for the market. An investor is able to create this so-called "positive alpha" by identifying and extracting value from individual companies or securities, or by choosing other professionals who have this skill. This is a rare and highly refined wealth management competence. Those who do it well have highly developed instincts. They also have deep investment expertise and resources to measure investment performance. But you don't know who these people are because they try to keep what they do secret. The last thing most of them want is competition.

You might think that if you could see into The Secret Society, it would be filled with euphoria and hubris. After all, these are people who have made it big with their investments, right? This isn't the case. Most of the residents of The Secret Society are on edge. They are driven investors and wealth advisors who are aggressively looking for new opportunities. But they are defensive, even a bit paranoid, at the same time. Although personalities run the gamut, the residents of The Secret Society are surprisingly modest and very self-assured, a rare but useful combination.

Those who operate in the investment world of The Secret Society display other unusual investment traits. For example, they are always looking for what is wrong with their investment perspective. George Soros, one of the great hedge fund investors and manager of the Quantum Fund, puts it this way: "By and large, I found managing a hedge fund extremely painful. I could never acknowledge my success, because that might stop me from worrying, but I had no trouble recognizing my mistakes."[7] How many advisors that you run across think like that?

Secret Society investors are also constantly on the hunt for what's wrong with other people's perspectives and for ways to take advantage of those misperceptions. Remember that alpha is a zero sum game. To create alpha, you have to take it from someone else. No one willingly gives away alpha in a market economy.

Most of the strategies that create alpha are sophisticated and involve complex analysis and (sometimes) execution. The plans devised in The Secret Society are highly confidential, customized, and sometimes proprietary. They're hard to replicate, and they usually command high fees. Investors and advisors who operate in The Secret Society don't want to publicize their success or discuss their investment approaches. They recognize that they are in privileged company and that too much public recognition of how they make money will actually make it more difficult for them to continue producing stellar investment results.

As such, there is no formal entrance to The Secret Society. Sometimes investors arrive in this investment world but don't know it. More often, people think they've arrived but really haven't. The signs of entry are elusive, subtle, and, at times, contradictory. There are a lot of imposters (both advisors and investors) who claim to have discovered a secret doorway into The Secret Society, but they're often fooling themselves as well as others by saying they've arrived. Most imposters take excessive risk and then are lucky for a time. They call their good performance alpha when it's not. When their luck runs out, the extra risk causes the investments to fall more violently. Therefore, the cost of thinking you're in The Secret Society when you're really not can be very high. That's why it's important for travelers looking for an entry into The Secret Society to possess highly developed wealth management skills, instincts, and resources—and to pick their advisors extremely carefully.

Most private and institutional investors who navigate the world of The Secret Society try to identify people like Soros who can create alpha for them. They look for money managers who have what it takes to add alpha to investments and who are looking for additional capital to manage. These investors ask prospective managers to discuss what they do in hopes of evaluating the depth of their investment expertise and whether they can add enough value to cover their fees and still return some of the benefit to the investor. It's a tough job, and it carries with it a lot of anxiety.

Besides shrewd investing, there are still other ways to enter The Secret Society. You can do it by leveraging your past career success and social prominence to pursue new business ventures or to start and build a new business. These aren't easy ways to gain entry to The Secret Society—and they can certainly create anxiety. But some people are better suited to creating wealth in these ways than through shrewd investing. You be the judge of what might be best for you!

The Capital Kibbutz

Finally, after The Enchanted Forest and The Secret Society, there's a world of investing I call "The Capital Kibbutz."

For those who don't know what a kibbutz is, it is a form of communal living practiced in Israel in which everyone in the community shares in the resources and wealth that come to that community. There are actually kibbutz-like communities in many other parts of the world, including the U.S.

The Capital Kibbutz is an investment zone in which everyone who participates shares in the rewards and risks of investment together. It is populated by institutions and individual advisors that can help clients who want to participate in the growth of the global economy but who recognize that they don't have sufficient expertise or resources to engage in Active Alpha Investing. It thus provides the perfect sanctuary for these investors to reside in.

For all practical purposes, The Capital Kibbutz is the world of indexed mutual funds, exchange traded funds, and term life insurance. It is a rather safe and tame investment world—one where the investor is taken care of but in which the investor rarely if ever gets a chance to take big risks.

To operate effectively in this world, you don't need to compete against institutions with highly developed competencies to extract alpha from the market. You don't need to think about which securities are cheap or expensive, and you don't buy or sell much. Most of the time, you sit passively and let the economy work for you. For these reasons, the costs of market participation are quite low.

In The Capital Kibbutz, there aren't many decisions that clients have to make. There isn't much opportunity to make big mistakes, and there is little incentive to abuse the system. Therefore, the amount of vigilance clients must exercise to protect their own interests isn't very great. Clients have time available to pursue interests other than investing and can sleep well at night. In The Capital Kibbutz, investments don't earn the kind of returns that one experiences in The Secret Society, but so long as the economy performs relatively well, the average investor earns a better return than in The Enchanted Forest.

Occasionally, there's an innovation in The Capital Kibbutz that everyone can share in. The growing interest in indexing by individuals has led some firms to create new tax-managed, index-linked products that try to add a little value to indices. Whatever "value added" is realized, however, comes not from advisors being better stock pickers, but by advisors managing their clients' taxes very efficiently. They do this by selling stocks that generate losses while letting the gains of others keep growing unrealized (and untaxed).

Meanwhile, "harvested" losses can be used to offset gains and make a portfolio even more tax efficient than a standard index fund would be. The added turnover from realizing losses does cause a portfolio's performance to diverge slightly from the index, but not much. Other times, this divergence is slightly additive, while sometimes it detracts slightly. But with improved tax efficiency, some Capital Kibbutz firms are able to generate alpha *after tax*, and they can do so with reasonably high probability. I include this kind of strategy in the domain of The Capital Kibbutz because even though it is a little more complicated than standard indexing or mutual funds, the investor's goal is still to participate broadly in financial markets.

As a wealth advisor, I encourage my friends, clients and colleagues to thoroughly explore the world of The Capital Kibbutz because it is a relatively safe investment harbor. Even though many people have tremendous ambitions for their wealth, most affluent and wealthy individuals, families, and institutions simply don't possess enough wealth management expertise and resources to operate in The Secret Society. What's more, The Capital Kibbutz is a wonderful place to get one's feet wet, investment wise. You can operate with a safety net so that you're never financially over-leveraged or locked into a high-risk investment strategy with only slight chances of yielding big returns.

A Travelogue: Helping a Friend Get Out of The Enchanted Forest and Into The Secret Society

Some years ago, a friend who had been wandering around The Enchanted Forest and had ended up being attacked by bandits and then a bear came to me for help. He is a smart businessman, but like most smart businessmen, he didn't understand the financial world. He had been sold a large number of specialized high-fee products in the mid-1990s. The general rise of the financial markets had hidden the wealth transfer that was taking place from him to his advisor. But this client was diligent enough to measure what was going on and to eventually recognize that things were not going according to his plans.

When he came to me, I recognized that trying to get him into The Secret Society right away was not a wise choice. He had become disenchanted with The Enchanted Forest and wanted out fast! But to get him into The Secret Society, he needed a more thorough education about wealth management, and this would require time. I also needed to earn his trust and understand how he responds to the volatility of financial markets and to the inevitable periods of underperformance that even the best investors have.

What did I do? I recommended that he leave The Enchanted Forest and enter The Capital Kibbutz. This would give him time to regroup and give us time to build a strong foundation to our professional relationship. He made this move five years ago by selling most of his high-fee, actively managed investment assets and moving them into index funds. We moved immediately from a largely equity portfolio to one that had a more balanced blend of global stocks, bonds, and cash. We then began an education program and built a better performance measurement system.

Within a couple of years, he was ready to consider additional asset classes and the occasional opportunity to invest with an active manager. Over time, we have supplemented his indexed portfolio with a modest amount of well-chosen, actively managed accounts.

My friend runs a business that has considerable assets in real estate and collectibles as well as significant cash flow—three good diversifiers. We periodically discuss the risk and return profile of the business and how it complements the risk and return profile of the investment portfolio. We have integrated the two elements of his asset profile for purposes of executing a holistic investment strategy.

Over the course of about five years, my friend has tasted The Secret Society, but he still has most of his financial assets in The Capital Kibbutz. With time, his education will improve and opportunities to create alpha will present themselves. His confidence that he can distinguish between The Enchanted Forest and The Secret Society will grow as well, ensuring that his position in The Secret Society will become more secure.

Mutual Fund Indexing: Why it's *the* Investment Path for Most Individuals

When push comes to shove, investing is a tough business. For that reason, it's probably best that *most* investors limit their investment ambitions to the world of The Capital Kibbutz. And there's nothing wrong with that.

Of all the investment instruments available to investors in The Capital Kibbutz, there is one that is ideal for most investors to consider using. It's not a glamorous, exciting solution. It doesn't mirror the bold impetuosity of the Country Club Gambler. Nor does it embody the secrecy and mystery of The Secret Society. Even the term to define it isn't terribly compelling. But it is truly the best way for most investors to go. It's called "indexing."

Briefly stated, indexing involves investing in a statistical composite of securities that mimics the characteristics of an entire investment market or asset class, like the S&P 500, the Russell 3000, the Wilshire 5000, or other well-known broad-based indices.

Because most index funds contain a broad and representative cross section of desirable financial markets, there's no portfolio manager trying to improve performance by buying or selling individual securities. For that reason, most of the well-designed ones create very little in the way of investment fees, brokerage commissions, or capital gains taxes—at least until the index itself is sold.

So, should you pin *your* wealth management strategy on effective use of index funds? Consider this: Approximately $3.5 trillion of America's pension plans are indexed, or about a third of the total. This is up 400% since 1990.

Corporations know the value of indexing. In the last 20 years, most large pension plans have gone from having dozens of portfolio managers with various risk strategies to having a core stock portfolio that is indexed to a broad market benchmark.

What's more, there's broad agreement that indexing makes sense for a wide variety of investors.

"Most investors, both institutional and individual, will find that the best way to own common stocks is through an index fund that charges minimal fees. Those following this path are sure to beat the net results (after fees and expenses) delivered by the great majority of investment professionals," notes Warren Buffett, Chairman of Berkshire Hathaway, and considered by many people to be the world's most astute investor.[8]

There are a couple of things worth noting about this quote. First, Buffett talks here about *most*, not all, investors. He recognizes that a few investors—he, for example—do belong to The Secret Society. There just aren't a lot of people like him. Second, he states that both institutions *and* individuals will benefit from indexing, even though institutions have far greater clout in the marketplace.

But despite Buffett's advice, individual clients have been surprisingly slow to embrace indexing. After all, most individual investors don't have the expertise to build the Four A's needed for Active Alpha Investing. What's more, the case for indexing is actually stronger for individuals than it is for institutions for two reasons:

1. *Indexing is tax efficient relative to active management.* This can save taxable investors a lot of money, but is of no benefit to pension plans or endowments.

2. *While most private investors can't compete with institutions for access to the best active managers, they do have access to the same indexed products as institutional investors do at almost the same cost.* Indeed, for index products the fee differential between institutions and individuals is a mere .2% or less. By contrast, in the case of active management, the fee differential (between individual investors and institutions) is often a half a percent or more.

Indexing really is the way most individual investors should go. It may not be the most exciting route to take, but it can bring with it predictable and consistent investment returns. And in a volatile business and marketplace environment, this is undoubtedly the course most people will want to consider taking, if they lack the stomach to pursue alpha in The Secret Society or The Enchanted Forest. In Chapter 6, "Picking Your Investment Strategy," I'll have recommendations for you on how to index successfully, as well as ideas you can use to explore the worlds of The Enchanted Forest and The Secret Society, if you wish.

A New Perspective on the Wealth Management Industry

The financial services world is a world in transition. Distinct lines separating mutual fund companies, brokers, bankers, life insurers, and trust companies no longer exist. For the last ten years or so, all of these business models have been on a path to convergence. Today, you can buy mutual funds in a trust, get brokerage services from the same company that manages your mutual funds, and your broker most likely has a trust company. Life insurance and annuity products look a lot like mutual funds. Banks do a lot more than lend money. This blurring just adds to the complexity of the industry and confusion around the merits of the ever-growing array of products you can buy.

Open architecture is also here to stay. Traditional stock and bond portfolios have been sliced and diced in infinite ways. Alternative investments like venture capital and hedge funds are becoming more elaborate every day. The administration of wealth management businesses is also becoming more complicated, as previously distinct financial industries merge and we have to deal with the realities of terrorism and globalization.

All this change continues to make the work of a financial advisor complicated. Ten years ago, you could make a good living advising people about stocks and bonds, maybe in a mutual fund, maybe in a trust, maybe in a brokerage account. Today, financial advisors have a hard time just keeping up with all of the products that are available to their clients. Everyone is asking about hedge funds, commodity trading, venture capital, and timber. On top of that, the Patriot Act, passed by Congress in the wake of 9/11, mandates that financial advisors comply with numerous new "know your customer" provisions, which adds significant administrative responsibilities to an already staggering amount of advisor paperwork. Finally, wealth advisors today face time pressures to achieve specific sales goals and must often attend sales and operational meetings that further cut into their time to be active advisors to their clients.

Traveling the Investment Landscape

As an investor, it isn't necessary to visit only one investment world because, depending on your investment skills and interests, you can achieve investment success in any of the places I've just described.

If you tire of the safety of The Capital Kibbutz, or the pressure of The Secret Society, or the costs associated with the fun and excitement of The Enchanted Forest, you can move around.

If you are just getting started on a journey through the financial services world, I recommend you start by visiting The Capital Kibbutz. It is by far the easiest investment world to figure out, and it won't cost you much to learn from your mistakes. You can also establish a solid benchmark of success from which to determine the potential "value-added" profits that can come from increased complexity and fees as you navigate the other investment worlds.

You are less likely to get lost or confused in The Capital Kibbutz than in The Secret Society or The Enchanted Forest. If you establish a strong base there, you can travel to the other worlds with only a small part of your financial assets to see how much you like the experience. If you enjoy the complexity of The Secret Society and you possess the skills to navigate your way successfully there, you can shift your wealth management objectives to pursue more aggressive, growth-driven financial goals. On the other hand, if you are by nature entrepreneurial and are willing to watch your back a bit, exploring the world of The Enchanted Forest may be more to your liking and a good foray away from the safety and predictability of The Capital Kibbutz—with its focus on broad market participation and indexing. Just keep one thought in mind if you go into the forest: Keep your eye out for bulls. And beware of lions, tigers, and especially bears!

Conclusion

Now that you've learned a little bit about the three worlds described in this chapter, ask yourself: Which is the best match for me?

This chapter has focused extensively on the nature of the wealth management industry today and on the importance of matching your investment skill set (The Four A's) with an appropriate strategy. I have discussed the relative merits of open architecture and mutual funds, indexing and alternative investing, brokerage, and trust companies. I've also introduced you to "The Capital Kibbutz," "The Secret Society," and "The Enchanted Forest" in hopes that you can see more clearly where you should reside.

In upcoming chapters, we'll explore specifically what you should do to develop your investment prowess so you can successfully execute your chosen wealth management strategy to meet your needs and those of your family. The course you embark on will depend, of course, on where you see yourself positioned in the wealth management industry at this particular moment.

Before we proceed to the next chapter, answer the review and discussion questions I've put at the end of this chapter because they will help you put your thoughts in order for what's coming up next.

Chapter 5: Issues to Discuss with Your Family

1. How knowledgeable are you about investing? How hard do you want to work to become more knowledgeable?

2. Do you have that rare personality type that is suited for The Secret Society? Do you enjoy the thrill of The Enchanted Forest even if it is likely to cost you? Will you grow impatient with The Capital Kibbutz?

3. Does your wealth management competence match your investment strategy? If there's a mismatch, where is it?

4. To what extent do you "put yourself in the hands" of your investment advisor(s) rather than take charge of meetings with investment advisors? Do you trust your advisor because of his or her skill or because of his or her character?

5. Does your advisor's competence match the strategy he or she is recommending to you? What specifically are the "value added" services that your current wealth management firm claims it provides to you? Can you describe the specific services you receive?

6. Can you measure the value of your advisor's advice?

7. What makes you think that his or her investment advice is significantly better than average? Are you getting that advisor's best advice? That advisor's firm's best advice?

8. Do you have enough wealth to compete effectively in the world of alternative investments?

9. Are you pleased with the rate of return you are currently realizing on your investments? Do you know what it is?

10. To what extent are you aware of the fees, taxes, and administrative expenses that you pay as a percentage of your investment profits? Do you know the dollar value of what you paid last year in fees, taxes, and expenses? Can you estimate what these expenses are?

11. Do you currently use index funds? If so, what has been your experience with them? Are you interested in combining them with other kinds of investments? If not, why not?

12. What has been your overall experience with investment advisors or financial consultants? Is it generally positive or not? If not, what was lacking for you in the relationship? Be specific.

13. Where do you think you are with your investment strategy today? Are you in:

   The Capital Kibbutz

   The Enchanted Forest

   The Secret Society

14. What are your future investment and wealth management goals? Please be specific.

Endnotes

1 Bogle Financial Markets Research Center, "As the Index Fund Moves From Heresy to Dogma... What More Do We Need To Know?" Remarks by John C. Bogle, April 13, 2004, http://www.vanguard.com/bogle_site/sp20040413.html. *The 2004 Mutual Fund Fact Book*, published by the Investment Company Institute, and *ICI's Trends in Mutual Fund Investing*, January 28, 2005. *Financial Analysts Journal*, January/February 2005, "The Mutual Fund Industry 60 Years Later: For Better or Worse?," by John C. Bogle.
2 Barron's, February 7, 2005, page 22.
3 Bogle Financial Markets Research Center, "In Investing, You Get What You Don't Pay For." Remarks by John C. Bogle, February 2, 2005, http://www.vanguard.com/bogle_site/sp20050202.html.
4 Ibid.
5 "Tax-Efficient Investing Is Easier Said Than Done," by Robert H. Jeffrey, *The Journal of Wealth Management*, Summer 2001.
6 Barron's, February 7, 2005, page 21.
7 *The Crisis of Global Capitalism*, by George Soros, Public Affairs Press, 1998, page 24.
8 Berkshire Hathaway Inc., 1996 Annual Report, Chairman's Letter to Shareholders.

6

PICKING YOUR INVESTMENT STRATEGY

"Once you have made yourself rich, for gosh sakes don't lose it. The inconvenience of going from rich to poor is greater than most people can tolerate."

—*Fred J. Young, author of*
How to Get Rich and Stay Rich

icking an investment strategy and sticking with it through market ups and downs is essential to your long-term financial health. It's the single most important financial decision you will make! Like any long-term decision, it requires careful consideration. This chapter describes three options for constructing an investment strategy, each of which has specific benefits and requires specific actions on your part to implement.

Three Value-Added Financial Strategies for Managing Wealth

The investment strategy you choose will be based on how aggressively you want to grow your wealth, how much time and skill you're willing to allocate to managing your wealth, and your actual net worth. The three strategies are:

- Index Investing
- Barbell Investing
- Active Alpha Investing

Strategy #1: Index Investing

I introduced indexing when I talked about The Capital Kibbutz in the previous chapter. Indexing is the act of investing in a total financial market (i.e., the U.S. stock market, international stocks, or the U.S. bond market), rather than trying to select specific securities within that market that are likely to grow faster than the market as a whole.

I often recommend indexing because it is a proven method to secure a long-term annual rate of return of 6% to 8% on your financial assets, as long as you carefully control investment-related costs. Adopting this approach puts you squarely in the investment kingdom of The Capital Kibbutz. The actual rate of return you achieve, whether higher or lower, depends entirely on your asset mix and on how well financial markets perform. Study after study concludes that if you index, you are likely to end up with more money in your pocket than most people who choose more aggressive and time-consuming investment strategies. This conclusion applies whether your account is taxable or held in a tax-deferred retirement plan.

How Do You Implement an Index Investing Strategy?
Implementing an Index Investing strategy is quite simple and involves four Critical Success Factors (CSFs) that are essential to success. They include:

> **CSF #1:** Strategic Asset Allocation
>
> **CSF #2:** Index Selection
>
> **CSF #3:** Tax Management
>
> **CSF #4:** Rebalancing

The good news with indexing is that you only have to deal with each of these factors once, after which you can institute a process that puts the entire management of your assets on autopilot. I still recommend that you review your strategy once a year, but interim decisions can be formulaic. Your annual performance review is more focused on assuring that everything is on track rather than on making additional strategic decisions.

Let's briefly discuss the four CSFs in the context of an indexing strategy:

CSF #1: Strategic Asset Allocation. With indexing, strategically allocating your assets to different investment funds or pools is a long-term decision—one that may last unchanged for years or decades. Allocation is driven by a desire to optimize the return you expect to achieve for the amount of volatility that you feel you can withstand in your portfolio. In any diversified investment strategy, including indexing, you must invest in a blend of asset classes, each of which responds somewhat differently to economic stimuli.

For example, stocks, bonds, real estate, and commodities all tend to react somewhat differently to combinations of real economic growth, inflation, and interest rates. Emerging market stocks respond differently from large capitalization U.S. stocks. The stocks of energy companies respond differently from healthcare companies, and both respond differently to economics and demographics than automobile or paper companies do.

Optimizing a strategic asset allocation is something that wealth management firms do reasonably well. Most advisors who work for these companies have the training to help you determine the strategic asset allocation that's right for you.

It is my belief that everybody who pursues an Index Investment strategy should be well diversified. They should invest in most or all of the following asset classes: U.S. stocks, international and emerging markets stocks, commodities (especially energy)-related investments, real estate-related investments, high-quality U.S. bonds (either taxable or tax exempt), high-quality foreign bonds, and high-yield bonds. None of these asset classes should exceed 40% of your exposure. Someone willing to take reasonable risk might have a strategic allocation target that looks like this:

- U.S. stocks   35%
- International/emerging stocks   20%
- Commodities-focused   7%
- Real estate-specific   8%
- High-quality U.S. bonds   20%
- High-quality foreign bonds   5%
- High-yield bonds   3%
- Cash   2%

CSF #2: Index Selection. In the last five years, there has been a rapid proliferation of indexing choices. There are traditional index mutual funds and exchange traded funds (ETFs), some named after creepy animals like SPDRs (Spiders) and VIPERs, and even options and futures on indices that can be used to create "synthetic" index funds. Synthetic funds are index funds made up of derivative securities and cash—not actual underlying stocks and bonds. The number of funds that mimic a wide range of indices has proliferated in the last five to ten years.

Given what's available in the market, what would I own? Here's the breakdown by percentage of assets:

- A total U.S. stock market index mutual fund (35%)
- An international stock market index mutual fund (including emerging markets) (20%)
- A total U.S. bond market index fund—including high-yield bonds (23%)
- A foreign bond market index fund (5%)
- A money market fund or bank account (2%)
- A commodity ETF with an emphasis on energy (7%)
- A REIT (Real Estate Investment Trust) index fund (8%)

I only buy "no load" mutual funds and recommend that you do the same because the costs are lower. It reduces the universe of mutual funds you can buy and therefore makes choice easier.

CSF #3: Tax Management. By its nature, let me explain why an Index Investment strategy is the most tax-efficient investment strategy around:

A broad U.S. equity index fund has roughly 5% turnover in a year, mostly caused by merger and acquisition activity, so that the typical stock is held within the fund for nearly 20 years! Over most 20-year periods, stocks generate a lot of gains and, as long as they aren't sold, the gains aren't taxed. This is a valuable characteristic of some, but not all, index funds. Generally speaking, the more broadly diversified the fund, the lower the turnover.

By contrast, a very low turnover, *actively managed* fund buys and sells each stock in its portfolio about every four years, and the average mutual fund "turns over" once a year. Such rapid turnover means that your gains are taxed much more frequently and sometimes at higher rates. Not only does high turnover add tax cost, it also adds transaction costs, another reason to lean toward indexing.

CSF #4: Rebalancing. I recommend you periodically rebalance your fund positions so that their weightings remain consistent with your strategic asset allocation objectives. The fund mix can get out of balance when one or more of your funds does especially well or comparatively poor relative to the other funds. Whenever any of your funds differs from its strategic allocation target by 15% or more, it is time to rebalance. For instance, if your U.S. stock exposure rises from 35% to 41% (a 17% increase), I would rebalance the exposure back to 35%. If your exposure to commodity-related assets drops to 5% from 7% (a 29% drop), add assets to bring it back to 7%.

The best way to rebalance your portfolio is to use your cash flow rather than selling an investment (which incurs taxes and transaction costs.) For instance, if you want to reduce your exposure to U.S. stocks and you are adding to your investments with cash flow, buy other asset classes first to bring the overall portfolio into balance relative to your strategic asset allocation target. If you are withdrawing capital from your investments for spending or to pay taxes, draw it first from stocks. That way you don't create taxable transactions simply for the sake of rebalancing. If you need to shift assets from one fund to another to get back into balance, minimize the amount of net gains you have to realize by first selling shares in those index funds that have the highest costs associated with them. Obviously, tax-efficient rebalancing is not an issue in tax-deferred accounts, but due to potential transaction costs, you still want to make changes as efficiently as possible.

Sometimes, an index fund with an average cost that is well below the current price includes some shares that you bought above the current price. If you sell those shares and account for them correctly, you can realize a loss and use it to offset gains you have realized elsewhere. This is called tax lot accounting and is another useful, simple tool of integrated wealth management.

Buy Low, Sell High

Part of the beauty of a well-diversified portfolio is that individual asset classes perform well (and badly) at different times. Done systematically, rebalancing forces you to trim investments that have done well and add to those that haven't done so well in the recent past. Why do this? If an investment is going up, shouldn't you keep it?

In many cases, you'll want to keep high-performing investments because they *are* profitable. On the other hand, investors have a tendency to fall in love with their winners (that have gotten more expensive), and very few investments remain good investments forever.

Investors also get frustrated and sell the ones that have declined in value (and become cheaper). Periodically rebalancing your portfolio forces you to engage in counterintuitive behavior that is usually beneficial to investing. It also reduces potential downside risk and ensures that you don't become overly dependent on a few investments that have appreciated a lot in value. This is what happened to many investors who had great exposure to high-flying growth stocks in March of 2000 and who saw their portfolios decline a lot over the next several years. Think of rebalancing in terms of what the skipper of a sailboat does to catch the wind on the ocean. He or she periodically trims the sails to remain in the wind's favor, stay on course, and continue on a steady and smooth path toward the ultimate destination.

FINAL THOUGHTS ON INDEXING

By choosing an indexing strategy, you'll reap long-term results better than most investors. And you'll pay only modest taxes, assuming that the global economy continues to progress as it has over the last 100 years. This approach often outperforms more complicated investment strategies, whatever the economic and market environment looks like.

So why don't wealth advisors push this approach more with clients? There are four reasons:

First, indexing isn't very profitable for the wealth management industry. As is often the case, Vanguard's Jack Bogle[1] said it best: "The problem faced by low-cost, no-load index funds is that, as I have often observed, '(almost) all the darn money goes to the investor!'"

A typical diversified U.S. stock or bond index fund has annual costs of 0.25% or less. With this fee structure, an indexed portfolio of $10 million generates less than $25,000 in annual fees and expenses. A $1,000,000 portfolio generates about $2,500 dollars in fees. A $100,000 portfolio generates just $250 in fees. Furthermore, index funds have almost no transaction costs associated with them.

By contrast, the average equity mutual fund has management fees and expenses five times that of index funds. Separately managed account fees might be six or seven times that of an index fund. The extra $100,000, $10,000, or $1,000 you pay for the privilege of having your fund actively managed adds a lot to your investment firm's pockets.

On top of management fees, actively managed funds typically have annual transaction costs of 1% to 2%. In short, actively managed funds are much more lucrative for advisors than index funds!

Second, if you select an indexing strategy, it sets a higher standard for any active manager that comes across your path and promises to deliver to you an above-average rate of return on your investments. By gaining experience in indexing, you will know what "average" means and will hold active managers to a higher standard. They will know that they have to beat indexing (maybe even on an after-tax basis) to gain your trust and your business. That is a tough performance hurdle.

Third, wealth advisors don't push indexing because low index fund fees generate less revenue for firms to spend on marketing campaigns. Profit margins are low on index funds, so firms that offer them have little excess cash flow to spend on marketing. What's more, these firms have built trillion-dollar businesses by relying on sophisticated investors who understand the benefits of indexing to simply seek them out.

Finally, indexing isn't nearly as interesting for advisors to talk about as the other two strategies that I'll be covering shortly. After you make the decision to index and set up a structure to do so, the investment decisions move to autopilot. For people who live and breathe the markets, "being on autopilot" with your investments isn't a very exciting place to be.

All that said, if you absolutely must indulge the temptation to try something more "ambitious" than indexing, I suggest you do some research and then allocate no more than 10% to 15% of your assets to more complex strategies (outlined later in this chapter), and then see how you do over a three- to five-year period. If you're successful, then and only then add another 10% to 15% for several more years. This gives you time to experience different market conditions, sharpen your skills, and test your advisors.

Strategy #2: Barbell Investing

The Barbell Investing strategy is best for anyone who is still in their working years and isn't an investment expert. By looking at Figure 6.1, you can see why this strategy references the weights that many of us use to keep fit. One end of the barbell represents the management of your financial assets, probably using the Index Investing strategy. The counterweight is the energy and capital you have tied up in your career, an existing business, or a new business enterprise. Holding the two weights firmly together is sound cash flow management. Many people who engage in Barbell Investing maintain a high savings rate. For periods of time, others rely on investment income when their business is in a startup phase but then revert to a high savings rate when the business is stable.

Figure 6.1   Can you handle the weight and keep the barbell balanced? If so, it's a ticket to The Secret Society.

Barbells are heavy and need to be balanced. The left-hand weight should have most of your assets but require only a modest amount of your time to manage. This leaves you free to focus most of your time on the right-hand weight, which at least for a time should have only a modest portion of your assets. The right mix of time and assets on each side of the barbell keeps the weights in balance.

You will be working hard to manage the barbell. It is the most likely way for non-investment experts to gain access to The Secret Society because they leverage their skills, past business experience, and relationships to keep building wealth, yet they are also diversified in the face of an uncertain future.

What Can You Expect with a Barbell Investing Strategy?
The Barbell Investing strategy represents a powerful approach to wealth preservation and wealth building because it encourages you to keep working. Because you are (probably) earning compensation while you are building your career or business, your financial assets keep growing

without a drag from spending. This bolsters financial security and clears the way for you to take modestly greater risks with your investments. This, in turn, can help you earn more from those investments and enjoy more discretionary income in the future. This is a virtuous cycle if you can make it work. It means you can embrace a *growth-driven* financial goal instead of being forced to opt for a *distribution-driven* goal. As you now know, there's a quantum difference between the two! On the other hand, if you take entrepreneurial risk and the business fails (which businesses often do), you can rest assured that your financial assets will be there when you really need them.

Figure 6.2 shows the annualized rate of return you will achieve if you use a Barbell Investing strategy that invests 80% of your assets in index funds and 20% in a concentrated growth asset over a 10-year period. In this instance, there is no rebalancing between the two sides of the barbell over the entire 10-year period. The left vertical column shows various likely rates of return from the index funds; the top horizontal row shows the possible rates of return from the concentrated growth asset.

The shaded areas show those combinations of returns that will position you solidly in The Secret Society, even though most of your assets are indexed. For example, let us say that you earn 7% per year for 10 years on the assets that are indexed. You also allocated 20% of your assets to a business at the beginning of the decade. The business was successful and its value grew at a rate of 20% per year for 10 years. At the end of the decade, your combined assets have grown at a rate of 10.9% per annum, almost tripling in value.

Barbell Strategy: Annualized Rate of Return (ROR) Over Ten Years

		ROR Growth Assets (20%)				
		−100%	0%	10%	20%	30%
ROR Indexed Assets (80%)	6%	3.7%	5.0%	6.9%	10.3%	15.4%
	7%	4.6%	5.9%	7.7%	10.9%	15.8%
	8%	5.6%	6.8%	8.4%	11.5%	16.2%

ROR Blended Assets (100%)

Figure 6.2 Following the Barbell Investing strategy can achieve well above average rates of return while keeping your wealth prudently diversified.

Let's look at the two extreme examples of potential results that are represented within this chart.

Worst-Case: If you invest 20% of your assets in a growth asset that turns out to be a total write-off (−100%) after a decade's work and your return on indexed assets is 6% per annum over the same period, your combined assets will still have a positive return of 3.7% before taking leakages, if any, into account. This is because you've been prudent about the amount of capital (20%) you committed to the risky venture, you didn't dip in savings to cover your living expenses, and because the conservatively invested "indexed" portion (80%) of the barbell generated enough return to make up the loss.

Best-Case: If your indexed assets generate an 8% return per annum and your growth asset generates a 30% annualized rate of return, after 10 years (before any leakages), you will have generated a 16.2% rate of return on your combined assets. What the chart doesn't show is that even with solid results from indexing, after 10 years of compounding, your growth asset constitutes 57% of your total portfolio, up from 20%. You are really growing your wealth quickly, though you are running a larger and larger risk by owning a single concentrated asset. At this point, you should consider trimming some of your concentrated assets and investing the proceeds on the other side of the barbell to keep things in balance.

CRITICAL SUCCESS FACTORS FOR THE BARBELL INVESTING STRATEGY
To implement a Barbell Investing strategy, there are three CSFs. You must

> **CSF #1:** Target the right growth asset.
>
> **CSF #2:** Select the percent of assets to put toward your growth asset.
>
> **CSF #3:** Adjust the strategic asset allocation of your diversified investments to account for your concentrated growth asset.

CSF #1: Target the Right Growth Asset. For the 20% or less of your funds that you will allocate to the "growth" side of the equation, you have to decide what type of asset to target. You could:

Start, Buy, or Control a Company

Some people manage to have significant liquidity events while still controlling a profitable company. This is a great opportunity for those who can pull it off. They get diversification and continue to oversee a business they know very well. They know their employees, customers, suppliers, and competitors. They know the pricing structure of the industry and understand the regulations. Their "guts" are well attuned to the issues of the business.

Many wealthy people cannot engineer such a low-risk Barbell Investing strategy. After a liquidity event, they need to acquire or start a new business. In making new acquisitions, the further you get away from your field of expertise, the greater the risks. Most people who make the transition from one industry to another for the first time underestimate how difficult the transition is. You obviously want a business that has potential, but you also want to accurately calibrate your level of competence to evaluate and manage new ventures. It helps to stick with what you know.

One harmful pattern that I see regularly repeated is the successful business executive turned venture capitalist. Even business executives with substantial experience in acquisitions often discover (painfully) that their existing skill set and that of a successful financier are different. It is a much tougher transition than you expect.

Extend Your Career

If you have built a lucrative career, you may not have to invest any capital to build a growth asset (like a business) that substantially increases your net worth. Many people extend their careers beyond liquidity events by staying with their company after it is sold or by switching to another company. By working in a corporate environment, they earn stock options, restricted stock, and other forms of long-term compensation that defer tax and can grow significantly in value without putting up any capital at all.

Many lawyers, doctors, and dentists never have liquidity events. Instead, they keep putting a significant portion of their earnings into savings each year, manage these savings responsibly, and watch their assets grow.

The longer they stay in a well-paying career, the greater their opportunity to channel their earnings into savings and the longer those savings grow without being tapped for spending and monthly expenses.

If you love what you do, keep working into your sixties, seventies, or eighties. Do it for enjoyment *and* the extra income. Want more free time? Don't retire! Just scale back the hours you devote to paid work and begin to tap into your savings to make up the difference. You'll be happier, and from a financial planning standpoint you'll be better off, too.

The key to choosing the right growth asset is to take advantage of your skills, experience, judgment, personal contacts, and professional network to identify attractive opportunities to pursue. The "next act of your life" might very well focus on something that you enjoy with a passion, that you know a lot about, that leverages your expertise, that enables you to generate income, *and* that reduces your reliance on unearned income.

CSF #2: Select the percent of assets to put toward your growth asset. A key distinction of being wealthy is that you can afford to take bigger financial risks than most people can. A person with $100 million in assets, for example, can afford to put a larger percentage of their assets "at risk" without jeopardizing their financial security than a person who has accumulated $1 million in assets.

Still, the riskier the business venture you want to undertake, the less capital—as a percentage of your total wealth—you should put toward it regardless of the size of your assets. You may have a great idea for a new product or service, or want to launch a biotech start-up to create new drugs. But if that venture fails and you've invested all your disposable assets in that initiative, you won't be in a position to try again.

So, what should you do? If you feel comfortable allocating 20% of your wealth to the high-potential return side of your barbell, and your risky business idea has only a one in four chance of succeeding, consider allocating just 5% of your wealth to this particular venture. That way, if your venture fails, you will still have capital left over to try again—to take more "bites of the apple" through other endeavors—without depleting your total assets.

You should also consider your age when addressing this CSF. If you invest a large amount of your wealth in a new business in your late forties or older, it may be tough to recover financially if the business fails. You could find yourself living a more frugal retirement than you planned. However, the same situation in your thirties gives you several decades to rebuild your retirement nest egg.

Sidebar 6.1: The Pros and Cons of Leverage

Almost everyone who has investable assets also has debt or some other form of financial leverage. Leverage can take the form of credit card debt and home mortgages, but it also includes taxes payable, debt in a company, margin loans, or derivative securities. When things are going well, leverage can be a wonderful thing. During hard times, leverage undermines net worth, forces untimely asset sales, and worse, can increase the correlation among otherwise unrelated assets. A careful analysis of financial leverage on your personal balance sheet can improve returns or protect against a rapid decline in wealth caused by the spillover effects of excessive leverage.

The most dangerous form of debt you can have is "recourse debt" that can potentially lay claim to your entire estate. Recourse debt enables the lender to seize any or all of your assets if you don't meet the terms of your loan. Most personal loans, except mortgages, are recourse loans. If you get into an illiquidity crunch, you may be forced to sell your assets at distressed prices to meet payment terms.

But even non-recourse debt can have ripple effects. Non-recourse debt, like first mortgages, only has specifically named collateral—like a house or a car. In a diversified investment portfolio, two asset classes can each have discreet, non-recourse loans associated with them—for example, private equity and real estate. Under *normal* circumstances, one asset class may remain steady in value when another declines. These assets are uncorrelated, an expected benefit of owning a properly diversified

---

portfolio. However, if both are leveraged, a general move in interest rates could affect both assets similarly and simultaneously, increasing the correlation of otherwise uncorrelated asset classes.

Leverage in investment portfolios can also be hidden. If an investment manager buys stocks in highly leveraged companies, she adds leverage to a client's portfolio. But the client sees only a portfolio of stocks, not the debt and other leverage of the companies in the portfolio. If the manager is correct and the companies improve, their stocks will soar even though the combined value of the company's stock and debt (its enterprise value) increases just a little. But the reverse is true as well, adding considerable risk to the portfolio.

Modest amounts of the right kind of leverage may be attractive. Putting a million-dollar mortgage on your primary and/or secondary residence is very tax efficient because you can deduct the interest expense from your taxes. Furthermore, mortgage interest rates are much more attractive than most other forms of consumer debt, and the debt is usually non-recourse. I own a 30-year, fixed-rate mortgage rather than an adjustable rate mortgage because I want the security of knowing what my payment commitments will be.

As a general rule, I believe that the risks of leverage are substantial. Leverage can dramatically reduce your flexibility to respond, either defensively or opportunistically, to a stress environment. Leverage can also set off a contagion effect that can run out of control and quickly destroy wealth that took decades to build. Periodically, hedge funds unravel because of contagion effects. But individuals can be wiped out, too. I fear that many speculators in residential property will suffer this fate when the housing market slows from its current torrid pace. When it happens, opportunists will be standing by to acquire good properties at bargain prices from forced sellers.

CSF #3: Adjust the strategic asset allocation of your diversified investments to account for your concentrated growth asset. The 80% side of your barbell that contains your strategic asset allocation is generally designed by wealth advisors with the assumption that you don't have any concentrated growth assets on the 20% side of your barbell. Therefore, if you still have a career or control a business you need to adjust your asset allocation accordingly. For example, if you accumulate real estate investment properties, you can use your properties to achieve your real estate asset allocation target, instead of REIT (Real Estate Investment Trust) index funds. If you have a career in banking or the securities industry, you might want to consider reducing your exposure to stock market investments so that you don't experience losses in your investment portfolio at the same time your job is in jeopardy for precisely the same reasons. Finally, if you are in a job that isn't affected by economic downturns (you're an undertaker, dentist, or tax accountant, for example) your earned income stream is very stable and has "bond-like" characteristics. Consequently, you may feel comfortable with *greater* exposure to stocks.

FINAL THOUGHTS ON BARBELL INVESTING
Even if the scale of your wealth affords you the opportunity to devote yourself to investing full time, consider strongly whether you really want to do this. I've seen many people quit their careers to devote themselves to actively managing their portfolios only to find that they would have fared better if they stayed focused on what they were good at and indexed the rest of their assets! Barbell Investing makes sense for people who are good at business or who have successful careers in other areas.

Strategy #3: The Active Alpha Investing Strategy

The words "active" (read, aggressive) and "alpha" (read, dominant) suggest a strategy that is all about red Ferraris. Active Alpha Investing involves integrating a diversified portfolio of traditional securities like stocks and bonds with exciting, high-return potential alternative investments, such as private equity, venture capital, commodities, real estate, and hedge funds.

Most of the people who build such portfolios have bought the marketing hype and are thinking "Ferrari." Their goal is getting into The Secret Society, but they wind up instead in The Enchanted Forest. Indeed, for every 1,000 happy travelers to The Enchanted Forest, there may be just 200 people executing an Index Investing strategy in The Capital Kibbutz and only 150 people who add value through an Active Alpha Investing strategy.

Even then, the majority of Active Alpha seekers who succeed in their endeavors will beat the returns of those who employ an Index Investing strategy by only a small margin; yet they will put enormous amounts of work into it.

Given these odds, Active Alpha investors have a steep hill to climb. Why then do so many make the attempt? Probably for the same reasons mountain climbers climb Mount Everest—for the challenge! Beating the odds is at the heart of the psyche of most private investors.

What Can You Expect with Active Alpha Investing?
If executed well, an Active Alpha Investment strategy has the long-term potential to generate a 10% to 15% annualized return in a variety of market and economic circumstances. The key is to achieve modestly above-average returns consistently over a long period of time.

The Lucas Family Uses the Active Alpha Investment Strategy
Ten years ago, I convinced my family to undertake an Active Alpha Investment strategy that we still use today. It is similar to the strategy used by endowments of many leading educational institutions and a growing number of pension plans. After having extolled the virtues of an Index Investing strategy, why does my family stay dedicated to an Active Alpha Investment strategy? More than anything, it's because we:

• Pursue a long-term, multigenerational wealth management approach.
• Have the financial resources to develop in-house expertise.
• Have a family culture that supports it.
• Have a talented team in place to execute it!

Our style is more like my father's 1965 Plymouth Valiant—steady, long term, and understated. We didn't exactly embrace this strategy overnight. In 1982, we started the Lucas family office with limited investment experience, two CEOs from the most respected investment firms in the country who acted as trusted advisors, service agreements with a blue chip brokerage firm, and a well-respected trust bank.

Then, in 1988, I established a partnership financed with a small amount of family money, a quarter of which was my own. Its purpose was to serve as a "laboratory" in which we could build our investing competence, increase our confidence in our ability *to* invest, experiment with different asset mixes, and develop some core beliefs and best practices around successful Active Alpha Investing. It performed well, and we learned a lot about alternative investments in the early years.

In 1994, I scrubbed and analyzed data on the core Lucas family asset base and found that we weren't even realizing returns achieved by the indices. At that point, with 13 years of investment experience and six years experimenting with our "laboratory," I convinced the family to embrace an Active Alpha Investment strategy for managing our entire portfolio with the goal of achieving an annualized rate of return of 12.5% over a long period of time. After the decision was made, it took six more years to complete the big changes necessary to fully implement our new strategy.

HOW TO IMPLEMENT ACTIVE ALPHA INVESTING

Implementation of a successful Active Alpha Investing strategy depends on three Critical Success Factors:

> **CSF #1:** Choose a strategic asset allocation based on the right mix of traditional and alternative investments.

> **CSF #2:** Choose managers who add value net of fees and taxes.

> **CSF #3:** Use episodic dynamic asset allocation to increase asset value.

In addition to these CSFs, this strategy demands a foundation of strong, effective family values and culture to maintain structural integrity through a multigenerational timeline, and a roof that provides effective leakage management (cost control). The schematic in Figure 6.3 represents this strategy well.

Active Alpha Wealth Management

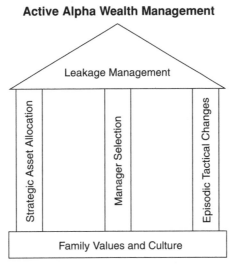

Figure 6.3 All the components need to be in place for the Active Alpha Investing strategy to work.

Assuming you have a solid roof over your head and a strong foundation on which to build your investment strategy, here are details on the three CSFs, weighted heavily toward the Lucas family perspective.

CSF #1: Strategic asset allocation must be based on choosing the right mix of traditional and alternative investments. You already know that traditional investments include stocks, bonds, and cash. But what is alternative investing?

Alternative investing is a catchall term to describe just about every investment strategy or asset that is *not* a portfolio of stocks, bonds, or cash. It includes private equity, venture capital, and hedge funds, as well as real estate, distressed debt investments, commodities, and emerging markets. Alternative investments generally provide useful diversification to stock and bond portfolios. However, performance results have been mixed.

A few years ago, I commissioned an informal study to estimate what percent of financial assets people with wealth in excess of $25 million had put into alternative investments. Feedback from the research suggested that, on average, about 25% of their financial assets were committed to these types of investments. But the dispersion around the average was wide. Some people didn't have any assets committed to alternative investments while others had committed well over half their assets.

If you ask people why they invest in alternative investments, most of them say they do it to achieve increased diversification and reduced volatility. But if you press, there's usually the expectation of generating better returns as a result of these investments. Given that these investments are usually illiquid and often entail more risk, an investor *should* expect to see additional return.

When you mix alternative and traditional asset classes, you obviously have a lot more choice than is available to indexing investors. The broad objective with Active Alpha Investing is no different than it is for an Index Investing strategy—to build a series of asset classes that, in combination, generate solid returns with acceptable volatility. For that reason, you may want to consider each of the following asset types if you are interested in embarking on an Active Alpha Investment approach.

PRIVATE EQUITY AND VENTURE CAPITAL

Private equity is, quite simply, equity capital invested in a private company. In some cases, the company can be worth billions of dollars when it is purchased. Often, these purchases are financed with a relatively small amount of equity and a large amount of debt. In other cases, private equity finances new companies or companies that are struggling to grow rapidly and are still generating losses. This type of private equity financing is called venture capital and it is usually 100% equity financed.

How wise is it for you to invest in private equity? Steven Kaplan, the Neubauer Family Professor of Entrepreneurship and Finance at the University of Chicago, and his colleague Antoinette Schoar, Assistant Professor of Finance at MIT's Sloan School of Management, produced a paper that evaluates the performance of actual cash flows that went into private equity investments (leveraged buyouts [LBOs] and venture capital) from 1980 to 2001 and compared this to the performance of the same cash flows invested in the S&P 500. They concluded that private equity fund returns (net of fees) are approximately equal to results achieved by the S&P 500.[2]

Many people (and some statistics) suggest that private equity is a diversifying investment that lowers the risk of equity portfolios. I disagree. Many portfolios of private equity investments have characteristics similar to public equities except that they are smaller companies, more heavily leveraged, and illiquid. These three characteristics make them riskier than public equities, more difficult to value, but not necessarily good diversifiers. Therefore, you should expect a significantly higher rate of return from private equities than from public ones, but not much diversification benefit.

Private equity managers charge high fees, usually 2% to 2.5% of committed capital per year. Plus, they take between 20% and 30% of the profits that they generate. Kaplan and Schoar say that the average private equity or venture capital manager does add considerable performance relative to the index *before* fees, but that nearly 100% of the excess goes into the manager's pocket. Considering the illiquidity and additional risk of private equity, this is a disappointing result for the investor. You take the risk and the manager gets the reward!

But Kaplan and Schoar made two additional points in their paper. First, they noted that there was a much wider dispersion of return around the averages than you might expect from a group of public equity portfolio managers. In other words, those LBO and venture managers in the best-performing quartile did much better than the averages, and they shared that added value with their clients. Conversely, managers in the bottom quartile did much worse, but they still got their management fees even if their clients got nothing.

In summary, the biggest risk with private equity isn't with the volatility of the asset class or its correlation to stocks. What's risky is doing a better job than 75% of investors in choosing the right manager!

Kaplan and Schoar draw another important conclusion. Their data show that, unlike in the public equity market, there is strong persistence of return in private equity investments, and returns improve with partnership experience. In other words, those managers who have performed well are likely to continue doing so in the future. This means that the small print that accompanies all advertising of the track records of traditional portfolio managers, "Past results are not an indicator of future performance," may not apply equally in the private equity world.

It's pretty tough for the private investor (and even "fund of funds" vehicles) to *consistently* gain access to top funds. Leading institutions have large budgets available to search out and hire attractive private equities managers, and they have many long-standing relationships with private equity and venture managers. They also talk with one another. So, if a respected chief investment officer finds an attractive first quartile fund with available capacity, a few phone calls can quickly fill it up. This means that even if you identify top funds, you probably can't get consistent access to them.

HEDGE FUNDS

Hedge funds aren't really an asset class. They are a whole group of relatively unregulated pools of capital that charge their investors a percentage of the profits generated by the investment strategies that they employ. Hedge funds invest in a wide array of asset classes, including but not limited to stocks and bonds. Many hedge funds also sell assets short. Simplistically, this means they bet that such assets will decline in value. In other words, a hedge fund manager has the potential to make money on securities that are rising (longs) and on securities that are falling (shorts) at the same time. Of course, they can also lose money on both their longs and shorts at the same time. Hedge funds have the ability to use leverage and alternative assets, including private equity. Because hedge funds often make significant commitments to illiquid assets, it's harder for them to be nimble in changeable financial markets and it will take longer for you to remove all of your capital if you choose to withdraw.

The universe of hedge funds is reputed to include many that have "fat tails." This means that a hedge fund's strategies can work well for years and then suddenly unravel. Some combination of losing money on both longs and shorts at the same time coupled with illiquidity and leverage periodically causes hedge funds to "blow up." When a fund blows up, it can lose 50% of its value or more in a matter of months. Investments with "fat tails" are riskier than they appear on the surface.

Some hedge funds stick to one strategy all the time. Others shift strategies depending on where they see opportunities. Most hedge fund managers trade their portfolio aggressively, making them relatively tax inefficient. When they were first designed, the conceptual idea behind hedge funds was to use a combination of longs and shorts and varying strategies to hedge out, or reduce, the risk of investing while still participating in most of the upside. This is certainly a laudable goal, but not an easy one to execute. With the growth that has taken place in hedge fund assets over the last seven or eight years, it's hard to generalize any more about their behavior. Some hedge funds have high risk but shoot for big gains; others aim for steady, stable returns. If you are going to use hedge funds, it is important to understand what you own.

My family has invested in hedge funds only sparingly, despite their popularity. The combination of high fees, low tax efficiency, and tricky risk evaluation leave us with two big concerns. First, only a few managers will generate *net* alpha. Second, we won't be able to discriminate early enough in the funds' lives between the few superior managers and the rest, to access the good ones while they're still open to new money. Intensifying competition in the industry is only making these challenges tougher to overcome. Ten years ago, hedge funds were in an esoteric corner of the market. Today, there are thousands of funds and over $1 trillion under management.

It's very difficult to get valid information on the performance of hedge funds because there is no consistent measure of performance when looking at a single fund or when evaluating funds more broadly. Strategies vary among funds and can vary within the same fund as well. But one thing is clear: Hedge funds that build up high performing track records over five or ten years are very difficult for new investors to access. Investors, institutional or individual, really like the combination of great returns and low volatility. Some think it's like having your cake and eating it, too. When hedge funds are performing as advertised (though they are not allowed to advertise), they can be excellent diversifiers.

Several firms now produce composite benchmarks for hedge fund strategies that combine the performance of a broad cross section of the market. However, these composite benchmarks have serious flaws. For one, hedge fund managers do not have to participate in these composites. As you might imagine, there is little incentive for a manager who is performing poorly to continue reporting his numbers. Likewise, some managers who do really well aren't interested in attracting additional assets, so they don't report their numbers either. As a result, the composites have real sampling problems. I think that the indices probably overstate the actual performance, but a few composites may actually understate performance.

Regardless, you are unlikely to get access to the good-performing managers whether or not they report their numbers. In 2004, a talented group of managers left Harvard Management Company to set up a hedge fund. They didn't crisscross the country conducting marketing meetings or talk with the consultants who are gatekeepers for wealthy individuals, foundations, and pension plans. They didn't speak at conferences about alternative investing. Harvard Management agreed to be a cornerstone investor, and before the fund opened on its first day of business it had raised several billion dollars from a handful of sophisticated institutions. Unless you were part of the "inner circle" and could write an eight-figure check, you stood no chance of entry.

REAL ESTATE

Real estate takes almost as many shapes as hedge funds. Houses, hotels, rental apartments, raw land, office buildings, and industrial facilities are all real estate assets. Managers of real estate are diverse. Some acquire and lease only very high-quality properties with very high-quality tenants. Others develop raw land into buildings, office parks, and communities. Still others redevelop properties that have not been well managed, are losing tenants, or are even vacant. Depending on your strategy, your expected return on real estate and the risk associated with achieving it will vary.

Real estate is often considered an inflation hedge. Yet over the last decade, inflation has been benign while the prices of urban residential real estate and some vacation properties have been skyrocketing. If real estate can boom when there's no inflation, it can also under perform when inflation is rising.

Many real estate investors finance their properties with significant amounts of leverage (borrowing). Leverage adds to the risk of a property investment and may further subject the asset to changes in interest rates and the availability of credit. If interest rates rise significantly and/or credit tightens, the value of real estate may be impaired, even if the property is financed with fixed-rate debt. All other things being equal, potential buyers of the property will have a harder time attracting credit and will have to pay more for it. As a result, their net cash flow will decline, even though the performance of the property itself hasn't changed. Declining cash flow adversely affects property valuations. Obviously, this scenario can work in reverse, too.

It's hard to generalize about the behavior of real estate because it's the quintessential local investment market. Any manager of real estate should have demonstrated capabilities to effectively evaluate local market conditions, to select those that are favorable, to shun those that aren't, and to manage effectively all the properties in the portfolio. "Local" in this case means evaluating traffic patterns in the community, knowing where people are shopping, and understanding what vacancy rates and lease terms exist in a local area. A real estate manager's knowledge and influence becomes as granular as knowing which side of a residential street has access to the good public schools, gaining the support of neighbors for redevelopment plans, and even knowing whether the property owner adjacent to you once spilled contaminants on their property that have now leached into *your* soil.

Including real estate in a portfolio can provide needed diversification, but because real estate is so diverse, it is important to understand the type of diversification you want. Many people like real estate because they see it as a safe, secure alternative to high-quality bonds, with the added bonus of inflation protection, and some tax shelter on the income they produce that comes from depreciation. If you want this kind of asset, it is best not to use much leverage.

Other people like to buy speculative real estate. There is a whole county in Florida (Collier County) named after a family that was smart enough to buy vast amounts of land when most people thought it was useless swamp land. Now the land is covered in orange groves and vegetable farms that grow high-value crops year round. Northward, there are a few families that for generations have owned tens of thousands of acres of rich, black farmland in the states of Illinois, Iowa, and Indiana. By renting the land to tenant corn and soybean farmers, they continue to reap the benefits of the vision shown by their forebears a century ago to acquire land that had to undergo the back-breaking work of being drained and tilled to grow anything but cattails. In southwestern cities like Phoenix, Las Vegas, and Santa Barbara, most real estate developers in the last 25 years have done extremely well because the demographic trends have been so powerful. In the industrial northeast, some people like to buy properties in old industrial cities that can be acquired inexpensively, fixed up, leased up, and sold for a tidy profit.

The characteristics of these property types and locations vary tremendously, and so do the insights necessary to turn them into profitable investments. One or all of them could be useful additions to a diversified portfolio, but each is sensitive to both general and local market conditions. The skill of people "on the ground" managing such properties is vital. Properties that require a lot of hands-on work to make them profitable add another dimension to the real estate analysis. You need to choose first-class operators because their skill is as likely to determine the success of the investment as general market conditions.

DISTRESSED DEBT

When a company starts to fall on hard times, the value of its equity usually declines because potential buyers of the stock are less willing to own it, and owners are more likely to want to sell. Prior to the 1980s, most corporate debt, especially that of small and mid-sized companies, was owned by banks that didn't have the ability to readily sell the debt they controlled if the company's fortunes were declining. Yet they had the benefit of being able to seize control of the company from the equity holders if the company was not meeting its obligations. Then, they could restructure or liquidate the company to try to recover their investment, often by forcing the company into bankruptcy.

In the 1980s, the world of distressed debt changed because of Michael Milken and his firm Drexel Burnham. Almost single-handedly, Milken and his associates created what is now called the "junk" debt market. They convinced institutional investors that it was good business to provide debt financing to companies that didn't have great credit. He also allowed them to buy and sell the debt in public, liquid markets, just like stocks. Milken also convinced companies that Drexel could raise financing less expensively than if they turned to banks. When some of the companies that were financed in this way inevitably ran into difficulty, the distressed debt market was born.

Some people, especially ex-Drexel employees, became experts in evaluating these fallen darlings. Many also became experts in bankruptcy law, enabling them to figure out when the sellers of distressed debt became fed up enough (with the companies they were financing) to sell their holdings at a cut rate. Then, these experts would snap up the debt at a fraction of what they expected it to be worth one day. Sometimes they would fight to take control of the company in bankruptcy. At other times, their analysis showed that the company would never enter bankruptcy and would simply continue to pay the interest on its debt and slowly recover its former strength.

This talent was well positioned in 1989, when Congress created the Resolution Trust Company to seize control of, and then sell, the loan portfolios of failing savings and loan institutions. Combined with the economic downturn in 1991, a perfect storm was created that played right into the hands of distressed debt buyers. At the time, there was an abundance of sellers of distressed debt and relatively few people who understood how to analyze these investments and consider them for purchase. Those in the know scooped up these assets at a fraction of what they believed to be their true value. When the markets recovered several years later, they were proven right with handsome returns.

In the 1990s, the distressed debt market developed further. Banks found there were willing buyers of the distressed loans they held on their books… at a price. Many felt that it made better business sense to sell these deteriorating loans than to get into the messy job of bankruptcy and restructuring. Meanwhile, the "junk" market continued to expand, creating the fuel for the next disaster in the distressed market. Sure enough, it came in 2001 and 2002, and again those with the skills and the strong stomach made out very well.

Distressed debt is not for the faint of heart. There are times when one can make a lot of money as a buyer of distressed debt, but for a number of years between 1993 and 2001, the market wasn't particularly attractive. Today, the know-how needed to evaluate distressed debt is much more widespread. Many more firms have gotten into the business, including hedge funds that invest in distressed debt when they see opportunity and get out when they see better opportunities in other asset classes. The fluidity of capital and broad access to investment know-how lead me to believe that the golden days for distressed debt investors have passed, at least in this country. That said, distressed debt has tended to do reasonably well when the stock market has struggled, so it may continue to be a good diversifier in broadly invested portfolios.

EMERGING MARKETS

Investing in emerging markets makes investing in distressed debt look straightforward. To be successful, you need access to all the analytical tools that a good investor in this country must have, and you must be able to adjust for variances across languages, cultures, accounting practices, legal systems, political systems, and national economies around the world.

Most investors that choose to tackle emerging markets do so with broadly diversified equity portfolios that invest across Central and Eastern Europe, the Middle East, Latin America, Asia, and Africa. Many of the emerging economies that are developed enough to have their own stock markets are growing at a faster rate than the United States and Western Europe. By investing in these countries, people hope to capture some of that additional growth in the value of their investments. In some cases, they also hope that, as these countries' economies grow, their currencies will strengthen relative to the U.S. dollar, creating another source of return.

Emerging markets equities are volatile. In a study of 13 major asset classes from 1993 to 2004, emerging markets equities were either in the top two performers or the bottom two in ten out of twelve years. Yet over the 10-year period from 1995 to 2004, they were the worst performing asset class in the group.[3] So investors got a lot of volatility (risk) and a poor rate of return, which is hardly a compelling case for enthusiastic investing!

However, all of this may be changing. Some emerging markets like China, India, and parts of the Third World are starting to have a much bigger impact on the global economy. China accounts for more than 25% of global consumption of aluminum, steel products, iron ore, and cement—even though it's GDP is only 4% of global GDP. India produces nearly twice as many new engineers each year as the U.S. and Europe combined. The size of these two countries' economies coupled with high growth rates are drawing upon and producing global resources at an unprecedented rate. It is possible that—in contrast to the last 10 years—the next decade will see positive financial returns to emerging market investors. However, I have little doubt that emerging markets will continue to be a volatile place to try to make money.

COMMODITIES

For centuries, the prices of most commodities have fallen steadily as advances in productivity have driven down the costs of production—even in the face of ever-increasing demand. In the last few years, we have seen a reversal of this long-term trend, specifically in areas such as energy prices and the prices for industrial metals like copper and precious metals like gold. Does this speak to a fundamental change in the price of commodities, or is it a cyclical rebound that reflects general economic activity?

It wasn't that long ago that oil prices were under $10 per barrel. Now with prices heading for all-time highs, the days of cheap energy are only a memory. For some years, major energy companies have found it difficult to replace their reserves with new discoveries of oil and gas. Yet as the global market continues to grow, and emerging economies like China, India, Korea, and Brazil consume ever-larger amounts of energy, some people think that we are at a fundamental turning point. I don't think so.

Back in the 1970s, some experts projected that the world would run out of food. There were forecasts of famine, and in some parts of Asia and Africa, global population growth was projected to accelerate while arable land remained a finite resource. Now, agriculture is more productive than ever as new seed stock and tillage techniques have increased productivity. Distribution systems are also more efficient, getting food to where it needs to be. It's true that famine remains a problem in many parts of the world today, but this is due mostly to issues of nationalism, ethnic conflicts, and dire poverty, not to the inability of the world to produce enough food.

If we look more closely at the energy market, we see some parallels. New technology will eventually bring us hydrogen fuel cells, a virtually limitless source of energy, as the scientific community makes new breakthroughs. In the meantime, Canadian oil sands that are not economic at $10 per barrel very profitably produce oil at $60 per barrel. On the supply side, at some point higher prices will drive people to change their energy consumption patterns and to purchase more efficient automobiles. The industry is also adapting. For example, some power plants that have produced electricity from oil are today switching to coal as their raw material, now that cheaper, cleaner technologies are available.

We will continue to see volatility in the price of commodity assets but, when prices rise, markets will continue to bring supply and demand back into balance. Eventually, competition and innovation will put downward pressure on prices and continually improve quality.

So how do you make money in commodities? Smart investors can do so by playing the cycles. Few financial investors actually ever buy and sell volumes of gold, wheat, natural gas, wool, pigs' feet, or copper. Most either buy financial futures that mimic the price behavior of the underlying commodities, or they own the stocks of companies that manufacture commodities. These securities often behave differently than conventional stocks or bonds, so they are often seen as good diversifiers. Unlike real estate, they are also liquid, so you can buy and sell them easily. This makes them particularly useful if you want to engage in active tactical asset allocation.

CONCLUDING COMMENTS ABOUT ALTERNATIVE INVESTMENTS

Alternative investments are like ninja swords. In experienced hands, they can be used powerfully to achieve dramatic results. But, it's also easy for unskilled users to hurt themselves.

Our family now allocates up to half of its assets to alternative investments when we think they are attractively priced, and we might go higher. Over the last 15 years, our allocation to alternatives has slowly but steadily risen as we've developed the skill to wield our ninja sword. We do our own research. We develop a thorough understanding of the strategies embraced by various alternative investment managers before we hire anyone. In some cases, we monitor a manager for a period of up to a few years before hiring him or her. Over the years, we have built our knowledge and constructed a network of sources for generating ideas and cross-referencing due diligence. We take educated risks on individual funds and asset classes with the goal of constructing a total portfolio that generates consistent growth with moderate volatility. We've had one hedge fund blow up on us, and several private equity, real estate, and emerging market funds perform below our expectation. On the other hand, through our commitment to alternatives, we have generated good returns and achieved broader diversification and lower volatility overall. We are pleased with the results so far, but we don't sleep all that well at night.

As you review various alternative investments, you may consider using a fund-of-funds as your investment vehicle. A fund-of-funds is a single entity that invests its assets in a range of other funds, typically with a specific focus. There are funds of hedge funds, private equity funds-of-funds, and real estate funds-of-funds. Even some mutual funds are funds-of-funds.

We recently hired our first fund-of-funds manager because it gives us the ability to diversify broadly in early stage venture capital, a place where we want to be invested at this point in time. We think the manager has unusually good access to top tier venture firms and his fees are reasonable by fund-of-funds standards. It remains to be seen whether or not we'll get that unusual access to top-tier venture managers.

If you want to invest in a fund-of-funds, it's important to understand that you give up information and direct contact with fund managers because there is an intermediary representing you and the other investors to fund managers. The downside is that you lose direct contact with people managing your assets and the flow of information that comes directly from those managers through their quarterly correspondence and annual meetings—two vital advantages to have when pursuing an Active Alpha Investment strategy. And, there are additional fees that the fund-of-funds manager charges you on top of the fees charged by underlying funds.

CSF #2: Choose managers that add value net of fees and taxes. Most people choose managers because they have good track records of performance. Performance is actually one of the *last* things I look at. Here's why.

For traditional managers investing in public markets, the evidence indicates that past performance is not a good predictor of their future ability to add value. As a case in point, I asked U.S. Trust Company and CTC Consulting, Inc. to do a study for me to test this thesis using data provided by Morningstar, Inc.[4] We isolated the top 25% of all equity mutual funds based upon performance over the period from 1997 to 2001. I then asked them how well these top-performing managers did for the subsequent three-year period (2002 to 2004) compared to all other equity managers with a track record over the full eight years. If the performance of these top-tier managers was entirely random, you would expect that 25% of them would fall into each of the four quartiles of performance. However, Figure 6.4 shows that nearly 40% of the "Top" managers ended up in the worst performing quartile. Over 50% were in the bottom half! If you'd wanted to pick top performers for the period 2002 to 2004 on the basis of their previous five years' experience, you'd have had a better chance of selecting from among the worst 25% of all the funds in the Morningstar database from 1997 to 2001 than from the top 25%.

For "non-traditional" managers specializing in alternative investments, the opposite appears to be true. There seems to be a correlation between past and future performance, but by the time a manager has a long enough track record to be meaningful, he or she usually isn't interested in adding new clients.

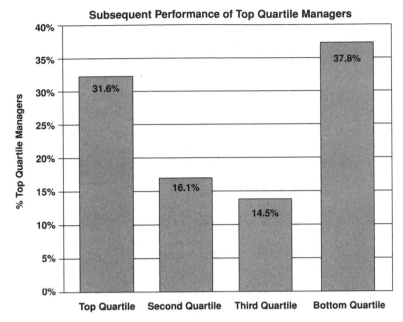

Subsequent Performance of Top Quartile Managers

Figure 6.4 shows a bar chart with the y-axis labeled "% Top Quartile Managers" ranging from 0% to 40%, and the x-axis showing four categories: Top Quartile (31.6%), Second Quartile (16.1%), Third Quartile (14.5%), and Bottom Quartile (37.8%).

Figure 6.4 Looking at the subsequent performance in 2002-2004 of managers in the top quartile from 1997 to 2001, we see that more than half performed below average and nearly 40% were in the worst-performing quartile.

So, how do you as an investor solve this dilemma? Over several decades, and after interviewing hundreds of managers and watching them perform, here are my well-weathered recommendations for selecting a good manager[5]:

• **Can I get access?** It makes no sense to get excited about a manager if you can't get into their fund. So early in the evaluation process, I check for two critical items: minimum investment sizes that the manager will accept and whether the manager is open to new investors. These two criteria eliminate many funds that might otherwise be attractive. What you're left with is typically smaller and newer organizations looking for new investors. Occasionally, a well-established investment firm will try to raise money in a tough fund raising climate by allowing access to new investors. Ironically, often the best time to invest is when it's really hard for a good manager to raise new money in an asset class that everyone is shunning.

- **Do I like the manager's investment approach?** A prospective manager has to differentiate him or herself when it comes to managing risk, buying well, adding value when they own an asset, and having a set of contacts, operational resources, or proprietary knowledge that sets them apart. That prospective manager also has to add value to my investment, net of fees and taxes. This is all "smell test" stuff. Does the manager have the right stuff to manage my assets? I want to know. What's more, the firm's resources and competence have to be matched with their ambitions, private assurances, and public claims.
- **Is the manager in a niche (and planning to stay there) where lack of size is an advantage?** Alternative investment markets are getting more efficient. So much capital is going into them that excess profits are being squeezed out. But occasionally there are niches that remain too small for large institutional investors, and therein lies potential to create alpha. Unfortunately, managers who start in small niches often outgrow them because the economics of their business reward growth in assets under management more than good investment performance.
- **Am I certain the manager will be good at execution? Does he/she have a competitive advantage?** Finding an attractive investment niche is only valuable if you can capitalize on it through access to a competent manager in that niche. Alternatively, some managers build competitive advantages that translate into sustainable top quartile performance in large and competitive asset classes. In my mind, you need access to both.
- **Is the manager making a big financial commitment?** I like to hire managers who have incentive to make more money from returns generated on capital that they invest in their funds than on fees and carried interests. In other words, I look for managers who have "skin in the game." Unfortunately, the hefty fees that many active managers earn usually outpace earnings from the returns they generate for clients. I generally start to feel comfortable with the manager who puts up 5% to 10% of a fund's assets. With this amount of "skin in the game," the manager stands to lose as much from that investment if it's poorly managed as they are likely to earn in fees. This is a major motivator of conscientious manager behavior!
- **Is the manager a disciplined investor?** I like to watch a manager perform over a number of years or carefully study their track record,

investment by investment, to answer this question. In investing, there is a delicate tension between aggressively trying to find deals and waiting for the right ones (on the right terms) to materialize. Some of the managers I use haven't made an investment for up to two years in a row because they didn't see anything they liked. I've seen others persist on a deal through busted negotiations, lawsuits, changing legislation, due diligence revelations, and changing markets, doggedly pursuing an opportunity but not closing on it until all the conditions are right. In both cases, they served my interests well.

- **Who is performing due diligence on the manager?** Big, sophisticated institutions do extensive due diligence. When they invest $50 million or $100 million with a manager, they can afford to do all sorts of research to protect their investment, and to some degree you or I can ride on their coat tails. Managers in small niches don't have big, sophisticated institutional investors, so there isn't someone else doing the heavy lifting when it comes to due diligence. As a result, you have to take responsibility for doing enough due diligence to gain comfort that your investment is secure. Examples of due diligence might include doing reference/background checks on the advisor, evaluation of a manager's risk controls and his firm's decision-making processes, and being familiar with a firm's legal counsel, its custodian or prime broker, and its accountants.

- **Does the manager's fee structure align their interests with your own?** Fee structures vary widely with some being more attractive to the investor than others. None brings perfect alignment. I am skeptical of any arrangement where the manager's compensation isn't linked directly to the long-term performance of the fund, potentially resulting in poor-performing portfolios still making the manager rich. Most alternative managers earn at least 20% of the profits they generate in addition to an annual management fee of 1% or more of assets. If the fund has $500 million under management and earns 20% profit in a year, you can do the math. If you're not careful, it's very easy to create misalignment of interests between managers and their investors—if incentives are not in balance. A manager with large assets under management may be content with generating low stable returns because the fees are so attractive. Or, in trying to hit a jackpot, the manager might reach for excessive risk unnecessarily—thereby endangering your hard-earned capital.

- **Is the manager part of a financial conglomerate?** I rarely hire managers who are part of financial conglomerates because they have conflicting loyalties—to you and their own bosses, to their own proprietary products, and to other products that it might make sense for you to buy through open architecture. Trying to figure out the manager's compensation scheme, no matter how fair the arrangement, is a headache I don't need.

- **Is a financial intermediary involved?** There is so much capital looking for a productive home that most managers who meet the criteria I just mentioned don't have to hire an intermediary to raise money. Even so, there is a huge market of financial intermediaries who do just that. They raise money in small amounts of a few hundred thousand, or in big chunks of $5 million, $20 million, or $100 million per investor! And they charge the manager a fee for doing so. We have used intermediaries only sparingly, even though lots of institutional and individual investors justifiably rely on intermediaries for ideas and due diligence support.

CSF #3: Use episodic, dynamic asset allocation to increase asset value. What is episodic, dynamic asset allocation? It is a very specific form of tactical asset allocation. Tactical asset allocation is an agile investment technique that aims to build portfolio value by taking advantage of the changing outlook for different asset classes. When people practice tactical asset allocation by buying and selling stocks, bonds, and cash, it is often referred to as market timing. Most investment experts agree that it's impossible to market-time these three asset classes consistently enough to add value over long periods. I agree.

Like market timing, episodic, dynamic asset allocation involves selling asset classes that you think are overpriced and buying ones that are undervalued. But that is where the similarities stop. Instead of watching over just three asset classes (stocks, bonds, and cash)our family office watches over twenty asset classes and sub-classes. While this gives us many more opportunity sets that we can act on, we rarely do. We rarely make more than one big move per year, and some years we don't make any. When we do start to move, we tend to ease into a new asset class, slowly building it over six months to two years. For part of this time, it almost invariably looks like we are making a bad decision because the new asset class continues to decline in value. Usually our moves into an asset class coincide with sellers who are driven by non-economic stimuli to sell. Sometimes the stimuli are regulatory, sometimes they are structural, and sometimes they are driven by panic. Of course, in addition to identifying an attractive asset class, we also need to find a competent manager who will take our capital.

One person who understands episodic, dynamic asset allocation well (though he refers to it differently) is global uber-investor George Soros. In 1992, Soros gained global notoriety for betting against the power of European governments to maintain a managed value for the British pound. The pressure built for months due in part to Soros and others betting against the pound. The more he bet against the pound, the more the British Government had to spend to hold its value steady. Finally, the government's power was simply overwhelmed by the market. When that happened, the pound's valuation collapsed in a matter of hours after pegs for the currency were abandoned.

In ensuing weeks, there was a contagion effect throughout Europe as the pegs in other currencies fell. When Soros was proven right—that markets determined to change are more powerful than governments determined to prevent change—he made over $1 billion. In targeting the British Pound, Soros identified a situation in the financial market where governments were acting for non-economic reasons. They wanted fixed exchange rates for political reasons. Currency traders felt that the pound was overvalued but government structure had not allowed the free markets to define a clearing price. As time went on, pressure built and Soros seized the opportunity to invest. When the pressure built to an unsustainable level, the governments were forced to de-link the pound and Soros made a fortune!

It's easy to paint a rosy picture about the benefits of episodic, dynamic asset allocation, but it's risky. George Soros reportedly lost $500 million betting on the Japanese Yen in 1998, and my own family—operating on a much more modest scale—has had a tough time making the right allocation decisions in emerging markets, energy, and tech stocks.

The British pound example underscores how money-making opportunities can occur because prices or economic conditions move faster than regulation or market structures can adapt. In other cases, investors' perceptions regarding risk will change, causing an imbalance of supply and demand for certain financial assets.

For example, when defaults on junk bonds rose more quickly than generally expected in 2002, in part because of the unexpected collapses of Enron, Worldcom, and Adelphia, many investors started dumping junk bonds much faster than the market could absorb them. With a huge imbalance between supply and demand, prices plummeted. For those with strong stomachs and the research capabilities to sift through the bonds and determine which were worthless and which were highly undervalued, it was a once-in-a-career opportunity to make a killing.

Sometimes opportunity is created by a combination of politics, economics, and short-time horizons. Back in 1997 when oil prices eased below $10 a barrel and natural gas was going for about $1.50 per 1000 cubic feet (or "MCF"), a combination of near-term excess supply and constrained demand drove prices so far down that there was hardly any economic incentive for oil companies to drill for new sources of energy. At the time, the political climate in the Middle East and Latin America was also relatively benign.

Then, everything changed in the opposite direction. Growing global demand for energy in China and India, increasing challenges in finding new supplies of hydrocarbons, political insecurity in Venezuela (a major supplier of oil to the U.S.), stagnant domestic refinery capacity, the war in Afghanistan, and the second Iraq war all conspired to quintuple the price of energy with no end yet in sight.

Euphoria can be just as destabilizing as panic. Bubbles, like the recent "Internet bubble," are caused by "the madness of crowds." In the year 2000, Veritas Software Corporation had the same market capitalization as Weyerhauser, United Airlines, American Airlines, and General Motors *combined!* Today, GM alone is worth twice Veritas—and GM by all accounts has been a poor performer. There are many similar examples that in retrospect look equally ridiculous, but greed and a herd mentality can drive prices up to stratospheric levels that have no basis in reality.

In cases like these, one can and *should* use episodic, dynamic asset allocation to reduce, eliminate, or even bet against an asset class where people are buyers or sellers for reasons that have little basis in *economic* reality.

HAVING THE RIGHT STUFF

Opportunities to make money through episodic, dynamic asset allocation are based on an investor's skills in three areas:

- The ability to assess risk in a different—and correct—way relative to the hordes that are driving the markets way up or way down
- Access to liquidity when competitors don't have it
- Having a mechanism to capitalize on the opportunity

Opportunities sometimes exist to make dynamic changes to asset allocation because large numbers of people have assessed risk incorrectly. Sometimes people think something isn't very risky when, in fact, it is. Think of Enron when it was flying high or Internet stocks in late 1999. Nobody thought of these as financial train wrecks just waiting to happen. Conversely, people sometimes think things will be risky but they don't turn out to be. Investing in distressed debt in the early 2000s was considered a gamble when we undertook it, but it didn't turn out to be. Distressed debt investing has traditionally been the province of institutional investors, but we found that it made sense for us to get involved with it as a family office.

To be effective at episodic, dynamic asset allocation, you must have strong confidence in your skills as an investor to go against the grain and seek opportunities where most people see only danger ("buy low") or to walk away from situations where others see only riches ("sell high"). Good research and courage have to be accompanied by adequate cash to invest in such situations. Often, panics are accompanied by credit squeezes and weak economic results that make it difficult to quickly execute a sale and a subsequent purchase. One of the advantages of maintaining a broadly diversified portfolio is that you're always likely to have a highly liquid asset that you can sell quickly to take advantage of especially attractive buying opportunities.

But even if you see an opportunity and have the cash available to invest, you still need a mechanism. Our family office hires money managers to be our mechanism because we don't have the resources to develop that level of expertise in 20 or more asset classes ourselves. But we don't wait for a crisis to start looking for a manager that has expertise in the affected asset class. We have a "bench" of excellent managers who we haven't hired today, but who we might hire tomorrow if an opportunity for episodic, dynamic asset allocation intersects with our priorities and their area of expertise.

THE LUCAS FAMILY TRACK RECORD WITH EPISODIC, DYNAMIC ASSET ALLOCATION

So, how much success has the Lucas family had with our form of tactical asset allocation? Let's put it this way: We're pleased with our efforts in this arena over many years. As I indicated previously, we've been successful because of our ability to assess risk well. We also have access to liquidity when competitors don't have it, we have a mechanism to capitalize on the opportunity, and we've undoubtedly had some good luck.

As a family, we have made tactical commitments to emerging markets debt, small cap growth stocks, large cap value stocks, distressed corporate debt, collateralized mortgage obligations, energy stocks, and Asian private equity. Some of our early successes involved investing in "distressed debt" in the late 1980s and early 1990s as the Resolution Trust Company was trying to clean up the Savings and Loan debacle here in the U.S.

In 2001 and 2002, we again bought up distressed securities and made good money through the cycle. We had liquidity to make this commitment in a bear market because we had sold many of our growth stocks in 2000 ("selling high").

But not all our tactical bets are successful.

After the Asian meltdown in 1998, we committed to private equity investing in that emerging market region. We thought our timing was great and we found a superb manager, but it is not clear even now whether we will make money on our investment.

When oil was below $10 a barrel, we made a big investment in an energy hedge fund. We trimmed back our position a couple of years later after making excellent returns, but we did not anticipate the recent run up and were underexposed, at least relative to where we had been.

Episodic, dynamic asset allocation isn't for the faint of heart. It's also not our family's goal to capture every asset class that embodies uneconomic sellers. We try to identify one or two asset classes every few years out of the 20 or more we monitor that exhibit exceptional risk/reward parameters. If we're right, we'll significantly overweight them and then participate in their upward revaluation. That is all we need to generate favorable returns.

Sidebar 6.2: What to Do If There's Nobody to Replace You as Wealth Strategist

What if you have the investment skill to oversee an Active Alpha Investment strategy but there isn't anyone in the next generation of your family who can carry out these responsibilities? There are several possible solutions to this problem.

First, you can skip a generation. If your family is like most, you will have a numerically larger pool of potential candidates to take on these duties among your grandchildren than among your children. However, you may have to remain at the helm as Wealth Strategist longer than you originally hoped in order to assess the interest and skill sets of your grandchildren, as well as to develop their Wealth Strategist skills.

Second, you can find advisors who are capable of continuing your strategy. The risk here is that very little stays the same in the financial world. Companies get acquired, new investment strategies emerge, and people retire. Even though you are in a good position to assess potential advisors to continue your work today, you have no idea whether they will be equally capable 10 years from now; or, if they will even be in business then.

continues

Third, you can switch to an Index Investing Strategy. You are well positioned to make the shift, and it is likely to take a number of years to complete the transition if you are using alternative investments right now. The simplicity of an indexing strategy means you need less expertise and there are more wealth advisors out there that have the skills to execute it effectively. And if future generations want to get back into Active Alpha Investing, nothing prevents them from trying to do so.

Conclusion

At the beginning of this chapter, I told you that choosing among Index Investing, Barbell Investing, and Active Alpha Investing is the single most important investment decision you will make. It is more important than asset allocation or manager selection or any of the other investment related decisions you may consider.

If you choose the Index Investing strategy, you don't need to dedicate much time to the wealth management process or build specialized expertise. On the other hand, with a Barbell Investing strategy or an Active Alpha Investing strategy, an extraordinary commitment is required for either of these wealth management strategies to succeed.

All three investment strategies have merit. There is no right or wrong answer, but one of the three strategies should suit almost everyone. You can follow other riskier paths, but they will reduce your chances of success and potentially jeopardize the wealth you have created.

Since hiring a Financial Advisor is a pivotal move in helping you to identify the right financial path for you, let's move on to Chapter 7, "Making Your Most Important Hire," for information on how to proceed in finding the right fit for you.

Chapter 6: Issues to Discuss with Your Family

1. Do you enjoy investing, or do you see it as a necessary burden?

2. How would you characterize your ability to take risk? Are you:

    a) Very risk-averse

    b) Somewhat risk-averse

    c) Willing to take moderate risk for purposes of portfolio growth

    d) Willing to take significant risk to grow the value of your assets

3. What is your ability to assess risk accurately when it comes to allocating capital? Under what circumstances are your abilities enhanced or impaired?

4. If you are averse to indexing, why do you think you're more skilled than most other investors?

5. What special skills, insights, or resources do you and your family have that could support the concentrated growth asset in the Barbell Investing strategy?

6. Are you convinced of the merits of working into your sixties, seventies, or even eighties, as indicated in the discussion on Barbell Investing strategy? If not, what would it take to help you think more about doing this? How can you gain better access to alternative investments than the average sophisticated investor?

7. To what extent do you feel knowledgeable about alternative investments? What more would you like to know about them?

8. Do you see yourself pursuing an Active Alpha Investment strategy but feel you lack the skill set to do it? If so, what can you do to develop deeper investment skills, and then true insight?

9. To what extent do you think your investment managers' economic interests are aligned with your own?

10. What questions do you have for your own wealth management advisor, in light of reading this chapter?

11. Given your answers to the preceding questions, which one of the wealth management strategies discussed in this chapter is most in line with your wealth management goals and your tolerance for risk-taking?

    a) Index Investing

    b) Barbell Investing

    c) Active Alpha Investing

Endnotes

1 John C. Bogle, Remarks from the Gary M. Brinson Distinguished Lecture, "As the Index Fund Moves From Heresy to Dogma… What More Do We Need To Know." April 13, 2004, http://www.vanguard.com/bogle_site/sp20040413.html.

2 Steven N. Kaplan and Antoinette Schoar, "Private Equity Performance: Returns, Persistence and Capital Flows." Journal of Finance, August 2005.

3 "Leadership of Major Asset Classes." Produced by CTC Consulting, Inc.

4 ©2005 Morningstar, Inc. All Rights Reserved. The information contained herein: (1) is proprietary to Morningstar and/or its content providers; (2) may not be copied or distributed; (3) does not constitute investment advice offered by Morningstar; and (4) is not warranted to be accurate, complete, or timely. Neither Morningstar nor its content providers are responsible for any damages or losses arising from any use of this information. Past performance is no guarantee of future results. Use of information from Morningstar does not necessarily constitute agreement by Morningstar, Inc. of any investment philosophy or strategy presented in this publication.

5 These questions are experience based, not empirically based. Asking the questions without the experience to evaluate the answers effectively is of little value. If you insist on usingg and Active Alpha Investment strategy, this is just one more reason why you should expose only a small portion of your financial assets to the strategy until you become an expert. Also, keep acurate and complete performance records over three to five years to demonstrate your skill!

7

MAKING YOUR MOST IMPORTANT HIRE

"Recognize the skills and traits you don't possess, and hire people who have them."

—*Howard Schultz, Chairman, Starbucks*

Now that you've articulated your values, defined your financial objectives, and chosen a strategy to achieve them, your next step as Wealth Strategist is to make a key hire. You need to select a Financial Administrator.

A Financial Administrator (FA) is the practitioner that every Wealth Strategist should have as a partner in the integration and execution of an integrated wealth management strategy. Although the FA is an individual, he or she is usually affiliated with a financial company and, by extension, the financial industry. The company could be a small component of a large financial conglomerate with multiple sources of revenue or a fee-only boutique firm with only one or two employees. Firms come in a wide variety of shapes and sizes with widely varying fee structures that are only limited by people's imaginations. Some Wealth Strategists who employ a simple investment strategy like Index Investing opt to play the FA role themselves. Others with sizeable wealth establish family investment offices to serve this function.

The performance of the FA will be driven by his or her own skills and experience, of course. But performance is also dependent on the structure and resources of the firm for which the individual advisor works. Therefore, choosing an FA involves an analysis of both the individual and the firm, and both need to be first-rate to add value to the relationship. This chapter advises you on how to choose the right FA and how to do a thorough evaluation of the FA's firm.

Selecting the Right FA

An FA's job is to support and partner with you, the Wealth Strategist, to meet or exceed *your* financial goals using the investment strategy that *you* have chosen. In other words, the FA's primary job is to help you execute and measure your strategy and coordinate all the players involved. The issues the FA needs to manage include the following:

- **You—the client.** To help you keep good records, manage your cash flow, and stay on target with long-term financial goals.
- **Your other advisors.** To assure that investment managers, lawyers, accountants, and other advisors perform to expectations, individually and collectively.
- **The totality of your financial assets.** To measure your portfolio's performance, monitor your financial risk, and administer your wealth management activities.

It's not easy to select an outstanding FA. You have to find someone who is conscientious, of strong character, of high integrity, accountable to you, whose interests are aligned with yours, and who is able to strike a delicate balance between your needs and the demands of their employer.

With these qualifications, it's no wonder that even sophisticated Wealth Strategists struggle to select a single FA. Some Wealth Strategists give up on finding one person or team that can deliver all of these qualifications. Instead, they divide up their assets among different firms with the expectation that they can set up a competitive environment that will, after a year or two, highlight a clear winner. I urge you *not* to do this for a couple of reasons. It can become an unwieldy, time-consuming process, and even when you attempt to aggregate the performance of different FAs, it can be very difficult to accurately compare the performance of these individuals and their firms. Meanwhile, during the appraisal period, you're likely to take your eyes off of a big issue: your overall financial risk and performance!

Core Skills of an FA

What are the key skills that an FA must possess? Regardless of the investing strategy you choose—Indexing, Barbell, or Active Alpha— you need to find an FA with skills in a number of key areas.

For purposes of all three strategies (Indexing, Barbell, and Active Alpha), you need to find an FA with in-depth experience and expertise in the following:

1. Measuring financial performance.

2. Managing key client financial records.

3. Coordinating and recommending the work of specialists.

4. Strategic asset allocation.

To pursue an Active Alpha investment strategy, it's important to find support and expertise in two additional areas:

5. Selection of outstanding investment managers.

6. Episodic, dynamic asset allocation.

Responsibility #1: The FA Should Be Able to Measure Financial Performance

First and foremost, the FA is charged with holding accountable everyone involved with managing your wealth, including you and your family. It's imperative to track your overall investment performance as well as the performance of each investment manager. The FA should also make sure that asset allocation is in line with your strategy and that leakages are under control.

Investment performance metrics can get very fancy and complicated. Typical portfolio performance metrics can include attribution measures, style analysis, risk measures, measures of diversification, and the list goes on. Some of these metrics can be useful to illuminate financial performance and risk. However, just because a performance measure is complicated doesn't make it useful. How many times have you reviewed a presentation from a financial services company, found the statistics impenetrable, uninteresting, or off target, and ended up tossing the presentation into a file cabinet, a shoebox, or even the wastebasket?

Make sure you understand what specific performance data you need to gauge investment performance. To that end, there are five critical sets of data that you should ask your FA to collect and evaluate on a regular basis. They include the following:

- **After-fee performance of each individual fund manager, using standard industry practices[1] compared with the most appropriate index**. Each fund manager can tell you the index gainst which you should measure performance. If the manager recommends using a compilation of other managers—such as Morningstar or Lipper—as the benchmark, also insist on using a passive index. A passive index is usually harder to beat than the Morningstar or Lipper benchmarks of other active managers and thus raises the bar of expectations for managers. In addition, comparison against a passive index is a truer measure of value-added growth.

When using Active Alpha managers, the most important measures are three-year or even five-year returns. Measuring the performance of a manager over shorter periods is more a measure of the vicissitudes of market behavior than of a manager's skills at generating value-added growth. But, short-term performance is still useful as a point of inquiry with a manager if their actual performance diverges from the index.

- **Your aggregate portfolio's performance against an appropriate composite benchmark.** A composite benchmark is a selection of indices weighted in such a way that in aggregate they are likely to have the performance and risk characteristics of your desired portfolio. A simple composite is 70% S&P 500/30% Lehman Aggregate Bond Index. Your FA can help you decide on the right composite benchmark. Again, use indices, not manager compilations.

If you're pursuing an Index Investing strategy, many firms have the necessary software to generate your aggregate performance. If you are pursuing an Active Alpha Investing strategy that includes illiquid investments like private equity or real estate funds, there are very few wealth management firms in this country that have the capability to provide what you really need: time-weighted aggregate returns compared with your composite benchmark.

I know of this situation quite well because, a few years ago, I evaluated 20 or more of the leading wealth management firms to see if they could provide me with time-weighted aggregate returns compared to a composite benchmark. Only a handful of them could do it. Today, a few software vendors offer the service, but it is very expensive for smaller wealth management firms to install and very complicated for the big ones to do so. This is a frustrating state of affairs, and one that's likely to change only slowly. I simply cannot condone an investor using a firm that can't provide aggregate performance measures of the investment products it recommends to its clients.

- **Measure your actual asset allocation relative to a target allocation.** Your FA can help you allocate your assets to be consistent with your wealth management goals and strategy. When you decide on a target allocation, you should regularly compare your actual asset allocation against the target and, when appropriate, rebalance your portfolio so that it stays close to your target. Also, be certain to reflect your target asset allocation in the design of your composite benchmark.
- **Measure cash flows relative to objectives.** The FA should track the family's spending rate (or savings rate) to assure that cash flow is aligned with family objectives and to assess its impact on investment results. For example, if a trust beneficiary is receiving 5% income annually instead of 4% annually, it affects the overall integrity of the family's financial plans. Effective wealth management can and should be measured in dollars and cents. If possible, the FA should also track other leakages including taxes paid, fees, and expenses.
- **Measure the long-term growth of your financial assets in dollars.** Each year, record the actual dollar value of your financial assets as of December 31 and the amount that you either added to or removed from your financial assets during that previous year. Measuring actual dollars is equally vital to measuring percentage gains and losses. Dollar measurements are also easier for most people to intuitively understand than percentages. After all, you can't spend percents!

  I have been tracking actual dollar data now for my family for nearly 20 years. It is *the* indicator that gave me the signal to restructure my family's assets. In recent years, it has been gratifying to see how our family's assets and distributions to family members have grown. Comparing the actual growth of assets relative to our long-term goal is a long-term indicator of success or failure that we evaluate over periods of 10 years or more. For shorter-term feedback, we rely on the percentage data, or we compare the percentage and dollar data to make sure they are sending the same signals. But if the percentage data look good and the dollar data look bad, that's a warning sign that deserves careful and immediate attention.

Ask your FA to give all five of the previously described metrics back to you in a form that ties actual performance to stated goals. If results and goals diverge, you can (and should) evaluate why. Were the financial markets performing particularly well or poorly, or were there problems in execution? Maybe your goals were too aggressive or are no longer appropriate because of changed circumstances. Collecting this data gives you the impetus to ask good questions of your FA and to keep your wealth management efforts on track. It synthesizes a whole series of decisions down to a few key facts that you can measure to stay on course and to stay focused on your most important financial objectives.

Responsibility #2: The FA Should Assemble and Manage Your Client Records

Having good investment, tax, legal, and administrative records, keeping them secure, and updating them as necessary is a critical service the FA should provide. Instead of sending a box full of unorganized papers to your accountant late in the tax season, ask your FA to assemble and manage the investment tax information you really need. Then have your FA send it to the accountant at the appropriate time (or to you if you're doing your own taxes). Work with your FA to keep important legal and administrative documents in a safe, accessible, organized location (possibly online) and a copy somewhere else. While some people insist on managing their own records, and others are fortunate to have trustworthy and skilled assistants who can be responsible for this task, I strongly recommend that your FA coordinate this function to do the following:

- Serve as the single point of contact for managing and coordinating all your financial records.
- Collect critical data about you for loan documentation.
- Satisfy the requirements of the U.S. Patriot Act passed in the wake of 9/11. (This act requires specific administrative due diligence of every client, no matter how well known to the financial firm. So be patient with your FA!)

- Provide performance measurement data on your investments.
- Maintain your trust documents, wills, healthcare powers of attorney, and other important personal documents.

Please keep in mind that the more complex your personal financial situation is, the greater the necessary burden you are placing on your FA. If you are using a Barbell Investing or Index Investing strategy, the cost and complexity of your FA's role is fairly low unless you have a complicated estate plan. But if you use an Active Alpha Investing strategy, the bar rises considerably on both counts.

Responsibility #3: The FA Should Coordinate the Work of Specialists

Most wealthy people rely on specialists to help them manage discrete parts of their lives. They use some combination of lawyers, accountants, insurance specialists, stockbrokers, trustees, bankers, philanthropic consultants, and even family counselors to help them manage. Much of the day-to-day work in each of these specialist areas is administrative. In addition, the work that one specialist does often influences the work of other specialists. Unless you are willing to take on the role yourself, the FA should be responsible for coordinating the work of these specialists and for following up with them to make sure that key tasks are completed correctly.

The FA can help you evaluate your wealth management/estate planning advisors. After you choose an FA, he or she should work at the epicenter of your wealth management process. This will help ensure that you're able to execute an integrated wealth management strategy.

A good FA typically has broad experience with a number of private clients and is in a good position to help you evaluate whether there are holes in your wealth management plan and whether the specialists you have hired are performing well. He or she can also provide valuable advice when it comes to reviewing, hiring, and possibly replacing wealth advisors.

This support can be especially valuable in the wake of a liquidity event. At the time of liquidity events, many wealthy people already have lawyers and accountants in place. For business owners in particular, these relationships may go back many years, and the relationships can be very close. Having such trusted advisors in place is a wonderful thing, but the issues that you face after a liquidity event are usually different than those that you faced previously. Thus, you'll need to evaluate how well your existing advisors' skills and temperaments are suited to the new set of demands that will be placed on them in the wake of your liquidity event. An experienced FA can often provide guidance to help you make the right decisions and can be a good source of leads for new hires, if necessary. Whether you keep or replace your accountant, lawyer, or insurance agent, make sure each of them has substantial experience relevant to your new circumstances.

The FA plays a critical role as a communications coordinator. I find that some of the biggest problems in implementing wealth management plans are due to poor communication between clients and their advisors. The best legal or tax advice can be rendered null and void if conceived in a vacuum or misaligned with your individual or family wealth management goals or investment strategy. Because wealth management advice is expensive, it pays to have someone ensuring that your advisors are working in tandem to help achieve *your* wealth management goals.

Your FA's ability to coordinate the work of various advisors is especially important when it comes to managing complex, long-term execution issues—such as implementing wealth transfer or tax reduction strategies. For example, family partnerships need to have a clearly documented business purpose, and if gifts are made from one family member to another, their value must be properly appraised and documented.

Some of these execution issues require assistance from a lawyer, an independent appraiser, or an accounting firm, but administrative and coordination functions are more appropriately in the domain of the FA. In my experience, (expensive) lawyers and tax accountants are more interested in inventing creative new strategies and generating new business than they are in managing the routine, ongoing administrative details of estate and asset management. So think carefully about whether the specific task you need to accomplish requires a lawyer who bills at $400/hour or can be handled just as easily (and far less expensively) by your FA!

Responsibility #4: The FA Should Be Involved with Strategic Asset Allocation

Your FA should guide you in allocating your assets to provide appropriate levels of diversification, risk, and growth potential. The goal is to maximize your return potential for the particular level of risk that you feel comfortable taking. Working with your FA, you can evaluate various models to find the asset allocation mix that's right for you.

The historic data that go into these models are used to characterize the return potential or volatility of particular asset classes, or to define how asset classes behave relative to each other. Just because an asset has behaved historically in a particular way doesn't guarantee it will continue to behave that way in the future. More sophisticated advisors address this problem by projecting the future, independent of the past, and include that information in their forecasting models. Because even the best models don't predict the future with absolute accuracy, make sure your portfolio is well diversified.

Additional FA Responsibilities #5 and #6 for Active Alpha Investing

Active Alpha Investing is much more complicated than Index Investing. The four FA responsibilities I've just described become more demanding. At the same time, two other concerns—*manager selection* and *episodic dynamic asset allocation*—become critical. Both of these functions add considerable execution risk to your portfolio, as well as upside potential. Our family focuses intensely on these functions because the stakes are so high.

Having said that, should you charge *your* FA with these responsibilities?

Many FAs claim to have skills in one or both of these areas. Financial consultants who work with institutions and very wealthy families also do this work. But in both instances, verifiable track records of people's performances are hard to come by.

Manager Selection—FAs like to recommend that their clients use investment managers—both in-house and third-party—who have

---

demonstrated track records of past investment performance. Clients also respond more favorably to recommendations of managers who have been doing well. But past results are not a good indicator of future returns. In business, you want to back a winner, but when investing, you should seek value for money. Often, this requires that you look for opportunities in places where others don't see them.

How do you work with your FA to transcend conventional market wisdom and correctly identify managers who are going to be winners, not just those who were winners in the past? You need to have the Four A's discussed in Chapter 5, "The Enchanted Forest, The Secret Society, and The Capital Kibbutz," to consistently and successfully choose them. Does your FA have these attributes of acumen, access, alignment of interests, and accountability? It's like horse racing: You can't make much money betting on the odds-on favorite. You have to see opportunity that others don't.

There are no easy answers when it comes to selecting top managers. In addition to reviewing your FA's experience and resources, make your FA prove to you over time that he or she has that rare skill of being able to move insightfully and consistently against the tide.

Episodic dynamic asset allocation—Experts in episodic dynamic asset allocation are extremely valuable and even tougher to identify.

Many wealth management firms only make episodic dynamic asset allocation recommendations within narrow parameters. If an FA or firm recommends a big move and is wrong, it costs their clients plenty and may encourage an exodus. If the recommendation is right, the clients do well, but it isn't particularly lucrative for the FA or his firm.

Some hedge fund managers use periodic, dynamic asset allocation (and other forms of tactical asset allocation) aggressively, in part because the incentive structure is tied directly to the investment profits they deliver to their clients. Hedge fund managers typically get 20% of the profits they produce for their clients (but not the losses.) So they get a big carrot if they make correct decisions and no corresponding penalty if they are wrong! For wealth advisors, this is good business if you can get it. FAs who truly have tactical asset allocation skill (or who can convince people they have it) can make ten times more money applying their expertise to a hedge fund.

Measuring the quality of an FA's insights into manager selection and periodic episodic asset allocation is hard to do, except with the benefit of a long relationship, the ability to measure resultsand your own expertise on the subject. For that reason, tread cautiously when relying on FAs and their firms to add value in these areas. Explore the facts in detail and ask tough questions. Assess whether your advisors have good judgment, as well as unusual market insight. Indeed, try to determine if the firm or FA has proprietary insights that are different from what other firms are offering to their clients. In the last analysis, manager selection and tactical asset allocation are as much art as science. If you are uncomfortable making these assessments you are better off using the Index Investing or Barbell Investing strategies.

Evaluating the Success of the FA

To determine how well your FA is performing the responsibilities outlined at the beginning of the chapter, meet at least once a year to do a comprehensive review of your wealth management plans. In these meetings, review your administrative procedures and your investment performance, update your FA on any relevant changes in your personal life, review any substantive changes in the FA's firm, look for ways to improve your results, write or update an action plan for the coming year, and review last year's plan. During these sessions, determine whether you are satisfied with the services you're receiving. Take the opportunity to ask your FA probing questions in the following areas:

- Is each of my investment managers performing as expected? If not, why not?
- Is my aggregate investment performance acceptable relative to stated objectives?
- How will changes in the ownership, management, or compensation systems in your firm affect my account?
- Is the administration of my assets working smoothly and accurately?
- Did I achieve other goals that we agreed on? What are the goals for my account next year?
- Has the risk profile of my assets shifted measurably? If so, what should we do about it?

- What's the likely impact of new tax or trust laws that have been enacted since we last met?
- Do I have the right insurance in place?
- How do changes in my life affect my estate plan?
- How can we improve our collective communication within my family about wealth management issues?

These reviews should *not* cover new products and services that the FA may want to sell you. Those discussions can take place at another time.

If you are implementing a complex Active Alpha Investing strategy, you will need to meet with your FA much more frequently. These meetings provide occasions not just to learn about investment opportunities, but also to probe the thinking and skill of your key advisor and his or her colleagues. With complicated portfolios, there are many issues to discuss and decisions to make. I encourage you to request and review written materials, including a written agenda, investment performance, asset class research, and manager recommendations (including supporting material) in advance of each meeting with your FA. The more prepared you are, the more prepared the FA will have to be, and the more productive the meetings will be.

Sidebar 7.1: Suggestions for How to Measure Performance

At a minimum, you and your FA should track the following on a regular basis and report results to appropriate family members at least once a year. You should track separately the performance of each entity in your estate that has a distinct investment strategy (i.e., personal investment portfolio, trust, family partnership, retirement plan):

- The aggregate time-weighted performance of financial assets, measured quarterly against a customized benchmark of financial assets over 1 year, 3 years, 5 years, and 10 years.

---

continues

- Aggregate net assets (in dollars) tracked annually and measured against the long-term absolute return goal defined in Chapter 4, "Defining Your Financial Objectives." Measurement periods of less than 5 years are not useful; a 10-year period is better.

- Actual asset allocation (in percentages and dollars) relative to target percentages, measured quarterly.

- Aggregate contributions to, or spending from, savings in dollars and percents relative to targets. Track this annually, and review the trend over time.

- Annual state and federal income taxes paid on investment assets (in dollars and percentage of assets) tracked annually. Review trend over time.

- The time weighted performance of each investment manager, benchmarked quarterly against a relevant index and/or benchmark and measured over 1 year, 3 years, 5 years, and 10 years.

- Debt to equity structure of each entity or individual, as well as the family as a whole, as appropriate, reviewed annually.

- The liquidity position of each entity or individual relative to contingent or prospective calls on that liquidity, reviewed annually or quarterly as appropriate.

- A quarterly (or annual) "To Do" list and a review of the previous one. This should include an annual list of accomplishments (qualitative and quantitative) as well as objectives.

In addition to the Wealth Strategist, family members and the FA can add additional measures to track other aspects of past performance. A good system of accountability is not only an invaluable financial tool; it also provides ongoing reinforcement of the key values and business principles established in the strategic wealth management process.

Sidebar 7.2: Common Wealth Management Implementation Errors

Be on the lookout for these common signs that your wealth management plan is not working as it should.

Near Term:

1. Your advisor hasn't worked with you to develop an investment policy for each of the discrete entities in your estate (e.g., personal investment portfolio, trust, family partnership, retirement plan) that includes performance goals and a target asset allocation.

2. You or your advisor adds alternative investments, especially illiquid ones, to your portfolio, and in doing so you lose the ability to measure your aggregate investment results.

3. You want to divide your assets among several wealth advisors to test them head to head. Dividing among investment managers is alright, especially when using an Active Alpha Investing strategy.

4. Responsibility for investment performance between you and your wealth advisor is ambiguous.

5. Your advisor compares performance against benchmarks of active managers rather than indices, uses indices that don't account for reinvested dividends, doesn't have a composite benchmark to compare against, or changes benchmarks without a major change in your investment policy.

6. Your advisor compares performance before fees, sales charges, or exclusive of cash in the portfolio.

7. You have high portfolio turnover either at the manager or the security level, you are not accruing unrealized capital gains in a rising market, or your investment tax bill consistently is more than 20% of your gains.

continues

8. Your advisors give you multiple options for investment but don't make a firm recommendation for which they are willing to be held accountable.

9. A prospective advisor describes 'unique attributes' in their marketing materials, such as asset allocation skill or the ability to measure portfolio risk, but the professed skill isn't measured in your regular performance reporting.

Medium-term:

10. Aggregate performance, net of fees, is below the composite benchmark for three and five year periods. The performance of active managers—net of their fees and sales charges—is below their index benchmark for three- and five-year periods.

Long-term:

11. Over five to ten years your assets, as measured in dollars, are significantly below your absolute return objectives, especially if markets have been relatively strong.

Should You Act as Your Own FA?

Some people decide to act as their own FA. If you are an index investor, your family and financial circumstances are fairly simple, and you have the time and inclination to act as your own FA, I encourage you to consider this path after assembling the critical information you need. Firms like Vanguard have a range of index investment products and the ability to offer aggregate investment performance as part of their core service. Alternatively, firms like Morningstar offer a service that allows you to measure the individual and aggregate performance of all your mutual funds. Morningstar charges a fee for performance measurement but it includes a robust package of research information on mutual funds and investing that is useful to advisors and private investors alike. Acting as your own FA can be time-consuming, but with the right tools and the dedication to follow through, it can be rewarding and inexpensive.

Some people with large and complicated asset bases hire a part-time or full-time employee to fulfill the FA role. People pursuing a Barbell Investing strategy often designate someone on their finance staff to play the FA role. Alternatively, they may set up a dedicated family office to fulfill the function. (Sidebar 9.2, "What Is a Family Office?" discusses family offices in greater detail.) If you opt for either of these choices, recognize that they require intensive oversight and that implementing good performance/accountability systems can be challenging but is critical to do when millions of dollars are at stake.

Final Words on FA Selection

Up to this point, I haven't suggested that you evaluate the investment management skills of an FA or their firm—even though most FAs work for wealth management firms that tout their investment capabilities. There's a reason for this. I recommend that you keep the role of FA clearly separate from that of the people who manage your investment portfolio. This is especially critical if you are pursuing an Active Alpha Investing strategy. You need your FA to be a score keeper, organizer, and possibly a judge of talent. If the FA must also manage money, it creates a conflict.

How important is this conflict to the future of wealth management? In a stunning move, in mid-2005, Citibank announced it was selling its investment management operations because it didn't feel it could both advise clients on investment management and be an investment manager. Time will tell whether other firms follow suit.

If you are Index Investing or are confident in your own ability to select good managers, choosing your FA and your investment managers from the same firm does have advantages. Administration is easier and often less expensive if everything is under one roof and can be tied together electronically. In addition, the FA doesn't have to judge investment talent, which can be a major source of conflict. Rock-bottom investment fees and low transaction costs also keep the financial relationships pretty transparent and aligned.

Selecting the Right Firm

Now that we've covered how to find the right FA for you, it's equally important to make sure that the right financial services firm is standing behind the FA.

It's difficult to separate the qualifications of the FA from the qualifications of the firm employing the FA. Nevertheless, there are a number of key issues to consider in evaluating different wealth management firms. For example:

1. What investment strategy did you select?

2. How transparent are the firm's fees?

3. How robust are the firm's administrative systems?

4. How are FAs measured and incentivized by their firms?

Selection Factor #1: What Investment Strategy Did You Select?

As I've already suggested, the type of strategy you select—Index Investing, Barbell Investing, or Active Alpha Investing—has a profound impact on the type of firm you'll want to hire. The complexity of your chosen strategy determines the robustness of the infrastructure you'll need in your FA's firm. It also drives the nature of the products, services, and third-party service agreements[2] you should expect from the firm.

INDEX INVESTING

One of the beauties of the Index Investing strategy (alone or as part of a Barbell Investing strategy) is that it makes the selection of the FA firm quite straightforward. You will want an FA firm to:

- Have administrative capabilities to handle index funds in their various forms.
- Measure their aggregate performance.
- Rebalance your strategy as different asset classes either perform well or poorly.

You do *not* need an FA firm to:

- Be well-versed in tax efficiency because index funds are already tax efficient.
- Specialize as a skilled selector of value-added managers because you are selecting commodity products.
- Be proficient in tactical asset allocation skills because you have sworn off this level of risk and complexity.
- Get you embroiled in brokerage-type fee structures because the number of transactions you will have is minimal.

Now, here is the bad news.

Fewer firms will want your business if you index because profit margins for Index Investing strategies are razor thin. Existing providers are loath to cannibalize their very profitable Active Alpha business with low-margin index business. New index-based entrants need huge scale in order for the investment company to make a profit.

What's the solution to this dilemma if you've decided to index? In addition to the direct fees (from less than 0.1% to 0.25%), you'll be charged to participate in the actual index, I encourage you to consider paying a modest fee to your FA firm of between 0.1% to 0.5% of your assets, depending on their size and complexity, to your FA firm if the firm can provide the necessary accountability to support an Index Investing strategy. With this arrangement, you will pay at most *half* the industry average for such services, but will likely get better performance and service with fewer headaches. If you pursue this approach, I'm confident that this strategy will provide you with an FA firm that will meet your needs for executing an Index Investing strategy or a Barbell Investing strategy.

ACTIVE ALPHA INVESTING

Hiring an FA firm to oversee an Active Alpha Investing strategy is much more challenging because your portfolio needs more specialized attention and requires higher-order investment skills to manage it properly. For Active Alpha Investing, you will want an FA firm to:

- Use outstanding accountability systems to track the performance of your diverse portfolio.

- Be well versed in tax efficiency because you are investing in assets that are highly sensitive to tax implications.
- Specialize as a skilled selector of value-added managers because you are selecting riskier products that require a mastery of their fickle characteristics
- Be proficient in tactical asset allocation skills because you will be taking additional risk and the relative attractiveness of asset classes will periodically create opportunities for additional return.
- Evaluate incentive fee structures because the number and type of investments you have will be highly variable.

The good news is that many firms will want your business because profit margins are lucrative with Active Alpha clients, especially if you use their in-house investment products. When you do this, most firms "bundle" your administrative costs into the investment management fee. There may be cases, however, when you'll want to insist that the FA recommend only third-party managers to avoid conflicts of interest. In such cases, you'll pay separate fees to your FA and to your managers. This is what the Lucas family does because it keeps the FA focused on serving our needs.

Selection Factor #2: How Transparent Are the Firm's Fees?

It's incumbent on you as the Wealth Strategist to evaluate a prospective FA firm's fee structures through what I call the "alignment-of-interests" filter. When applying the filter, I ask two key questions:

- Will I know all the ways I'm paying the firm?
- Will the fees I'm charged correlate with the "value-added" benefits the firm provides to my account?

The answer to both questions should be "Yes!" If the answers aren't forthcoming or either is negative, the firm in question doesn't pass the screen.

That's the easy way to evaluate prospective FA firms, but there are many nuances to this process.

Firms that employ FAs, as well as most other financial companies, are remunerated based on four primary compensation models. I've listed them here in order of their attractiveness to you as an investor.

- **Asset-based.** Advisors are paid based upon the size of the assets within their responsibility. Compensation is somewhat tied to effectiveness. If assets grow in value, compensation rises. If assets fall, compensation declines. But asset growth and value added may or may not be linked, depending on the strength of the general markets relative to a portfolio's performance. Investment managers are usually paid this way. It is also my preferred method of compensating FAs, even if it means having a separate fee arrangement with investment managers.
- **Time-based.** Advisors are paid hourly for their work on behalf of the client. Compensation is *not* tied to the effectiveness of the work. Consultants and accountants are paid this way.
- **Transaction-based.** Each time an advisor conducts a transaction on behalf of a client, a commission is earned by the advisor. Compensation may be tied to the apparent value of the transaction to the client, but it is *not* tied to the actual value of the transaction to the client. Brokerage firms typically charge on this basis.
- **Spread-based.** Advisors are paid based on the difference between what your funds earn and the expenses associated with managing those funds. A simple example of spread-based compensation involves banking deposits and lending. A bank pays a depositor 2% interest, lends the money at 5%, has 1.5% in costs, and earns a "spread" of 1.5%. But there are many other examples of spread-based compensation, such as "costless collars" and municipal bond trading. The wider the spread the advisor can create, the greater the profit potential.

When evaluating a firm's fee structure, there are other potential costs you may incur:

1. **Profit participations.** Some advisors get a share of profits that they generate for clients, particularly in hedge funds and private equity funds. Some tax strategies are priced in part on expected profit (or tax savings). So-called "profit participations" or "carried interests" enable managers to share in profits but not have to suffer losses. Because of the potential for large returns to the manager, without the commensurate risk of loss, profit participations do entice managers to take more risk.

2. **Switching costs.** You pay penalties if you sell some products before an appointed time. This penalty period can be one, five, ten, or more years from the date of purchase. Almost all investment products, except no-load mutual funds, have significant switching costs. Life insurance and annuity products are particularly prone to high switching costs because they incur high upfront sales commissions that must be amortized over time. Any investment with a significant unrealized gain has a switching cost because capital gains taxes become due.

3. **Hidden compensation.** Wealth management firms have other sources of "hidden compensation." They include mutual fund marketing fees (called 12b-1 fees), brokerage fees, fee-sharing arrangements with third-party separate account and hedge fund managers, and in-kind services in exchange for directing clients' trading activity to certain brokers. (The latter are known as "soft dollar" arrangements.) Still other fees can include corporate finance and merger/acquisition fees, directors' fees, and profits from engaging as a principal in a transaction (i.e., stock trades and derivatives trades). Don't be bashful about asking a firm to commit in writing to full fee disclosure.

Some financial service firms, especially large conglomerates, may charge their clients using several compensation models—*all at the same time.* If you analyze other fee components—performance features, switching costs, and hidden compensation—you'll find that these can either increase or decrease the alignment of interests. Suffice to say that the more ways a firm charges you for services, the more difficult it is to keep the interests of advisors and client aligned.

Selection Factor #3: How Robust Are the Firm's Administrative Systems?

An efficient administrative infrastructure is critical to managing the alignment of interests between the Wealth Strategist and his or her advisors, including the FA. A perfect meshing of advisor accountability and alignment of interests is hard to achieve in the wealth management industry today. Still, creating a culture of accountability is extremely important because it drives all parties involved toward alignment of their collective interests. It also signals when interests are diverging. Whatever the practical impediments are to creating accountability, work through them as best you can with your FA and his/her firm.

Here are some of the problems you will encounter. The firms that most easily pass muster on the alignment of interests test fail most easily on accountability. The reverse is also true. Small, specialized advisory firms that are less encumbered than big firms with managing conflicts of interests are typically not big enough to justify the capital outlay for complex, automated administrative and reporting systems. Therefore, more error-prone manual labor is required, and there are some things they simply can't do.

The financial conglomerates, especially investment banks, have the most sophisticated reporting capabilities and arguably the most sophisticated full-service product offerings, but there are potential conflicts of interests embedded in almost everything they do. It is hard for you to feel assured that they are consistently putting your interests first.

Issues of alignment and accountability aren't huge hurdles to deal with if you are indexing or investing only in mutual funds. You can find small firms that have adequate systems, and you can structure your relationship with big firms to avoid most conflicts. However, if you use alternative investments as part of an Active Alpha Investing strategy, finding a solution that gives you both accountability and alignment of interests is very difficult. In addition, very few firms, large or small, track long-term historic asset values and cash flows to help clients understand long-term, dollar-based trends. With a little arm twisting, you may be able to convince your FA or accountant to do this for you. In our family, we have to track this data ourselves and find it enormously useful. We also do "shadow accounting" to double-check the accuracy of our FA's systems and procedures, and our own.

We are all stuck with a difficult challenge of finding optimal administrative solutions. This problem represents a wonderful business opportunity for wealth management firms. Indeed, the standard for industry leadership is wide open here. I hope that one or more firms will aggressively address this opportunity in the next few years and that clients are wise enough to recognize its value.

How Are FAs Measured and Incentivized by Their Firms?

To be successful, FAs have to make money for their firms if they want to keep their jobs. At the same time, they *should* add value to their clients. In an ideal world, these two goals are symbiotic. However, most firms don't even measure the value that FAs provide to their clients, and if they did, the exercise would be complex and imprecise. Value can come in many forms—by the FA creating positive alpha for the client through good manager selection, identifying hidden risks in a client's balance sheet, giving the client good asset allocation advice for an Index Investment strategy, or pointing out to the client that he/she is spending too much money.

Most firms, however, don't spend much energy measuring their value added to clients. Some firms don't even measure how often clients leave the firm.

By contrast, measuring the revenue (or profit) contribution of FAs is simple, precise, and closely scrutinized. Firm managements typically track it at both the individual and/or team level. Often, this information is publicized within the firm to encourage competition among FAs. Recognition, bonuses, and discretionary awards are given for exemplary performance. These incentives create constant pressure to perform. To a greater or lesser degree, it is in every firm's DNA, and it needs to be for firms to succeed as businesses.

Fortunately, most FAs pride themselves on service to their clients and want to do the right thing for their customers. I've known a number of FAs over the years who go out of their way to get things done for their clients, despite the predictable institutional roadblocks that arise from time to time. Most of these advisors have served at their firms a long time and have developed loyal clients over the years. They build strong personal relationships, meeting with their clients at summer homes or joining them on fishing trips or for golf outings. In return, these loyal clients actually provide their advisors with an element of job security. Happy clients mean a stable revenue stream. Of course, because it is so hard to measure the value added to clients, good service and a strong personal relationship are often the best ways to keep clients happy.

The combination of company pressure to perform and the inability to provide strong accountability to clients presents a real challenge to highly conscientious FAs.

Below are three real-life examples of FAs from three different firms dealing with the peculiarities of their job.

FA #1: Eve was such a good client advisor that a few years ago she was lured from one major boutique wealth management firm to another. The terms of her non-compete agreement prevented her from soliciting her old clients, and she and her new firm actually abided by that agreement. The new firm promised her resources to build a team and to support her business development efforts. But then the economy suffered a downturn and, in the face of industry contraction and a new management team, profitability and cost reduction became the priorities of the firm. Each month, the firm compared the revenue and profit contributions of each client advisor and distributed the results to all the team leaders. Eve and her scaled-back team were always at the bottom. Despite the fact that Eve enjoyed high customer satisfaction ratings from clients, she decided to leave the firm after a year of ever-increasing stress to meet the firm's expectations for performance. Even though her employer didn't literally push her out the door, the pressure to meet performance expectations simply became too great.

FA #2: George was completely dedicated to his clients even though he worked for a huge financial firm. He carried two cell phones at all times and was always on the road. His clients could call him 24/7, and they received plenty of "face time" when they wanted it. George was careful about how he managed his book of business and would, from time to time, hand off smaller and time-consuming relationships to a colleague. This enabled him to maintain service levels *and* profitability.

George was a real stickler for process and timeliness, much to the chagrin of the middle and back office specialists at his firm whom he regularly chewed out because he knew how to expedite things for clients when staffers erected roadblocks. Years of working inside the firm before becoming an FA had taught him the firm's systems and processes backward and forward.

Even though George's firm had been subject to mergers, systems changes, and numerous reorganizations and "adjustments" to his compensation plan over the years, he managed to shield his clients from the turmoil. While the rest of his firm struggled to keep client attrition down to acceptable levels in the 2000–2002 bear market, George never lost a single client. In 2003, the firm went to a bonus system that was payable entirely at the discretion of management. Ostensibly, this was done to improve teamwork, but it also had the benefit of helping the firm to manage its earnings because bonuses were a line item in the firm's budget. Finally, managing the tension between serving the client and meeting the firm's expectations got the better of George. When the financial markets started to recover, he quit. I speculate he will turn up again as the founder or co-founder of an independent advisory firm.

FA #3: Martha worked for a large brokerage firm during the second half of the 1990s advising private clients on their portfolios. The firm has a highly entrepreneurial culture that offers advisors wide latitude on the advice they give as long as their revenue numbers look good. This firm is one of many that tracks advisors' performance on the basis of net new revenue, but does not measure client attrition.

Through a referral, Martha attracted a successful entrepreneur as a client. This client's firm had spun out several million in excess cash that the client needed to invest. In addition, the company had tax-deferred profit sharing and pension plans that needed to be managed. Martha recommended a selection of variable annuities invested in stocks. One of the expressed benefits of annuities is that the assets grow on a tax-deferred basis. She recommended variable annuities for the company's profit sharing and pension plans, as well as for her client's taxable accounts.

The cost of the annuities plus management fees approached 4% per annum, sucking up all of the tax benefit for the client in anything but the most robust stock market environment. By contrast, an equity index fund of equal amount would have been nearly as tax efficient and had an annual fee about 95% lower. Furthermore, recommending that variable annuities get placed inside a tax-deferred vehicle was inexcusable.

The sales commission on the annuities Martha sold to her client enabled her to make a very tidy sum upon closing the deal. Furthermore, when her client committed to the products, the switching cost to change to other alternatives would further cut into his profits, essentially locking him in for seven or more years.

For a couple of years in the late 1990s, the rapid rise in the stock market obscured the impact of the high costs the client was paying to be invested in annuities. But when the bear market hit, the full impact of the misguided strategy became apparent. The client suffered severe losses and fired Martha's firm. She, however, had already made out like a bandit and was ready to move on to the next new prospect. Four years later, the client is still trying to extricate himself from these highly priced, poorly performing vehicles.

All of the previous examples are true, though the names have been changed to protect privacy. All these advisors are, or were, at the top of their game and, with the exception of Martha, went to great lengths to balance the demands of their companies with their own very high standard of service to their clients. But despite considerable personal sacrifice, and in most cases financial success, each FA had a very hard time maintaining balance.

Most advisors are dependent on a single employer, but have numerous clients. When pressures to perform increase, all people, financial advisors included, tend toward economic self-interest. All other things being equal, this gives the employer the upper hand in molding employee behavior. The more aggressive the employer and the greater the level of advisor remuneration, the harder firm managements tend to push. In such environments, customers need to be even more protective of their own interests than normal.

It's the responsibility of the Wealth Strategist to provide a proactive counterbalance to the business pressures of firms and the natural human tendencies of individual employees. In some cases, the Wealth Strategist must stand up to the advisor, and in other cases, he or she needs to informally partner with the FA to pressure the FA's firm for better client support.

Sidebar 7.3: The Case for Corporate Trustees

Many wealth management strategies involve the establishment and management of trusts. On the assumption that trusts will be part of your integrated wealth management strategy, how should you choose a trustee?

Being a trustee is a serious responsibility that can be technical in nature and carries with it substantial potential liability. There is inevitably a significant administrative component as well. Trustees can either be corporations or individuals. I am a strong believer in using corporations, especially for trusts that are for anything other than your own benefit. Corporate trustees are usually more expensive than individual trustees, but the professional expertise and the administrative capabilities you receive are usually worth the cost. Corporate trustees embed a notional liability insurance charge in their fees because they do get sued by disgruntled beneficiaries. Individual trustees can get sued, too, but they usually accept the role as a favor to a friend or family member. They rarely have the experience and structure in place to protect themselves legally in cases of disputes. Do you want to saddle a friend or family member with this responsibility?

There are two additional benefits to using a corporate trustee, benefits that I would argue are even more valuable. The first is that they have "infinite lives." They don't die unexpectedly, get sick, or leave town on extended vacations. They provide a sense of stability and long-term perspective that is useful. Their other great benefit is their ability to say "no" to beneficiaries in a dispassionate, unemotional way. Family relationships are complicated, and corporate trustees can act as objective and legalistic arbiters of disagreements or misunderstandings. Most people don't expect them to have a heart if it conflicts with their fiduciary duty to fulfill the grantor's wishes or to execute administrative responsibilities within the law. If there are family feuds, spendthrift children, or financial guardianship issues, and even if the family is functioning well, inserting a corporate trustee into the mix adds valuable perspective, professionalism, and administrative skill.

To guard against trustees becoming complacent, I recommend that you put a process in place to remove the trustee without cause at any time during the life of the trust. In our case, a majority of selected family members may remove a trustee without cause. A trusted lawyer, accountant, or family friend can also be a good "trustee remover."

Hiring an FA

As I said at the beginning of the chapter, hiring an FA is your most important wealth management decision. Assuming that you have followed the Strategic Wealth Management Framework to this point, you're ready to write a fairly detailed job description for your FA in the context of your values, family situation, and financial strategy.

After you have written a job description, the next step is to identify firms that are most likely to meet your needs. If you are looking for an FA to help you with indexing, firms like Vanguard, Barclays, State Street Global Advisors, or PIMCO may be places to start. Sometimes you have to dig deep within a firm to learn about its indexing capabilities. U.S. Trust, Northern Trust, Goldman Sachs, and J.P. Morgan also have indexing capabilities, but they aren't well advertised. Also, there are smaller wealth management boutiques and banks, such as M&I Bank in Wisconsin or Parametric Portfolio Associates in Seattle, which have specialized indexing capabilities.

If you are looking for an FA to help you with Active Alpha Investing, almost all of the aforementioned firms offer active management, as do many more large and small firms.

Regardless of the strategy you are pursuing, I suggest building a list of six or eight firms that you think can meet your needs. Make sure your list includes different types of organizations, including independent fee-only financial planners, not just big brokerage firms or mutual funds companies or banks. Try to identify a few smaller, specialized wealth management firms or independent planners so that you can study a range of offerings. If possible, get good references for specific advisors within those firms. Review your list, go to each firm's Web site, and try to narrow it down to three or four preferred providers.

After you've compiled your preferred list, prepare a written Request-For-Proposal (RFP) that includes the FA's job description, information about yourself and your financial and family circumstances, and a series of questions that you would like each firm to answer. To help you out, I've included a list of sample questions in Sidebar 7.4. When the RFP is complete, assemble the names and contact information of specific individuals within each firm, preferably a business manager in wealth management, to whom you'll send the RFP. Because wealth management firms aren't used to receiving RFPs, insist on written replies so that you can compare the firms' responses, and don't meet with any of them until you have a chance to review several responses. If one provider declines to respond, add another to your list. Will they look out for my interests first, even in tough times?

When you get an acceptable, written response, set up a meeting with the person or people who will be assigned to manage your relationship. You can ask some of the same questions that you listed on the RFP, and you will undoubtedly have other questions to ask in person. All the while, ask yourself: Are these people I can work with? Will these people be the ones who will actually work on my account, or are they salespeople or senior managers? Are they comfortable with the way I want to manage my assets and with the job description I have for them?

If you don't come away from these meetings with positive feelings, don't hesitate to send out more RFPs or to meet other FAs within the same firm.

Sidebar 7.4: The FA RFP

Putting together an RFP is a key step in identifying prospective FAs. Here are questions and requests you should address to prospective service providers as part of that process:

1. Can you provide brochures describing your wealth management services and financial products? If possible, please include the firm's annual report, including financial

---

statements. (Getting several years' reports will give you insight into the stability and priorities of the organization. Read between the lines; these are polished marketing documents.)

2. Who owns the firm?

3. Can you provide relevant organizational charts for the firm and the private client group?

4. What constitutes a typical team serving each wealthy client? How many clients does the typical private client team serve? Who do you recommend for my relationship? How long has this team been working together at your firm? How many new clients have been added to this team in each of the last five years? How many have left in each of the last five years? (Please send a resumé of each of the key people that you recommend to work on my relationship.)

5. How does the firm track the amount of value-added that the client service team provides to its clients? What does it do with the information it collects?

6. How do you make strategic asset allocation decisions on behalf of clients? How do you evaluate risk? Are your models based on forward-looking or backward-looking information? Before-tax or after-tax information?

7. How do you help clients choose managers? Do you receive any incentives to recommend certain managers over others? If so, what are they? What track record do you have to demonstrate your manager selection skill?

8. What fees do I pay the firm? Does the firm receive any other income from my assets other than fees, including but not limited to brokerage fees, banking fees or spreads, sales charges, 12 b-1 fees, or indirect compensation from service providers that you recommend to me?

continues

9. How much professional personnel turnover has there been in the private client group in each of the last five years? How are your key client advisors compensated? On what basis are their bonuses calculated? How do you measure client satisfaction?

10. Please send a sample of your typical client-reporting package. Can you calculate the time-weighted total return for a total portfolio of public assets including stocks, bonds, and mutual funds? If alternative investments, including illiquid investments, are included, does your system still have the capability to measure aggregate time-weighted rates of return?

11. Can you create customized benchmarks using market indices to compare against the actual performance of each manager and the aggregate portfolio? Are there any upgrades to your accounting and performance measurement systems planned within the next two years? If so, please describe them.

12. Describe the administrative services offered by the typical client service team other than portfolio administration and performance measurement. Summarize your procedures for ensuring accurate and timely execution of administrative services. Do you have online administrative services that I can access?

13. Can you provide at least five client references at the appropriate time?

The Lucas Family Experience of Selecting an FA

Before we chose our new FA in 2001, we had the same individual serving us for seven or eight years. He was almost part of the family, and if he had received better support from his organization, we would probably still be working with him. He had developed strong personal relationships with each member of the family. He got his firm to do things for us that it did not do for anyone else—using third-party investment managers, putting alternative investments into irrevocable trusts, and creating a partnership with our family to make investment decisions.

But he couldn't fix his firm's reporting infrastructure, and even with his support we were always fighting the system. Because he had built such strong personal relationships, my family trusted him. This made it particularly difficult for me to convince the family to take action. But finally I prevailed, and the search ensued for a new FA.

We needed an FA equipped to handle an Active Alpha Investing strategy, complete with alternative assets and tactical asset allocation. We wrote up a detailed description of our wealth management strategy and the capabilities we sought to implement it. We wanted a corporate trustee that embraced complete open architecture, could provide the necessary support for accountability, and was comfortable with multiple asset classes, including alternative investments.

We sent out RFPs to eight carefully selected firms. Most were large banks with well-established trust departments; a few were large family offices that were trying to attract additional clients (multi-family offices). We also approached several investment banks that had trust departments. We explicitly told each firm that, if selected, we would ask it to sign a detailed Memorandum of Understanding (MOU) committing it to deliver on those things it promised in the RFP.

The search for a new FA proved to be eye-opening. First, when the marketing people realized we were serious about the key stipulations in the RFP, most said they could not deliver both the complete open architecture and the accountability structure we sought. And several insisted on managing up to 50% of the assets internally, a proposal that we rejected. Eventually, we did find three firms in this elite group that claimed they could fulfill all of our specifications. After interviewing two of them in detail, we chose to negotiate with one. In the late stages of negotiation, this particular firm backed away from claims it made in the marketing presentation about its performance measurement capabilities. (We ultimately agreed to pay an extra fee to an affiliated consulting firm to get what we wanted.) The second surprise was the takeover of this firm in the midst of our negotiations, even after representatives had assured us they intended to remain independent.

Despite the surprises and mid-course adjustments, out of this process we retained a new FA firm that delivers to us today in many ways:

- There is alignment of their interests with ours (if our assets do well, their fees rise; if our assets do poorly, their fees fall).
- I know precisely how they are paid.
- The accountability systems in place are adequate.
- The firm has a sophisticated suite of services that support our Active Alpha Investing strategy.
- The firm pays its people better than our previous FA firm did.
- Because the firm is in New York, the prospective hiring pool is plentiful and competitive.
- They oversee a tax-managed index portfolio for us.

The new FA firm does have one key deficiency: turnover of personnel has resulted in four relationship managers in the last three years. Fortunately for us, we have a stable family office, so when our FAs turn over it is less disruptive than if we didn't have our own infrastructure or if we had to change firms each time. Overall, our current FA team is really superb, and we hope we can keep it. Unfortunately, it is hard to predict when good people in this business are going to turn over. Going back to the first core principle of wealth management, if you take charge, the almost inevitable turnover of your advisors will be less disruptive for you to deal with when it occurs.

Conclusion

This chapter has described the pivotal roles that the Financial Administrator (FA) and his or her firm play in helping the Wealth Strategist implement wealth management plans and strategies.

Most potential FAs will tell you they are great investors. But what you need is a great administrator who has *your* interests, not an employer's interests, as their top priority.

Now, let's move on to Chapter 8, "Taxes Can Be Your Ally!" where we'll discuss taxes and how best to minimize them for purposes of optimal wealth management results.

Chapter 7: Issues to Discuss with Your Family

1. How do you track the performance of your investments? How can you improve upon your current process?

2. Do you currently employ financial advisors to help you implement your financial goals? If so, do they have the requisite qualifications outlined in this chapter?

3. Have you had experience with financial advisors that proves they have your best interests at heart? If not, can you imagine selecting new advisors to assist you?

4. Are you convinced that the more advisors you have, the harder it might be to fulfill your financial goals?

5. Have you ever measured your asset base at the end of each year? If not, are you compelled to do so after reading this chapter?

6. Have you ever known what fees you actually pay to a financial services firm? Has this chapter helped you to better discern how fees should be charged to you?

7. Do you think it's possible for a financial administrator to put their client's interests first, while still serving the firm in which they are employed?

8. After reading this chapter, do you have enough confidence to issue a Request-For-Proposal (RFP) to financial services firms seeking professional assistance?

9. Have you changed your mind regarding your preferred investing strategy after reading about the varied qualifications required of an FA to implement each of the three investment strategies?

Endnotes

1 The CFA Institute is a member organization of investment professionals committed to leading the global investment profession by setting the highest standards of education, integrity, and professional excellence. As part of their program, they have established a standard for how to measure investment performance in this country, and increasingly around the globe. The standard in this country is referred to as the AIMR Performance Presentation Standards, or AIMR-PPS. These standards are regularly reviewed and periodically updated to allow investors to measure performance in the fairest possible way and to accurately compare the performance of various managers. For more information about AIMR-PPS, go to: http://www.cfainstitute.org/cfacentre/ips/pps/aimrpps.html. For more information on the CFA Institute, go to: http://www.cfainstitute.org.

2 Many firms that sell third-party products negotiate service agreements with the firms whose products they sell. Agreements often include revenue and cost-sharing clauses, as well as terms for handling client information and joint marketing efforts.

8

TAXES CAN BE YOUR ALLY!

"Over the long term, benign neglect really does pay off."

—*Charles D. Ellis, Managing Partner,*
Greenwich Associates

I t should come as no surprise to you that taxes rank as either #1 or #2 on the list of expenses for the wealthiest Americans. In 1998, for example, my family paid seven times in taxes what we earned in profits in one of our investment entities! Today, taxes are our second biggest leakage behind spending, and without careful planning they would be the biggest.

By comparison, many institutional investors—pension funds and endowments, for example—that have billions of dollars in investments don't pay any taxes at all.

So what can you do to responsibly minimize your taxes?

While tax efficiency is a critical element in your investment strategy, most investment managers don't concern themselves much with tax minimization because doing so doesn't reap them any bottom-line benefits. After all, they are evaluated on pre-tax performance by almost everyone. But I'm here to tell you that evaluating your after-tax results is important. I will also tell you that, managed well, taxes can be your ally in the wealth management planning process.

The way the U.S. Tax Code works, the wealthier you become, the more control you have over how much you pay in taxes and when you pay them. There are also numerous incentives in the tax code that work in your favor to reduce risk and to help your assets grow more quickly.

This chapter gives you the framework you need to ensure that taxes stay front and center in your wealth management strategies, resulting in the highest net level of return possible on your investments.

Where Do You Begin?

There are enough tax regulations out there to fill a library. U.S. taxpayers are subject to the U.S. Tax Code with its federal regulations, fifty different state tax codes, and thousands of county/city/town tax codes. I simply cannot address the minutiae of all of these different rules, and you certainly didn't buy this book in search of mind-numbing tax analysis.

To keep your "eye on the big prize" (tax minimization and tax efficiency), I can tell you that the structure of the U.S. Tax Code offers some very attractive incentives for wealthy investors and creates disadvantages in other areas. Consequently, for you, the Wealth Strategist, there are five key takeaways from this chapter:

1. Understand that U.S. taxing authorities are, in fact, your investing partners. I'll explain why.

2. For taxable investors, it's valuable to be a long-term, equity-oriented investor.

3. You can add value to your bottom line through tax management.

4. Retirement and deferred compensation plans are great pre-tax savings tools, but don't over-commit yourself to these vehicles.

5. Don't put after-tax money into tax-deferred savings vehicles, such as annuities and life insurance policies.

It's worth exploring these key takeaways with your financial administrator and your accountant and incorporating them into your wealth management strategy. In the rest of this chapter, I will explore each of these points in detail. Sometimes the math is a little complicated, but it helps more numerate readers to understand the issues more clearly. In these cases, I separate the detail from the concept so you can choose how much you want to immerse yourself. For better or worse, a significant part of wealth management is quantitative.

Take-Away #1: U.S. Taxing Authorities Are Your Investing Partners

In previous chapters, I've talked about your partners in the wealth management process—accountants, lawyers, and investment managers.

I have not included the Internal Revenue Service or your local taxing authorities in this list of wealth management partners—until now.

Personal income taxes were legalized in the 16th Amendment to the U.S. Constitution, and the first modern income tax law was enacted in October 1913. Since the end of World War I, the top marginal tax rate has been volatile, with a high above 90%, a low of 28%, and a current rate of 35%. In its early years, the top marginal rate affected only the super-rich, but today the majority of people reading this book are likely to pay taxes at the top marginal rate, even in retirement. For sound economic reasons, the short-term capital gains tax rates now mirror income tax rates. This coupling is likely to continue unless there is a major overhaul of the federal tax code.

By contrast, since 1929, the top marginal long-term capital gains tax rate has ranged from a high of 40% to a low of 15%, which happens to be the current rate. This is a much narrower and lower range, particularly when you consider that the rate has been meaningfully above 30% only for brief periods. Since 1929, the long-term capital gains tax rate has been lower than the top marginal income tax rate in all but two years.

Today, federal income taxes are the largest source of federal government revenues, about 45% of the total. This is over 10 times the revenue typically generated by capital gains taxes. If the government needs a large revenue boost, it traditionally (and will likely again) raises income taxes significantly. It may increase capital gains taxes at the same time, but the likelihood that they would ever equate with income tax rates is highly unlikely. Most likely, capital gains taxes will continue to be significantly lower than income taxes.

All that said, I prefer to think of U.S taxing authorities as investment partners, as opposed to adversaries. I also view that partnership in unconventional ways, which I describe in the following paragraphs.

First, when designing a wealth management strategy, it's important to remember that, although the government sets the rules for how to calculate taxes in the tax code, the government in fact acts like a silent partner. Each taxpayer is left to apply the code's rules to his or her own advantage. (More on this in Take-Away #2.) Our actions and decisions have an enormous impact on our tax liabilities!

Second, unlike accountants, lawyers, and investment managers who make money off your assets through fees regardless of how well your investments do, tax authorities only benefit if you generate profits. If there are no profits, or profits are deferred, Uncle Sam doesn't get paid.

Third, in exchange for taxing you, the government provides you with a wide range of services including defense, emergency services, a system of law, economic management, social security, and community infrastructure, such as roads, schools, and the like. All these are critical to ensuring a stable society, guaranteeing free commerce, and enabling you to get wealthy in the first place. Just how many billionaires do you know in the Sudan? Even in Western Europe, the rate of wealth creation isn't nearly as high. I rest my case.

Take-Away #2: Be a Long-Term, Equity-Oriented Investor

The tax code offers strong incentives for investors to think and act long term.

Long-Term Investments Are Taxed at the Lowest Rate

Today, the top short-term capital gains tax rate is 35%, which means that if you sell a profitable investment one year or less from the day from its purchase, you are taxed at this rate.

By contrast, today's top long-term capital gains tax rate is 15%, a full 57% lower, and you don't pay the tax on the long-term gains until you sell. Also, most dividends on stocks are taxed at the same low rate, even in the first year, but you pay tax every year on dividends.

The longer you hold an appreciating investment, the more advantages there are:

- Deferred capital gains taxes are like interest-free loans.
- "Benign neglect" pays off.
- Deferred capital gains taxes provide downside risk protection.
- You never have to pay capital gains taxes.

- Investing in equities lowers the tax rate on "spending money."
- Declining capital gains taxes are a bonanza to long-term investors.

The combined benefits of holding assets for the long term are substantial, so long as the assets are appreciating in value. To explain the details, I must delve into some basic accounting theory and a few numbers. I encourage you to try to follow along, even if they are not your strong point. After all, it is *your* money, and taxes are a big leakage.

CAPITAL GAINS TAXES ARE LIKE INTEREST-FREE LOANS

Taxes on long-term gains can be deferred until an asset is sold, even if it's 86 years later, as in the case of my family's ownership of Carnation stock. The unrealized gains over 86 years of ownership meant that there was a large accruing, but unpaid, liability to the IRS on our family's balance sheet.

It's like getting no-interest loans from the government! It also has some other attractive features. First, at no point does the government have the authority to say, "We are calling your loan." You have the right to let the free "loan" continue to be unpaid for as long as you want, as long as you don't sell the underlying asset. Second, in most cases, the size of the loan varies proportionately with the success of the investment. The bigger the gain, the bigger the loan.

BENIGN NEGLECT PAYS OFF

The concept of benign neglect is best portrayed by a mathematical example. Let's start by looking at two investors who pay federal taxes on long-term capital gains at the full 15% rate. Each buys the same asset for $100,000.

The first investor holds it until it is sold for $1,000,000, for a 900% percent increase in the original investment. He pays taxes on the $900,000 gain (15% capital gains tax rate times $900,000 equals $135,000) and is left with $865,000.

The second investor gets impatient, sells early, and generates $200,000. He pays the $15,000 in taxes on his $100,000 gain and is left with $185,000. He then realizes he has sold too soon, but manages to buy back $185,000 of the asset at the same valuation. It then increases five times in value for a total of a 900% return, just like the first investor. After paying federal taxes of 15% on the $740,000 gain, the second investor is left with $814,000.

The second investor's impatience cost him $51,000 (the difference between $865,000 and $814,000).[1]

Additionally, if the second investor had executed his first sale within one year of buying the asset, he would have paid a 35% tax ($35,000) instead of a 15% tax ($15,000). After reinvesting, participating in the rest of the price appreciation, and paying the 15% long-term rate on the rest of his gains, the total value of his investment would be $726,000, a far cry from the already diminished $814,000. Clearly, the cost of paying short-term capital gains is high, which is why long-term investing is almost always better for taxable investors.

Lastly, let's look at two more hyperactive investors who sell (and repurchase) every time the stock increases by $100,000 in value. In other words, over the course of the 900% increase, they each buy and sell nine times. One investor only pays long-term capital gains tax at the 15% rate because he always waits at least one year to sell and repurchase. The other investor pays short-term capital gains tax at the 35% rate because he always sells and repurchases within one year.

How much are they left with after the 900% appreciation? The first investor is left with $742,318. The second investor generates only $489,793! Interestingly, the second investor's major loss is not because of the higher tax rate. It is the lost opportunity to earn profits on money that is paid each year to the government.

Figure 8.1 provides a summary of these five examples.

The Cost of Acting Short Term

	Investment	Pre-tax Return	Net Return	Cost of Acting Short Term
Long-term Hold	$100,000	900%	$865,000	$0
Intermediate Sale	$100,000	900%	$814,000	$51,000
Short-term Sale	$100,000	900%	$726,000	$139,000
Multiple Long-term Sales	$100,000	900%	$743,963	$121,037
Multiple Short-term Sales	$100,000	900%	$490,668	$374,332

Figure 8.1 High turnover adds a lot of cost to the portfolios of taxable investors.

You can clearly see the benefit of being a long-term investor. Most investments are not likely to return 900% over two, five, or even ten years. But over 20 years, a 900% return equates to 12.2% per year and over 30 years to 8% per year. Many investments over a longer time frame can and do generate these types of returns. So the costs of not thinking long term are very real.

The flip side of the long-term incentives offered in the tax code is that investment income and short-term capital gains are expensive luxuries. Before investing in assets that generate high levels of current income and short-term gains, it is prudent to compare the estimated after-tax performance of these assets relative to other more tax-efficient alternatives.

Sidebar 8.1: Alternative Minimum Taxes Complicate Everything

The Alternative Minimum Taxes (AMT) law uses a different methodology for determining your taxes, that eliminates a number of (usually favorable) adjustments to your taxable income (state income tax and property taxes among them). If your AMT liability exceeds your regular tax liability, you will be subject to AMT. Millions of taxpayers are getting hit by the AMT each year.

The AMT rates are still somewhat lower than standard rates. They are 26% on the first $175,000 of AMT income and 28% for income over that amount. The standard 15% rate on long-term capital gains and dividends also applies under AMT. So, even under AMT, you are given strong incentives to be a long-term investor.

Before a liquidity event, many people generate enough earned income and have few enough deductions that their standard tax rate is above the top AMT rate of 28%. After a liquidity event, many of the same people have higher itemized deductions that don't qualify under AMT, lower salaries, and more unearned income. Also, they may own certain investments that have income subject to AMT that are not subject to the regular tax. In short, it's tougher to avoid AMT after you have accumulated significant and diversified wealth.

Many private investors allocate a portion of their assets to municipal bonds because they are tax exempt. There are, however, many different types of "muni" bonds, and not all of them have the same tax treatment. Bonds that are general obligations of a municipality ("GO Bonds") are exempt from federal tax—including alternative minimum tax. For bondholders residing in the same state, GO Bonds are usually exempt from state tax. However, another common class of muni bonds called Private Activity Bonds, which typically fund specific qualifying projects, are not exempt from alternative minimum tax. These bonds often trade at higher yields than GO Bonds, but for those who are in the alternative minimum tax bracket, the net of tax yields are lower. Many muni bond funds invest in Private Activity Bonds as a way of increasing their stated yield. It is important to make sure that the tax strategy of the fund is consistent with your own tax position.

DEFERRED CAPITAL GAINS TAXES PROVIDE DOWNSIDE RISK PROTECTION

The U.S. Tax Code provides downside protection for the investor. Realized losses from one investment can be used to offset gains from another investment. There are some details that complicate this generalization,[2] so it is important to work with an accountant to make sure that the offsets are appropriate. Generally speaking, profits and losses from stocks, bonds, hedge funds, and other vehicles that invest in public companies can be used to offset each other.

My family and I review our assets every Fall to see if there are losses that we want to realize to reduce our net tax liability for the year. Sometimes, we can replace one mutual fund or stock with a similar one, lowering our tax burden without significantly changing our overall portfolio or incurring significant transaction costs. It's an easy thing to do. It can save real money and it involves insignificant risk if executed prudently.

Another benefit of downside protection that is rarely discussed is that your silent partner, the government, loses disproportionately when highly appreciated securities decline in value. Taxes are payable only on profits, not on the total value of your investment. If one of your high-performing investments has a reversal and declines, say, 30% in value, the deferred tax liability declines by more than 30% because the profit has declined more than the total value. Your share of the profit (net of deferred tax liability) declines by less than 30%. This phenomenon only happens in taxable accounts. In a retirement plan or annuity, a 30% decline means a 30% decline no matter what.

The downside protection offered by the tax code is more powerful for stocks than it is for bonds. Bonds almost always trade in a range that is within 25% of their $100 par value. As such, the level of capital gain or loss, and the associated capital gains tax, is fairly small. Stocks, on the other hand, can grow many times in value, accruing huge unrealized gains in the process.

Equity mutual funds and hedge funds that frequently turn over their portfolios also get much less benefit from the downside protection than investment vehicles with buy and hold strategies.

I have never seen a wealth management firm incorporate the downside protection of taxes into their asset allocation models. If they did, they would recommend that their clients increase exposure to long-term equity-type investments (including real estate) relative to bonds, hedge funds, or other tax-inefficient investments, especially as unrealized capital gains build within the portfolio.

For a few years after a major liquidity event, most people don't have many unrealized gains in their investment portfolios. If this is your situation, this has the effect of increasing your risk because you can't get the downside protection from taxes. Any losses you incur cannot be used to offset realized gains until you generate additional gains sometime in the future. In earlier chapters, I have urged you to be methodical when putting money into investments in the wake of a liquidity event. This is just one more reason to take your time, increase your risk profile in parallel with your own experience, and resist the temptation to put your newly liquid assets to work quickly.

YOU DON'T EVER HAVE TO PAY CAPITAL GAINS TAXES

If you play your cards right, you don't ever have to pay capital gains taxes. Here are four techniques that are straightforward and simple to execute. They are solidly embedded in the tax code (though obviously subject to change), and they can save you millions of dollars:

1. *Don't sell*: Neither my great-grandfather nor my grandfather paid capital gains tax on the majority of their Carnation stock because they didn't sell it! Forward-thinking estate planning enabled them to pass the stock from generation to generation, continuing the tax-free compounding of the stock's value. It was only when the company was sold in 1985, 86 years after the first case of evaporated milk rolled out of the factory, that capital gains taxes on the stock became due!

2. *Invest in tax-managed equity mutual funds*: I recommend that people invest in "tax managed" equity mutual funds offered by Vanguard and others that have never triggered a capital gains tax liability—even though a number of the stocks in the fund have been sold. The managers of these funds make an active effort to sell the stocks that have declined below cost. They then use those losses to offset against gains in companies that had to be sold because of a merger or takeover. The Lucas family employs a similar tax-managed index portfolio to do the same thing, but it is structured as a separate account, just for us. The entry ticket is higher but, unlike a mutual fund, we can use the losses we generate in the portfolio to offset against gains that we generate

in other investments. So long as we don't sell, and especially if new cash comes into these vehicles, we are likely to pay little or no capital gains tax on these investments for decades.

3. *Donate*: Rather than selling a stock and paying tax on the gains, we periodically donate it to either a non-profit organization or a family foundation, and take a tax deduction. Then the non-profit sells the stock. Because it is a tax-exempt institution, no capital gains taxes are owed.

    Donating appreciated securities is significantly more attractive than donating cash because you get the tax deduction on the amount you would have received, net of tax, if you had sold the stock yourself. Plus, you get a deduction on the amount that would have gone to the government in the form of taxes. In short, you don't pay taxes on the gain, and you can use a "super-sized" deduction to lower your taxable income.

4. *Death and taxes*: If one owns an appreciated asset at the time of death, there is a further capital gains tax benefit. When the asset is distributed out of the decedent's estate, it receives a "stepped-up basis." (The stepped-up basis may disappear in larger estates when Congress reforms the estate tax, but Congress may also significantly lower the applicable tax rate.) Essentially, the accrued capital gains taxes are not payable by the estate, and the recipient of the asset receives a cost basis equal to the value at the time of death. The asset is subject to estate taxes, but they are calculated without regard to unrealized capital gains. Smaller estates will suffer no estate tax bill. However, the tax can be substantial in multi-million dollar estates.

INVESTING IN EQUITIES LOWERS THE TAX RATE ON "SPENDING MONEY"

If you are spending money from your investments, how much you spend and what types of investments you use to finance spending will affect how much you contribute to government coffers.

If your spending money is generated by realized long-term capital gains or dividends, it is taxed at 15%. If it comes from interest income, a variable annuity, or a retirement plan, it can be taxed at 35% or more if you include state and local taxes. In places like New York City or California, the combined rate can approach 50%.

The tax efficiency of your investing will dictate the tax efficiency of your spending. By investing in stocks and accruing the capital gains, you can substantially lower the drain on your assets from spending. For example, on $100,000 per year of spending there is a net benefit of roughly $36,000 if your spending money comes from long-term profits and dividends on stocks rather than from corporate bonds, distributions from social security, annuities, or 401k retirement plans.

DECLINING CAPITAL GAINS TAXES ARE A BONANZA TO LONG-TERM INVESTORS
Today, if the government were in the marketing business, it would be touting the current capital gains tax rates as a great "bargain sale." When rates were dropped from 20% to 15% a few years ago, they became the lowest since they were instituted 76 years ago.

This cut in the capital gains tax was instituted at a time when the economy was really struggling to get back on its feet. It was intended to have a stimulating effect and, for wealthy Americans, it did. When the tax rate dropped, the size of the "loan" from the government to an investor with a million dollars of accrued, but unpaid, taxes (before the decline in rates) immediately dropped by $250,000 (a five percentage point [or 25%] drop on a 20% base times $1 million). This money went from the government straight into that investor's pocket. Talk about free money! For investors who suffered through the bear market of 2000 to 2002 and didn't have any gains, there was no immediate benefit from the tax cut. But it did encourage them to look favorably on being equity investors because they would get to keep a higher percentage of future profits. Not surprisingly, the stock market rallied strongly.

In the future, it is likely that tax rates will rise again. Under these circumstances, the math in the previous paragraph works in reverse. But the power of the "free loans" is so great that capital gains taxes would have to rise considerably to negate the benefit of the free loans, *so long as your asset continues to grow over the long term.* My bottom line here: If you own securities with large unrealized gains, only sell if you are a seller for fundamental reasons or if you think there is going to be a major hike in rates.

Take-Away #3: Improve Investment Results through Tax Management

Though it seems counter-intuitive, you really can add value to your investment portfolio by managing your taxes well. And you can do it with a high degree of certainty. Here's how:

Sidebar 8.2: Aggressive Tax Strategies Are Risky

The tax code is open to interpretation; the greater the complexity of someone's tax situation, the greater the room for interpretation. Aggressive tax strategies can keep a great deal of money in an individual's pocket that might otherwise go to the government, though at the current low capital gains tax rates, the benefit is less than it has been in many years. Even though the IRS audits less than 1% of all tax returns, and the odds of losing in an audit are smaller still, aggressive tax strategies are usually complicated. They also restrict your flexibility to deal with the unexpected and carry a substantial administrative burden.

Before embarking on aggressive strategies, do your homework thoroughly and choose selectively. I would start by asking some questions in the context of a potential IRS challenge:

1. Why do I need the extra money? Are the dollars big enough to matter?

2. Is there a less risky way to accomplish most of my objective?

3. Can I defend my position robustly? Documentation and process are really important. Also, carefully negotiate the wording of any opinion letters from lawyers or accountants to limit the caveats. If the caveats are too broad to make you comfortable, your interests are not aligned with your advisor. He or she will be paid up front while the risk burden falls largely on you.

4. Can I afford to lose a challenge?

---

5. Will other family members affected by a challenge or adverse ruling be my allies or become my enemy? Consequences can include lost time, stress, legal fees, back taxes, interest, and penalties.

If your answers sound equivocal or negative, the red flags should go up.

There are other potential risks of aggressive tax strategies besides IRS challenges. Any tax strategy is risky that requires you to establish a tax liability today that must be paid for with a volatile asset at some point in the future, particularly if the assets and liabilities involved are significant relative to your total estate. The outcome is terrific if the asset's value keeps rising, but if the opposite happens, it can be disastrous. In extreme cases, people have had to declare personal bankruptcy. Unfortunately, income tax obligations are not eliminated in the bankruptcy process.

Complicated tax strategies are administratively intensive. During the process of setting up the strategy, lawyers and accountants are usually very good at defining the infrastructure required to justify and support the strategy. However, someone needs to implement the infrastructure and keep it operating, often for a decade or more. Over longer time spans, lawyers, accountants, and administrators change or get busy doing something else, or clients balk at paying high hourly rates for essentially administrative duties. However, the viability of the strategy and the conditions set out in legal opinion letters are dependent on effective administration. Before executing such a strategy, be prepared to see through the mundane details over its complete life.

After a complicated strategy is put in place, it is expensive or impossible to turn back the clock. Yet, as we have already discussed, tax rates are unpredictable. What appeared to be a good decision a few years ago may, with a changed fact set, no longer be attractive. In fact, it may create all sorts of new, expensive, and time-consuming problems.

Hire Only a Few Broadly Diversified, Tax-Efficient Managers

If you use an Active Alpha strategy, most wealth advisors recommend that you hire a number of different managers. As part of a complete portfolio, you might be offered a large-cap growth manager, a large-cap value manager, a small-cap manager and an international manager, and four or five others as well. Your advisor may explain that each manager is an expert in his or her particular space, and that with multiple managers you have the ability to shift your asset allocation opportunistically, or if a manager doesn't work out you can simply replace the name in that "box." Even if your advisor advocates an Index Investing strategy, he or she may still recommend this approach to investing, which is often referred to as "style box" investing.

Institutional managers have been successfully pursuing the style box approach to investing for decades. But most institutional investors don't pay taxes and you, of course, do.

Let's take a look at what happens if you invest using this approach. The value manager buys a stock that has come on hard times. Then the company starts growing again, and its stock recovers. Now the value manager sells the stock at a profit about the same time that the growth manager thinks, "Hey, this is an attractive growth stock," and buys it. Your portfolio hasn't changed, but you have paid taxes and transaction costs unnecessarily. While these costs may be immaterial for a large institution, they can be quite substantial for an individual investor. If you keep selling your winners, you don't accumulate accrued taxes. If you don't accumulate the accrued taxes, you eliminate much of your ability to share investment risk with the government.

How do you combat this problem? When you assemble a series of tax-efficient managers—whether active or indexed (passive)—don't choose very many. The more managers you choose, the less tax efficient your overall portfolio will be because there will be more buying and selling going on. In particular, don't choose a growth manager and a value manager if you can choose an appropriate alternative that does both. Likewise, don't choose a large-cap and a small-cap manager if one will do. As the previous example attests, companies regularly move between growth and value portfolios as their fortunes change. In fact, if you own growth and value index funds, it is almost inevitable. The same is true of small- and large-capitalization portfolios.

Frankly, if you are using an Index Investing strategy, you need and want only one U.S. equity portfolio that replicates the whole market. However, it does make sense to own separate international and domestic portfolios because companies rarely change their country of domicile.

As you can plainly see, one of the beauties of maximizing tax efficiency is that it actually simplifies your investment strategy considerably while simultaneously adding a lot of value.

Save Early

Why do I encourage young college graduates earning modest salaries with outstanding student loans to put money into their retirement plans that they won't use for 40 or 50 years? It all has to do with what Einstein called the "eighth wonder of the world"—the power of compounding. And it has a lot of implications when it comes to paying your taxes.

Every $1,000 that you put into a retirement plan in your twenties, and has the ability to grow for 50 years free of taxes in an equity investment, could be worth $100,000 when you retire. If you don't start saving for retirement until you are 45, the value of that $1,000, compounding at the same rate, may only be worth $10,000. As you can see, there is a ten-fold difference in return simply by starting 20 years sooner.

In my own case, I am just about halfway through my career, if I work until 70 years of age. In the first six years that I worked after graduating from college, I deposited as much as I could afford into my retirement plans, about $50,000 in total. I put the maximum amount allowed into my IRA and my 401K plan. Fortunately, I didn't have college loans to pay off, had a reasonably well-paying job, and had an employer that offered an attractive retirement plan. After I left the company, I kept the money I had saved in a segregated retirement savings plan. Today, only halfway to retirement, the asset is worth about $700,000. If it grows at an average of 10% per year from now until I turn 70, the original

$50,000 investment will be worth $7 million! Those first six years of savings, from age 21 to 27, will have taken care of all my retirement spending needs, and then some.

Like Carnation, my retirement plan is an investment that grows consistently over many decades and is not held back by spending or the payment of taxes. Even better, my retirement plan is not investing in a single company but in a broadly diversified portfolio consisting largely of equity securities. The only unfortunate thing is that I will most likely have to pay income tax rates on the distributions rather than comparatively low capital gains tax rates.

Today, however, the government offers a great savings tool for retirement that wasn't available to me in my 20s called a Roth IRA. It doesn't give you a tax deduction when you invest (which isn't such a big deal if you are in a low-income tax bracket), but after your money is invested you don't pay any taxes, even at the time of distribution! If you're young, financially capable, have a low tax rate, and otherwise meet the eligibility requirements, I would invest first in a Roth IRA, up to the full amount available. If your tax rate is high, take a more balanced approach, employing your regular IRA or 401k plan and your Roth IRA.

High Management Fees and Low Returns Are a Bad Combination!

No one likes to pay an investment manager high fees in return for poor performance. When this happens, you suffer doubly because your taxes are calculated before subtracting fees. Most individual investors cannot deduct investment management fees from their gross income for tax purposes.[3] For example, if you invest in a fund that earns 5% (gross of fees and taxes), you pay tax on the full 5%. At a 30% tax rate, this leaves you with a return of 3.5%. Subtracting investment management fees of 2% of assets leaves you with a measly return of 1.5%!

This is exactly what happened to us once. We hired a technology manager who picked stocks and held them for the long term. Portfolio turnover was very low. For a while, the manager performed well and accrued large unrealized capital gains as he let his winners run.

Even though the manager's fee was 2%, we thought he had special insights that, coupled with good tax efficiency, more than made up for the high fee. But then the market reversed and the manager suffered along with the rest of the sector. Finally, after almost eight years, we sold the investment. Over the period, the gross rate of return, before fees, was a little more than 6%—acceptable under the circumstances of a down market. But net of fees and taxes, the return was a pathetic 2%. The manager earned as much from our money as we did! And because the fees were high and our returns were low, the government also took a disproportionate share of our meager profits. If we had sold this investment when the technology sector was performing well, the poor tax treatment of management fees would not have been a big deal, and the tax efficiency would have looked very attractive. But we got crushed. High management fees and low returns are truly a bad combination!

Take-Away #4: Don't Over-Commit to Retirement and Deferred Compensation Plans

Many people use retirement plans and deferred compensation plans because they assume that the tax deferral benefits make them superior investment vehicles regardless of all other factors in the decision-making process. They are conditionally wrong.

Many retirement plans and deferred compensation plans are great savings vehicles because they allow you to delay paying taxes on what would otherwise be taxable income for years, sometimes decades. In addition, gains are not subject to tax until they are distributed from the plan. When assets are distributed, they are taxed at the income tax rates (not capital gains tax rates) that apply at that time in the future.

This creates an analytical challenge. Is it possible to be worse off for having put assets into a retirement plan or deferred compensation plan than to have simply paid the taxes at the time money was earned and then invested the net proceeds? The short answer is yes, if income tax rates rise significantly between now and the time that your tax-deferred assets are distributed. Answering how much they have to rise is less straightforward. There are a number of variables that are extraordinarily difficult to predict, like whether the investments outside of a plan will perform better or worse than those in the plan or when you will withdraw the assets. But the most important variable is how tax rates will change. If the top marginal income tax rate rose by just 10 percentage points, the rise would negate the benefit of many retirement plans.

In addition, there are issues about liquidity. When you put assets into a retirement or deferred compensation plan, there are often penalties for removing them prematurely. These plans are much less flexible when it comes to handling the vagaries of life than if you own the assets directly. That's why I propose that you diversify your tax vehicles, just as you diversify your investments.

A Framework for Making Decisions

The following factors influence the attractiveness of specific tax-deferred vehicles:

- *The tax status of contributions*—It is better to contribute pre-tax earned income to a tax-deferred vehicle like many retirement and tax-deferred compensation plans. However, some tax-deferred vehicles like annuities, Roth IRAs, and life insurance savings plans cannot be funded with pre-tax dollars.
- *The tax status of distributions*—You have to weigh the tax treatment of each tax-deferred vehicle. For example, because Roth IRAs can only be funded with after-tax dollars, growth in value and qualified distributions from the Roth IRA are *not* taxed. This is a pretty good deal if you qualify, and management fees are low. When annuities distribute, part of each distribution *is* taxable as income while part is considered a return on capital and is not taxed. Beneficiaries of life insurance proceeds are not taxed, but if your life is the one insured, it doesn't help you very much (though it could prove lucrative for members of your family). If you surrender a policy for its cash value, the difference between the gross cash value and the net amount contributed to the policy is generally subject to income tax. Retirement plan distributions are entirely taxed as income. If distributions are taken earlier than intended (usually before age 59?), an additional penalty is levied by the government.

- *Future tax rates*—Given the current state of government finances and U.S. demographics and historically low federal tax rates, the odds are good that the tax rate applied to your tax-deferred assets at the time they are distributed will be higher than the current income tax rate. Most readers of this book are likely to be in or near the highest marginal tax rate after retirement. For them, high post-retirement income tax rates make tax-deferral plans less attractive, especially if long-term capital gains tax rates don't climb as much as income tax rates. If you own assets in a tax-deferred plan, the cost of unwinding the plan (in anticipation of future increases in tax rates) before you reach retirement age is high.
- *Investment strategy*—If you are using an Index Investing strategy, the value of a tax-deferred plan drops significantly because you are already deferring most of your taxes. But if you are an Active Alpha investor in The Secret Society or The Enchanted Forest and you are regularly buying and selling, these vehicles allow you to defer any tax payments until the time of withdrawal.
- *Age*—The closer you are to retirement, the lower the value of the deferral mechanism. Many plans require you to begin liquidating by the time you are 70 years old. If you are within 10 years of retiring, weigh carefully the tradeoffs between putting more money in a retirement plan versus paying the income tax now. You may prefer to have your money in a completely flexible form rather than maybe saving a little tax.
- *Expenses*—Some retirement plans have administrative costs that taxable accounts do not have. These costs counteract the tax benefit, especially in portfolios that generate low investment returns.
- *Switching costs*—If an investor needs access to cash or the investments in his or her tax deferral plan are not performing well, it may be desirable to access cash within that plan. Many plans have some flexibility for investors to withdraw or borrow assets without penalty. However, withdrawing more than a limited percentage of the assets can be expensive. The government taxes people (sometimes with penalties added) who withdraw assets from a tax deferral plan prematurely.

There is a real tradeoff between the flexibility of owning assets directly versus owning them in a tax-deferred plan. This is a complicated subject, even for wealth management experts. Unfortunately, there are lots of incentives in our financial system to encourage people to overuse tax-deferred vehicles and not a lot of incentives for advisors to encourage a reality check. Therefore, you must take charge to get good advice.

Take-Away #5: Don't Put After-Tax Income into Tax-Deferred Vehicles, such as Variable Annuities and Life Insurance Savings Plans

If I am an advocate of retirement and deferred compensation plans, why do I discourage people from investing after-tax dollars in tax-deferred savings plans like annuities and life insurance savings plans? There are a couple of reasons.

First, even a modest hike in income tax rates can eliminate the benefits offered by a retirement plan, deferred compensation plan, or annuity. Second, many of these structures have high administrative costs (on top of investment fees) that hack away at your investment return. Life insurance is a little different because there is no tax payable when a policy distributes a death benefit. And there may be some estate tax benefits, unless Congress repeals the estate tax completely. However, the cost of life insurance savings plans usually eats up all of the tax benefits with which they have been imbued, especially in an environment where investment returns are modest. For years, I have been pestered by aggressive insurance agents to buy life insurance savings plans. Although I think that term life insurance is a valuable product, and I own some myself, my recommendation is to "just say no" to life insurance savings plans.

If you show the last few paragraphs to an insurance agent (annuities are also sold through insurance companies), he or she will tell you that I am biased against his products. He or she will likely give you the following arguments against my view:

- The beneficiaries of life insurance don't have to pay tax on the benefits they receive.
- Capital gains taxes may go up.

- Bonds have been good investments, and you should own bond-like investments.
- You will be in a lower tax bracket when you retire.

After you hear all of these arguments for buying life insurance, ask the insurance agent to compare the returns from his or her products (after fees and taxes) against diversified index funds (with or without tax loss harvesting). Have the agent do various scenarios, check the math, analyze the assumptions, and decide for yourself whether you think there is value in these products.[4] I think you will still come to my conclusion.

If you still think that the tax deferral benefits of these products are good, read the fine print about surrender charges if you decide to cancel the policy. Then turn to the section that discusses insurers' unilateral ability to raise your costs. Although there are limits on their ability to raise your costs, there is still a lot of flexibility in the contracts I've seen. The agent will tell you that they have never raised the costs to their clients, at least in their memory. But remember, we have been in a 25-year bull market in bonds. Because bonds are the primary asset on life insurance companies' balance sheets, they have had the wind at their back throughout the careers of most insurance agents. If interest rates rise and times get tougher for life insurance companies, some insurance companies may feel compelled to raise their fees to policyholders in order to keep their shareholders happy. The way that policies are written means that the costs to switch vendors can be prohibitive.

With many types of insurance, you also become a general creditor of the insurance company, even though your money is invested in a diversified investment portfolio. In the last quarter-century, a defaulting insurance company has been a rare event. But it has happened. Ask a life insurance salesperson about Executive Life, Mutual Benefit Life, and Monarch Life, all of which became insolvent in 1991 during the last major recession. What happened to these insurance companies was similar. Their bond and real estate portfolios performed poorly, and then policyholders started to surrender their policies in large numbers, and finally the receivers had to be called in. If the bond market becomes bearish, we could see a similar scenario play out again.

Even if policyholders (or their named beneficiary) eventually receive the money owed to them after the bankruptcy is sorted out (it took eight years or more for Mutual Benefit), a delay in payment of months or years can cause significant financial hardship. If you have done all of your analysis and still believe that one or more of these products is right for you, don't put your personal balance sheet at risk by exposing it to a single general creditor, no matter how secure it appears to be.

Finally, don't put variable annuities into a retirement plan, IRA, or other tax-deferred vehicle. You don't need the tax-deferral benefits of an annuity in these vehicles. And there are many other ways to access high-quality investment vehicles that are cheaper and have no surrender charges. In short, a variable annuity in a tax-deferred vehicle is a high-cost redundancy, regardless of what happens to future tax rates.

Conclusion

As you can see, my perspective on taxes and their implications is quite different from many in the financial services industry.

Most wealth advisors encourage you to buy lots of investment products, choose multiple investment managers, buy low and sell high, use bonds to diversify risk, and encourage the use of annuities and life insurance as savings plans.

My goal in this chapter has been to convince you to manage your taxes efficiently when you invest, limit the number of investment products you own, sell low and hold high, de-emphasize bonds, and avoid annuities and life insurance savings plans.

If you do these things, you will pay less in taxes, make more money than the majority of people who invest in financial assets, and get good value for the money that you pay to your advisors and the government.

With the extra time and additional resources you have as a result of more efficiently managing your taxes, the next three chapters should hold appeal for you. I'll be talking about what I consider to be more important than anything I've been discussing so far—using your wealth to contribute to your community and empower your children.

Chapter 8: Issues to Discuss with Your Family

1. Overall, do you think that the U.S. tax structure is fair, or do you consider it to be a game of the survival of the fittest?

2. Are you convinced that a buy and hold investment strategy can reap substantial tax benefits, or do you think that active trading is more lucrative?

3. Do you ask your advisors about the after-tax effects of their investment recommendations? Do you measure whether the results actually come through as expected?

4. Are you bearish or bullish on the long-term health of the economy? How does this affect your tax management strategy?

5. How can you use the power of compounding to improve your financial circumstances?

6. Are you committed to life insurance savings plans as a sound investment? If so, why?

7. Are there opportunities for you to donate appreciated stock instead of cash to support your philanthropic objectives?

8. Have you asked your retirement consultant or insurance agent how their recommendations would be affected by an increase in income tax rates?

9. Do you use various portfolio managers with different investment styles (for instance, large cap growth, large cap value, mid-cap, and small-cap)? What's the likelihood that some of these managers are selling just as others are buying, creating unnecessary turnover, higher transaction costs, and lower tax efficiency?

10. Do you approach taxes aggressively ("I am determined to go to great lengths to pay as little as possible in taxes")? If so, how has this benefited you or been to your detriment over the years?

11. Is your family prepared to support you if your strategy is contested by the IRS?

Endnotes

1 The $51,000 cost is far more than just the difference between getting an "interest-free loan" from the government and having to take out an interest-paying bank loan for the same amount. It comes from the foregone profits on the $15,000 of accrued put unpaid taxes to the government. Alternatively, the second investor could take out a bank loan for $15,000 and reinvest a full $200,000 in the company. If the stock continues to rise, as it does in this example, then the only cost of selling early would be the interest cost on the loan.
  However, if the stock declines in value the first investor's liability to the government declines accordingly while the second investor's liability to the bank remains at $15,000 plus interest.

2 "Passive activity" rules prevent matching the losses from certain investments, typically related to oil and gas exploration and production or real estate, that generate passive losses against gains from the sale of stocks or bonds. Generally, passive losses can only be used to offset passive gains.

3 This is true of separately managed accounts, limited partnerships and most other commingled funds. However, mutual funds are taxed differently: taxes are calculated on profits generated net of fees. This has the effect of making mutual fund management fees fully deductible.

4 Some agents may decline to project mutual fund returns, citing that it is illegal under federal securities law for securities salesmen to make return projections for mutual funds. In most cases, life insurance is governed under separate, state laws that allow such projections. If the agent refuses, do the calculations yourself or ask an accountant to help you.

9

PROMOTING ENTREPRENEURIAL STEWARDSHIP

"My keenest desire is that the country's opportunities and its possibilities remain open and available to my son and to my grandchildren and to their children after them as well as to all other young men and women who have high ideals and are willing to make sacrifices for their attainment."

—*E. A. Stuart*

As you've learned in previous chapters, the Lucas family's financial goals are firmly multigenerational in focus. To that end, I've described what it takes to achieve ambitious returns on your investments. I've also talked about how to develop tax strategies and pursue other proactive steps to ensure that your family's wealth is preserved not only for your lifetime but for multiple generations.

The missing subject so far in our discussion—a critical factor in preserving and growing wealth over time—is something I refer to as "entrepreneurial stewardship." Entrepreneurial stewardship involves striking the right balance of risk taking, wealth preservation, and family leadership to ensure that a family can deal successfully with threats to family economic prosperity and harmony. It is the essential key to retaining and building wealth across generations.

Accumulating great wealth just to have it managed irresponsibly after you die is an abrogation of responsibility and a waste of assets. If the next generation isn't prepared to take on the responsibility of entrepreneurial stewardship, maybe you're better off making your assets available for the betterment of society the moment you die.

If, on the other hand, you do a good job of preparing the next generation of your family for the responsibilities of wealth management, you (and they) will have accomplished a great thing. You will bequeath strong values to your children and convey both the responsibilities of wealth with the privileges it contains. You will pass on to your heirs both the inherent advantages of wealth and the proper financial discipline to ensure the preservation of that wealth, not just for one lifetime or two, but for multiple generations of your family to come.

This chapter explores what I mean by "entrepreneurial stewardship" and how the Lucas family has incorporated it as a value and operating principle into the way we manage our own wealth. By way of introducing this topic, let me tell you a quick story:

Not long ago, I was at a meeting of family office executives. We get together periodically to discuss issues and exchange vital information about how to manage our wealth effectively. At one point in our discussion, we went around the room describing what "generation" of the family each of us represented. Some attendees at this conference gave two-word answers to the question, such as "second generation."

Since I have a propensity to go beyond one or two word answers to questions I'm asked, I wanted to give as thorough a response as possible. So, when my turn came, I described myself as fourth generation, because I am a beneficiary of the fortune that my great-grandfather initiated.

"But I am also second generation because my father passed along the mantle of responsibility for the Lucas family's wealth to me," I added. "I'm also first generation because to increase that wealth, I'm taking measured entrepreneurial risks, bearing the responsibility for their success or failure, and training future family leaders."

I then concluded by saying that, along with several cousins and uncles, I'm also entrusted with responsibility for managing Stuart family foundation assets and the distributions made from those assets to worthy causes and individuals.

To me, entrepreneurial stewardship is really about five things that I just alluded to in the preceding example:

- As a wealthy person, I am a *beneficiary*—of my parents' and grandparents' generosity and remarkable good fortune.
- I must be a *steward* of that wealth if it is to last beyond my lifetime.
- To ensure this, I must be an *entrepreneur* when it comes to growing my wealth.
- I also want to be a *philanthropist*—using my wealth to assist and benefit others and to improve the lives of people less fortunate than I.
- I want to pass wealth on to my children, but with it I also want to pass the values and skills they'll need to manage that wealth carefully and productively throughout their lives.

You Have to Take Risks

Preserving and growing wealth, as I noted early in this book, take as much discipline, imagination, and persistence as is required to amass wealth in the first place. There are multiple forces at work in our economy all the time—taxes, inflation, spending, and stock market volatility—that can rapidly erode your wealth. Therefore, it's important to search wisely for investment opportunities, to seek risk when good opportunities avail themselves, and to be appropriately cautious when the environment is dangerous. This is the only way your family's economic engine will perform well enough over long periods of time to overcome all the leakages.

To generate adequate returns after your own working years are over, it's also important to nurture successful entrepreneurs and wealth stewards in the next generation of your family. As Wealth Strategist, this entails instilling values of entrepreneurialism and self-sufficiency in all family members, nurturing a select few to assume hands-on responsibilities of wealth management, while finding ways to support all family members in the pursuit of their individual passions and goals. Doing this is the key to ensuring that all your children live vibrant, useful, and fulfilling lives, while ensuring your family's continuing legacy and heritage.

How do you get started? It begins with awareness of your own unique circumstances.

Reorienting Yourself

With wealth, you soon discover how it changes your life circumstances. For example:

- You now have investment income to pay for life's necessities, so you don't need to worry about "making a living" to put food on your table or to pay for the kids' college tuition.
- You have access to capital—maybe not enough to launch a multi-million dollar start-up by yourself. But you're not financing your business on a credit card either!
- You may have a track record of business success and a wide-ranging contact network—both of which can be platforms for future financial, social, and business success.

- You have the luxury of time. If you don't find a great opportunity this month, there's also next month—and next year! The luxury of time also enables you to pursue non-financial interests like helping others, writing poetry, becoming more physically fit, or collecting art.

In short, life as you know it has changed dramatically. You're now materially comfortable—perhaps more than you ever imagined you'd be. You're now in a unique position to pursue your personal goals and desires, help others, and contribute to society. So what will it be? You can use your good fortune to create more wealth or to make your mark in the arts, science, culture, good citizenship, or social advocacy. You have untold opportunities now, so go for it!

Growing Up

Where did I get my passion for "entrepreneurial stewardship?" It began early.

As every young person does, I had to find my way through the ups and downs of adolescence and young adulthood. Being from a wealthy family does not change those rites of passage. In high school, I worked hard, got good grades, and had a good shot at going to an elite college. But I was also overweight, couldn't hack "hell week" on the freshman football team, and was socially awkward. But I persevered. By senior year, I was chairing a ski racing league and competing in the expert class. I even had a date for the senior prom!

I applied to, and was accepted at, my father's alma mater, Princeton. But I took a great liking to Dartmouth. At the time, my father was a Trustee of Princeton, but when I was fortunate enough to be given the choice, I opted for Dartmouth. My father was very disappointed. I didn't fully realize it at the time, but this was the first major independent decision of my life. I wanted to own it and to know that I deserved it. By choosing Dartmouth, I knew that my successes and failures would be my own and would in no way be influenced by my father's position at Princeton. I wanted to compete on an even playing field with the best.

Many of us who are raised in privilege and want to succeed try to test ourselves independently of our family history and circumstances. I don't know whether my being born into a family of privilege ever made my classmates or colleagues talk about me behind my back or wonder about my capabilities. But I've always felt an urge to prove myself independently as a way of feeling comfortable being the beneficiary of my parents' wealth.

In my own way, I was starting on the road of entrepreneurial stewardship with my parents supporting my desire to prove myself in my own right. Other wealthy children graduate from college and go directly into their family business to work beside their fathers or uncles. I think this is often a mistake. This early life choice tends to stamp out entrepreneurial fires and restricts the development potential of those young people. In many cases, it'd be better if such individuals created lives for themselves outside the "family orbit" and perhaps built careers and track records of success in other businesses or other arenas of life. Doing so enables them to discover who they really are and to own their own lives, achievements, and failures. If they ultimately do return to a family business at some point, they do so with a lot of valuable life experience under their belts and with greater authenticity and ownership of the lives they have chosen to embrace at that point.

Education

Getting good grades while taking on leadership roles outside the classroom is an important part of our family's culture. It was a high priority in my house when I was growing up, and my own children know that we expect them always to do their best in school.

It is widely known that one's college or university is also a club through which connections are forged and lifelong friendships are established. Whether they come from privileged backgrounds or not, many people who attend elite colleges and universities have already exhibited the stuff of success before they are granted admittance. But the bonds of friendship and social networks they establish in college often provide a critical platform for their future careers, happiness, and success.

Sidebar 9.1: Do Your Children Need to Be Prodigies?

As hard as we try, all of our children aren't going to be good wealth stewards. Some will develop extraordinary talents that have no economic benefits and, in fact, could be talents that are expensive to nurture. Some will be spendthrifts without the sense or the self-control to exhibit financial discipline or to hold a job. Others may be gullible, marrying the wrong spouse or trusting an incompetent or deceitful advisor. A few may have physical, mental, or emotional issues that prevent them from taking care of themselves.

As these situations arise, it's important to handle them on a case-by-case basis. Sometimes the challenge is temporary; other times it is lifelong. Often, it is impossible to tell what the timeframe will be. Situations like these demand flexibility, creativity, and patience.

An effective management structure can be created by a combination of family emotional support plus the rigidity and objectivity imposed by a corporate trustee to provide needed financial steward-ship. That way, the role of financial disciplinarian gets separated from family emotional support. In rare cases, it may be necessary to exercise the family's right to walk away because one member is unwilling to fulfill his or her part of the contract to participate constructively with the rest of the family. When walking away, it's always best to leave a door open in hope that the future will be better.

Sometimes entrepreneurial talent skips a generation. If you are the Wealth Strategist and this turns out to be the case, you may have to rely temporarily on a trusted advisor or corporate trustee to act as interim Wealth Strategist. Or you may simply continue in the role until your grandchild (or grandchildren) is ready to take on the mantle of responsibility.

Think back on how you created or inherited wealth. What characteristics made you a success? What are the characteristics of other successful people around you? Maybe you really do have the makings of entrepreneurial stewards in the next generation. Your challenge, and your opportunity, is helping your children to discover their true talents. We all have them!

Education, however, means more than formal schooling or peer networking. Wealth Strategists need to supplement formal education by teaching young family members how to save and manage money—even to save for retirement. In our society, there are enormous incentives to spend money today rather than to save it for tomorrow. Yet, as I discussed in earlier chapters, there is great value in starting to save for retirement early in life. Encouraging young people, especially young entrepreneurs, to accumulate retirement savings fosters great discipline and can create strong values of responsibility and accountability in one's family. If you can pass on the value of financial responsibility and prudence to your heirs, you embolden them with a sense of the power of money and the importance of using it wisely. That's why I'm such a passionate believer in the importance of introducing young people to the power of investments, saving, and compound interest at the appropriate age and why I've made this a focus of conversations with my own children.

It's also why I think it's important to give young people the chance to experiment with small sums of money at a relatively early age and even to make some mistakes with it. This way, they can learn that it is a finite resource that must be protected and used wisely to last a long time—a lifetime!

Blending Career and Community

For many wealthy people, choosing a career means establishing your credibility independent of your privileged upbringing and finding focus and empowerment in meaningful work. It's also about proving that you have special qualities that the world needs while creating a place for yourself outside your immediate family circle. For many, it's about responsibly using one's privilege to contribute meaningfully in their community.

I admire those wealthy people for whom it would be easy to live quietly and leisurely who imbue their children with strong values about public service, social responsibility, and the need to serve or give to those less fortunate. They know that life is about more than wealth and success.

It's about reaching beyond yourself and your material good fortune to live a life of significance and service to others.

Being wealthy also means having the opportunity to pursue your personal passion or professional interests, unfettered by the need to make early, often conventional, career choices, and to go to work simply to put a roof over your head. For example:

- Several friends of mine run successful private equity firms, helping small businesses to grow and prosper. Knowing that they are influencing the fortunes of the newest entrepreneurs by passing on their economic savvy to fledgling companies and promoting new technologies is profoundly satisfying to them.

- My brother is an M.D. who works in a free clinic and also teaches elementary school science. He does both because he knows he adds great value in these places where it is very difficult to attract highly qualified professionals. He schedules his time carefully so that he can be totally committed to his wife, four kids, two dogs, and three cats. He's passing on desperately needed medical care to an underserved population and intellectual wealth to the next generation.

- My cousin is a dedicated philanthropist who chairs two well-run foundations. He's passing on wealth in the more traditional sense, as well as championing causes that are dear to his heart.

- In my case, in addition to managing my family's wealth, I play leadership roles in two organizations focused on strengthening primary and secondary education and community support systems for children. Through these roles, I'm trying to pass on my family's love of education and of children so that our society can be better equipped to compete and so individuals will have the educational tools to lead more fulfilling lives. I also use my investing skills for the benefit of these institutions.

Most of us are trying, in our own personal and private ways, to leverage our inherited wealth to make the world a better place. Each of us realizes that our lives would be very different and possibly less significant if we didn't have wealth that allows us to pursue socially significant passions. We have all faced the "dilemma" of overwhelming choices, felt a commitment to act rather than defer, and pursued our own entrepreneurial passions in focused and productive ways.

Family

The stereotypical image of a wealthy family is that of a closed system, only open to those who are born into it. This simply isn't true. With each new generation, every family is refreshed and sometimes redefined through marriage, and sometimes adoption.

Most wealthy families are the products of a strong-willed wealth creator, a seminal figure, who even if long dead may still strongly influence the family's shared values. Having said that, family culture changes with each generation. With every new generation, long-established cultural norms evolve. Generations radiate out and away from the founder. Each new marriage of a family member causes one's family tree to be interwoven with that of other family trees, bringing outside influences into the original family, forming new values, and reinforcing or replacing existing ones. These choices invariably dilute the founder's influence with ever-increasing numbers of family trees merging into the fold. At the same time, the founder's expanding lineage broadens his or her influence. Extended families must accept and adapt to, and even embrace, the addition of new family trees and all the richness they bring to the discussion of choice.

The patriarch and originator of the Carnation family, E.A. Stuart, set the tone in our family. That tone was reinforced and sometimes modified by E.A.'s son, E.H., who adopted my mother. Needless to say, my life would be entirely different had E.H. not made the choice to accept my mother and her sister as his own. When "the girls" married, E.H. accepted their husbands into Carnation. As they proved themselves, they became valuable members of the company's senior leadership team.

Following in this tradition of bringing "new" people into the family business fold, my sister-in-law Melissa joined me as investment advisor to the Lucas family's investments. As a former investment analyst at Capital Guardian, one of the world's premier investment firms, she has a strong technical background in pharmaceuticals, medicine, and technology. She is a great partner. The whole family has accepted her into this position of responsibility. She earned it, and we're lucky to benefit from her involvement.

Within my own generation, our families have expanded in ways that add richness and texture to our lives. All my siblings have married, and our spouses have brought to the family their own histories, heritage, and ways of doing things. We have carried on the tradition of creating families that go outside the narrow orbit of the biological family system. One of my brother's children with complicated health issues was adopted. At the time of the adoption, I worried for my brother and his wife because of the demands I thought they were imposing on themselves and their young family. They didn't see this as a risk, but instead as a great opportunity. Watching their kids today, I know they were right, and we are all better off because of their decision.

My nuclear family has broadened its religious and ethnic boundaries in ways that are wonderful. My wife (and soul mate) Susan had grandparents who were Jewish immigrants from Eastern Europe. They came to this country with stories of struggles to overcome adversity, in part because they were immigrants and in part because of prejudice against Jews in this country and the Old World. In the two generations her family has been American, they have added to their heritage stories of hard work, devotion to family, small business successes, commitment to education, and service to their communities. By celebrating the lessons from her heritage, we encourage our children's own ambitions and reinforce a standard for us all to live up to. I am as grateful for her traditions as I am for my own. In fact, we have made a conscious decision to raise our children in the Jewish faith, even though I was raised, and remain, Episcopalian.

We are not the perfect family (I've never run across one, except possibly as a Hollywood creation). As a large, complex family, we have periodically struggled with changing circumstances and our inability to satisfy all members. We act in insensitive ways, get mad at each other, and even fight. At times, people have chosen to opt out. My Aunt Ethel used to say that people are toughest on those to whom they are closest. Different times and circumstances have also presented opportunities for family members to reconnect. At some points, choice enabled people to pull apart, and at other points, it brought them back together. Reconciliation can be powerful, and it's my hope that all readers of this book will stay open to its healing nature.

Parenting

When I was growing up, I was fortunate to know a woman who raised four boys living in privilege in New York. I used to call her "Mrs. B" instead of her first name, as a sign of respect and admiration. She was the daughter of a minerals tycoon. In the summers, she used to take her four young boys to a fabulous lodge on a private lake in the Adirondacks when they weren't traveling to Europe to explore another branch of their family tree. Each of her boys is very different, but they are all industrious, creative entrepreneurs. They are also just great people and good friends.

One day, a year or two before she passed away, I asked Mrs. B what her secret to great parenting was. Her answer was simple and elegant. She said that she was totally and completely dedicated to encouraging each of her children to be a unique, independent person. She endeavored to support each son in the pursuit of his *individual* passions. She looked past the privilege, past the "important" people in her life, the fancy dinners and exotic vacations, and focused intensely on each of her children as individuals. She tried to understand them and support their agendas, not use them as an instrument of her own.

Another friend, Howard Stevenson, a professor at Harvard Business School and co-author of the popular book about success, *Just Enough*, has seven thriving adult "children." With all his responsibilities as an entrepreneur, professor, fundraiser, and author, he makes sure to set aside the time and energy necessary to be a good father as well. He knows that the gifts of his time and presence are more important to ensuring the future success and happiness of his own children than is any monetary reward or professional fame he achieves in his own highly successful and fulfilling professional life.

My greatest parental mentor is my mother. She has four children and she has been, and continues to be, there for us. She was very involved in our schools when we were growing up. She easily put 100 miles a week on her car shuttling us to and fro, even though she actually only drove carpool once a week. She kept mum when we put Alice Cooper or Black Sabbath in the 8-track tape deck. When my brother was in the fifth grade, she made a friend of his walk the last several blocks home for swearing too many times in the back of our station wagon.

At age 68, Mom is still showing up a lot. Even though we have lived at least 1,500 miles apart since I was 17, she still helps me when my father and I aren't communicating. And now she's showing up for my kids too. Not long ago, she took two of our three children to the Galapagos Islands in Ecuador for two weeks.

Yes, Mom has always been good at showing up for us. And I want to do the same for my kids, and eventually my grandchildren.

Following the example set by our parents, Susan and I are determined that our family be centered on our children. I joke to friends that our weekends are so busy that I go to work on Monday to rest and that we almost need a household supercomputer to keep up with our children's activities. Among our three children, a typical weekend involves soccer games, choir practice, swimming lessons, puppy school, music lessons, birthday parties, and sleepovers. Even with both of us acting as chauffeurs, we still occasionally need a helping hand. We have not imposed these activities on our children; these are the things (mostly!) in which they want to be involved.

To me, doing things that demonstrate our love and dedication to our kids is critical to nurturing the next generation of the Lucas clan. In figuring out when to give them support, when to encourage—and when to limit—their freedom, and when to bring them back into the fold, lies the key, I believe, to encouraging entrepreneurialism in an environment of privilege. Identifying and igniting passions is what it is all about. Directing each child to productive activity and nurturing an interest in a key activity or hobby may very well lay the groundwork for that child's life work in ways you can't imagine at this moment.

When it comes to parenting, a lot of what is important to Susan and me as parents is what was also important to my own parents when I was growing up. Even though Dad was on the road a lot, we still had lengthy summer vacations together, and my mother was always involved as a volunteer in the schools that my siblings and I attended. Both of them "showed up" a lot—certainly for the most significant moments of my life, and those of my siblings. But we also had dinner together almost every night. Family meals were the times when we all talked about our victories and frustrations of the day. It was such an important time of being together that my parents almost never went out to dinner when I was growing up.

When it comes to giving things to one's kids, I think most parents would agree that they would rather instill the will to excel in their children than transfer wealth if they could only do one or the other. In the Lucas family, we as parents are indebted to our children, and this indebtedness is of greater importance to us than any debt of gratitude that the children should have for us as parents. Our children mean everything to us. The more we can help them succeed at whatever they choose to do with their lives, the greater our sense of purpose fulfilled. That's why we owe them!

Family Stewardship

In multigenerational families that choose to combine their assets for purposes of efficient wealth management, it's not enough to instill a sense of entrepreneurial stewardship in just a few individuals. Instead, the whole family must accept a culture of entrepreneurial stewardship. Those family members who demonstrate interest and skill to manage family wealth face a difficult challenge. It's a tough job because there is a lot to lose. You can lose the family's money and the social standing that goes with it, and you will be held responsible by those family members who entrusted you with their assets. You can be extraordinarily successful, significantly enriching relatives who are along for the ride but who don't truly appreciate your skills as a Wealth Strategist.

One of the best ways to address the challenges of being an entrepreneurial steward in this position is to combine a culture of openness with the opportunity for individual family members to opt out of family wealth management activities, if they wish. These two things, in combination, enable adult family members to become informed and to make a choice between sharing the benefits of commingled management of their assets on the terms offered and acting independently.

Family Meetings

When was the last time you had a "family meeting" to discuss finances, complete with written agendas, flip charts, and bottled water? These meetings are key to communicating, educating, and maintaining stewardship over your wealth.

Because the Lucas family has a culture of openness, adult family members and their spouses are all invited to participate in regular family meetings so that a wide variety of views can be expressed openly as part of the family's wealth management activities. Everyone understands that his or her interests are well served by the family office and recognizes that there are tremendous benefits from working together to manage our collective wealth.

The Lucas family office adds value. As noted elsewhere in the book, it has been responsible for generating significant portfolio gains from Active Alpha Investing in recent years, and it has built competitive advantage that accrues to the benefit of each family member.

In order to benefit from the family office, there are certain expectations of each family member. First, each of us is expected to participate in an annual family meeting where we discuss the family's affairs in an open and informative way. Second, we are all expected to contribute to the costs of running the family office, including compensating those family members who work in the office on a full-time basis. Third, we share a common belief (one supported by facts) that our long-term interests, both individual and collective, are being served by the family office. We are willing to sub-optimize personal, near-term desires that could adversely affect the family's common goals. That's because we regularly prove that the long-term benefits of working together to manage our wealth far outweigh the costs. Plus, it's fun—most of the time!

In addition, the family office has a responsibility to listen to, and be sensitive toward, the individual circumstances of family members and, where practical, to support them.

Sidebar 9.2: What Is a Family Office?

At different points in this book, I allude to the fact that we have a family office. Somewhere between 2,000 and 3,000 families in the United States have a dedicated family office to coordinate the financial administration, and often the investment, of some or all of a family's financial assets. Most family offices get involved in organizing tax, legal work, and even bookkeeping. Some of the larger offices provide concierge and other support services for some or all family members. I've seen family offices responsible for as little as $50 million (though at that size they rarely make economic sense), and I've seen them with 50 or more employees and billions of dollars to oversee.

Family offices usually get established for two reasons. First, they are deemed to be prestigious. If you've become successful enough to afford a family office, you've become *really* successful. Second, a wealth owner sees them as a useful construct through which to organize a complicated lifestyle. However, I think this way of thinking really misses the boat.

Almost by definition, a Wealth Strategist who establishes a family office is thinking multigenerationally. To be successful over multiple generations, you need to maintain a strong economic engine, and you need to promote entrepreneurial stewardship. Many family offices encourage exactly the opposite behavior. They encourage dependency and risk aversion. Dependency is encouraged because the office is there to help, to take the burden of financial responsibility out of the wealth owner's hands, and even to make airline reservations for that person. There's risk aversion because most families hire professional management to run the office, but most families are unwilling or unable to compete for top (money-making) talent. What's more, they don't accept the responsibility (or set the example) for driving the family's economic engine as hard as it must be driven to maintain wealth across generations.

I think family offices need to think differently. First, they can benefit enormously from family leadership. Family leadership makes the job of professional managers more interesting and satisfying. Second, they must view themselves as economic engines, not as administrative hubs. Third, they must build, maintain, and protect competitive advantage to produce an adequate economic return. Fourth, they must be the epicenter of family communication, but they should subcontract as many administrative functions as possible. Finally, they should encourage each family member to be financially self-sufficient for the day-to-day management of their own affairs.

My family's office infrastructure currently costs us between 0.6% and 0.8% of assets per year before adding asset management, tax preparation, and legal fees, all of which we pay for separately. Our requirements are pretty complex, but we add value to our financial bottom line that is worth many times its cost. Over the years, we have strengthened our asset allocation capabilities and our ability to identify and access superior managers across a much wider range of asset classes. And we have strengthened our ability to measure our performance and the performance of our advisors. All this brings us competitive advantage and sets a good example and a stronger foundation for the next generation.

We spend a ton of time on communication with the family. My brother William plays the lead role here. He coordinates our quarterly communications about all our activities and prepares an annual report for the family that is second to none. Every report weaves together family culture and values, humor, financial results, discussion topics, and education. This report forms the basis for our annual meeting for the family and for a strategic review for the members of the family office. But he also spends a lot of time helping other family members to think through their personal financial issues. *He does not do their work for them*, though I know that in some cases this would be easier. Instead, he plays the role of educator and troubleshooter. He's not building dependency, he's promoting self-confidence, independence, and (subtly) a fuller appreciation of the value that the family office brings to managing the family's combined assets.

A successful family navigates a balance between the needs and aspirations of the individual and those of the whole family. This is where instilling a sense of stewardship is so important. Leadership by example is critical. A parent who is not a good steward of wealth is unlikely to pass a sense of stewardship on to the next generation. Good stewardship is about managing financial assets well, defining the culture, and living up to the values that suggest the importance you place on family. In doing so, you must strike a balance between the desires of the individual and the collective benefits to the family.

Nepotism

Nepotism, the favored treatment of one's relatives, can mean bailing out a relative or pushing a relative to new heights. The former implies some weakness; the latter bestows a sense of confidence to achieve. I have seen many parents—wealthy or not—misuse nepotism. Creating a sense among family members that they can expect nepotistic favors to get ahead fosters a sense of dependency and dampens entrepreneurial fires. This behavior often reveals itself in the way money is distributed in a family. Encouraging adult family members to be dependent on the family's wealth is a classic example. This arrangement reinforces negative, dependent behavior that can deepen over time, with both parties buying in. It ultimately weakens the family.

A healthier form of nepotism involves helping a family member explore new opportunities. In this form of nepotism, there is often an implied or stated contract that spells out what is expected in the hopes of accelerating the family member's trajectory forward. Beneficiaries of this kind of nepotism recognize the need to prove to the family that they are capable of achieving what they pursue. They are, after all, asking for family support in achieving their dreams or realizing their passions. With success, they can be assured of gaining the respect and admiration of family and colleagues who supported them in their endeavors from the beginning—financially and/or emotionally.

Using nepotism to share entrepreneurial risk or to help increase the odds of success stimulates entrepreneurial behavior while simultaneously exhibiting the power of family stewardship. We see the power of this healthy form of nepotism quite visibly in two political families of national prominence: the Kennedys and the Bushes. Powerful economic engines support both families, and in both cases a powerful older generation has been instrumental in propelling a younger generation forward to fulfill personal and family ambitions for the Presidency of the United States. Neither John F. Kennedy nor George W. Bush is likely to have experienced the political success that he did without his family playing an active nepotistic role behind the scenes.

This type of healthy nepotism expresses itself in America's financial and industrial families as well. However, it is less visible in the public eye. From the Mars family (makers of M&Ms, Snickers, and Uncle Ben's Rice) to the S.C. Johnson family (maker of a wide variety of household consumer products), many of America's largest family businesses are private. So too are the family offices and individual wealth owners that control vast financial assets in this country. There is nothing newsworthy about successfully practiced nepotism. Unfortunately, the media have an appetite for failed nepotism, which just reinforces the cynical view of this practice.

Fairness

Is nepotism granted to one child fair to another? This important question has no simple answer. In the fascinating book *The Millionaire Next Door*, there is a chapter titled "Economic Outpatient Care." The authors point out that in many millionaire families there is an inverse relationship between the amount of financial support that parents give each of their children and each child's skill in managing their finances. As a result, those with the least ability to manage money often receive the greatest benefit. If this practice is established early in a family's life cycle, occasional bailouts become regular handouts and repeated mistakes with money on the part of certain family members sap those individuals of self-esteem and foster life-long dependencies. Economic outpatient care can become chronic and debilitating, both to the donor and the beneficiary.[1]

As one of four siblings and a parent of three children, I find the fairness issue very difficult to deal with. Just how do you want to position wealth with your children? How do you foster an attitude of empowerment in a child versus an attitude of entitlement? It's a tough call.

The healthiest way I can address the issue is to think of it this way: It is the giver's responsibility to determine fairness. It is the recipient's responsibility to use any generosity that he or she receives in an appropriate way. If I bothered to struggle with whether the actions of my parents toward me have been fair or not, I would tie myself up in knots. I also realize that I simply do not have an adequate perspective to understand the whole picture here. Who am I to judge how my parents have interacted with me around the issue of money and how they use their *own* resources? Frankly, I have more interesting things to think about.

Today, my wife Susan and I are regularly accused of being unfair by one or more of our children, the oldest being just fourteen. As parents, Susan and I don't believe that fair means equal. We think our job is to help each of our children grow and flourish in his or her own way. Because they are each different, we expect to treat each one differently. If we do our job well, our fairness will eventually become apparent to them.

Time

Wealth gives you the luxury of time in making most financial decisions. When it comes to fostering an attitude of responsibility about money, one of the tricks I've found to achieving good stewardship is to extend the time horizon over which we make wealth management decisions, teaching family members to evaluate carefully the tradeoffs between short-term and long-term financial goals. In the past several years, for example, I've been trying to convince my family that the rate at which we spend money is too high if we want to maintain our goal of maintaining per capita wealth across generations. On the one hand, I feel like a "fun sponge" by proposing that everyone give up something very concrete today to meet an abstract goal that may be 30 to 50 years in the future. On the other hand, with the best information we have, it is what prudent stewardship suggests we do.

Fortunately, we have all worked hard to understand the context within which this decision to spend at a certain rate annually needs to be made. We have historic data going back more than a decade so that people can see what the long term means in concrete terms because our goals are framed with long-term outcomes in mind. Family members have learned to manage their finances responsibly. We took an incremental step about two years ago by modestly reducing our spending rate at an opportune time. We have been discussing the issue for several years and will probably discuss it for several more before we make another significant change.

Conclusion

In multigenerational families, developing one or more capable entrepreneurial stewards to stimulate and encourage the family's wealth-building capabilities is key to long-term success. The other key is a family that feels a shared sense of identity, heritage, values, and financial benefits that result from managing wealth collectively. Our family has found that, through its collective efforts, we have improved our financial circumstances significantly. At the same time, we have developed a capacity to work in tandem toward common financial goals, to respect individual needs, and to empower individual family members to pursue their own personal dreams and professional interests. The degree to which we continue succeeding in these endeavors will obviously dictate the degree to which we're able to systematically and continuously build our wealth, on a real per-capita basis, over coming generations.

In Chapter 11, "Putting It All Together: Multigenerational Planning and Wealth Transfer," I discuss how to transfer wealth from one generation to the next while reinforcing the values of entrepreneurial stewardship. I describe simple actions that can have positive impact for decades to come—and even longer.

But first, in Chapter 10, "Making Philanthropy Part of Your Strategic Wealth Program," I address some of the opportunities and challenges of using your wealth for the betterment of society.

Chapter 9: Issues to Discuss with Your Family

1. What do you consider to be the pinnacle of success in your life as a wealthy individual?

2. Are you taking risks beyond the financial realm to encourage entrepreneurial stewardship within your own family?

3. What does the term "social capital" mean in your own life? How do you leverage it to the benefit of your family and the wider community?

4. How have you chosen to be involved in your family's/children's lives so that your entrepreneurial goals are communicated and values are transmitted? How do you create the glue to strengthen ties with and among your children and grandchildren as they become mature adults?

5. Who are role models for you in your community? How have you reached out to them to network and to learn more about their family culture and values?

6. Do you believe that nepotism can be a good thing, or do you perceive it with suspicion? Why?

7. Have you charted your family trees, and what have you learned by performing such an exercise?

8. Is your family culture a closed system or more of an open system? What are the pros and cons of your current family culture, and are you open to changing it? How do you reinforce the positives and deemphasize the negatives?

9. Are there members of your family who cannot or will not assume independent financial status? If so, what are you doing to deal with this situation?

10. Do you agree with the concept of fairness meaning treating each person on their own individual terms, or do you think that fairness means treating everyone equally?

Endnotes

[1] Thomas J. Stanley, Ph.D., and William D. Danko, Ph.D., *The Millionaire Next Door: The Surprising Secrets of America's Wealthy*, (Longstreet Press, 1996), pp. 141-174.

10

MAKING PHILANTHROPY PART OF YOUR STRATEGIC WEALTH PROGRAM

philanthropy: 1. good will toward all people; esp: effort to promote human welfare 2. a charitable act or gift; also: an organization that distributes or is supported by donated funds.

—The Merriam-Webster Dictionary[1]

P hilanthropy is a deeply rooted value in our family's culture and is a significant aspect of the Strategic Wealth Management Framework. Given that in the next 50 years people with trillions of dollars in assets will have to part with them, a tradition of giving to others that goes back to the origins of our country will be strongly enhanced.

From a young age, E.A. Stuart, a practicing Quaker, gave generously of both his time and money, in good times and tough times. So when in 1937, in the midst of the Great Depression, he formed The Elbridge Stuart Foundation as a charitable trust, it was simply a continuation and formalization of a lifelong mission. Four years later, he established a second foundation in memory of his wife, Mary, to whom he was married for 55 years. From then until the sale of the Carnation Company in 1985, millions of dollars in grants from these foundations were made to strengthen local schools, libraries, churches, and boys' and girls' homes in communities where Carnation operated. The company's leadership felt strongly that it had a responsibility to make these largely rural communities as vital as possible. A board of directors made up of company executives, including members of the Stuart family, was responsible for allocating the grants and following up with grantees to monitor and encourage their hard work.

Back when these foundations were formed by my great-grandfather, there were fewer than 12,000 charitable tax-exempt entities of any kind in the United States, and most of them were operating as charities, not foundations. Today, there are more than a million charitable tax-exempt organizations in the country. Of that total, there are 65,000 foundations in the U.S. that have accumulated assets approaching half a trillion dollars. They distribute $30 billion per year to social services organizations, educational groups, healthcare organizations, environmental causes, the arts, places of worship, and other philanthropic institutions.[2] Proudly, I say that E.A. Stuart was in the vanguard with other great entrepreneurs and philanthropists of his time.

Since the Carnation Company was sold in 1985, the two foundations cited previously, plus another one started by E.H. Stuart, have been merged into the Stuart Foundation. We have also narrowed the foundation's focus. Today the foundation is dedicated to children and youth in the states of California and Washington and funds educational programs in public school systems, child welfare initiatives, and youth-oriented community building organizations. We focus on these two states because they were the primary residences of Carnation and the Stuart family. There is now a professional staff of experts managing the Stuart Foundation, and since Carnation was sold, the foundation has given away more than $200 million. I invite you to visit the foundation's Web site at www.stuartfoundation.org to learn more about this organization of which I am so proud.

Why People Give

From Biblical times, there have been stories of wealthy people who decide to follow a life of poverty and give away all of their worldly assets. Possibly the most striking example is that of Buddha, for whom Buddhism is named. He was the son of a king who gave up worldly pleasures to seek enlightenment as a monk. Today there are some extraordinary people still following this course, Buddhist and otherwise. But, in many cases, their stories of selflessness and service to others aren't very well publicized.

Some people are philosophical about their giving, as expressed in some of my great-grandfather's memoirs. In a statement he wrote upon founding the first foundation, he notes: "It has been my privilege and pleasure to have led a busy, and I trust, a useful life…" Now, "My keenest desire is that its [America's] opportunities and its possibilities may remain open and available to my son, my grandchildren, and their children after them, as well as to all other young men and women who have high ideals and are willing to make sacrifices for their attainment."[3] He adds: "One of my profound observations during all these years is that communities are industrious, progressive, and successful when the individual citizens are industrious, progressive, and successful."[4] I'm sure that there are many other philanthropists who feel similarly to my great-grandfather, and I admire them all for proactively sharing their good fortune with others.

Recognizing that many individuals and corporations have increasingly pragmatic or even business-related reasons for giving, over the past 100 years, the U.S. government has created many financial incentives to encourage private philanthropy.

I think most wealthy people engage in philanthropy for one or more of the following reasons:

- They want to make a profound impact.
- They believe that privilege and good fortune demand responsibility to others.
- They want to acquire social capital.
- They feel some of guilt over their good circumstances.
- They are driven by the inspiration of others.
- They want tax relief.

Making a Profound Impact

Many wealthy people get great satisfaction from the impact of their gifts, and they rise to the creative challenge of making their gifts effective. Great institutions have been funded through philanthropy. The Rockefeller family was instrumental in financing the creation of our national park system and in founding Rockefeller University (one of the finest graduate research institutions in the country); the University of Chicago; and Winrock International, an international development organization.

Groups of people sometimes come together with a vision. In 1992, a small group of people came together to build an endowment for National Public Radio, which at the time had 9 million weekly listeners. Just a few years later, I bought into the vision and joined the effort, becoming a member of the board of the NPR Foundation. Together with other members of the foundation, we transformed a financially insecure foundation with no assets into one with $25 million in assets. This transformation caught the attention of Joan Kroc, the wife of the founder of McDonald's Corporation, resulting in a bequest of nearly $200 million to the foundation and greater financial strength for NPR.

Thanks largely to her gift and to the dedication of NPR correspondents and Public Radio stations across the country, NPR's weekly audience now tops 25 million listeners.

Mrs. Kroc's gift did more than strengthen the NPR Foundation. She created a platform upon which NPR today produces a superior news product that is available to more people—through both existing and new media—than ever before. And because of her inspiration, NPR has been able to set its sights high to support one of the cornerstones of our democracy: an informed public.

But you don't have to give a big gift to make a profound impact. Small gifts of time, energy, and resources can change people's lives just as profoundly!

Privilege and Good Fortune Demand Responsibility to Others

John D. Rockefeller proclaimed his family's commitment to social responsibility in a plaque located in the middle of Rockefeller Center in New York City for all to see. "I believe that every right implies a responsibility; every opportunity, an obligation; every possession, a duty." Many others share Mr. Rockefeller's belief that those of us who are fortunate have a responsibility to help others, as individuals, as communities, and as nations. And they act on it in small ways and large. For many people, this sense of responsibility is inextricably tied to their religious or ethical belief system. This was certainly true of E.A. Stuart.

Responsibility to others takes many forms. At one extreme, people fight to reduce disease and poverty. They support institutions like food banks, shelters for battered women, AIDS clinics, and children's hospitals. At another end of the spectrum, people recognize and support exceptional drive and talent that some people exhibit. The Pritzker Prize in architecture, the Golden Apple teaching awards, the Rockefeller Genius Awards, and the MacArthur Fellowships are just a few examples of philanthropy where people give back by identifying and rewarding greatness in fields that make our culture and humanity stronger. Money, public recognition, time, and compassion are all the tools of thoughtfully offering good will to others.

Acquiring Social Capital

There is nothing wrong with giving money away as a means to acquire social capital. Some people do this by giving money to support charitable organizations and accepting invitations to lavish dinner parties as a reward. (Typically, attendance entails getting your name and sometimes your picture in the newspaper.) Other people act as honorary chairs of charity fundraisers with which they have only modest hands-on contact, but whose causes they love dearly or to which they're sentimentally attached.

There are still other ways that societies reward the rich and powerful with social capital. In England, you are knighted. In France, you can earn the Legion of Honor. In China, you rise within the Communist Party. In Monaco, it's about gaining access to the right boat slips and parties in Monte Carlo!

While the motives for giving in such cases can be mixed, especially when a "reward" is attached, the end result is that such giving does support worthy causes. And I applaud the motivations of people whose generosity ultimately benefits deserving organizations!

Feeling Guilty

Among inheritors of wealth, some people are motivated (unfortunately) by a sense of guilt. Guilt-driven philanthropy often derives from a person's efforts to resolve inner problems, not to serve the public good. But, ironically, if a person's inward focus can be turned outward, both the donor and the grantee are likely to benefit from the donor's act. Philanthropy at its best starts from the soul. From there, it typically radiates outward in expressions of exuberance, passion, and compassion for those who are less fortunate.

Being Inspired by Others

Sometimes committed leadership inspires people to give because they admire people who "live a cause." Lance Armstrong, Christopher Reeve, Mother Teresa, Nelson Mandela, and Princess Diana are all examples of exemplary public figures who have inspired people to support worthy causes with time and money—whether to cancer and spinal cord research, the elimination of poverty, political freedom, AIDS education, or the elimination of landmines. But you don't have to be a famous figure to inspire others to give. You just need a vision and the heart to see it through.

Wanting Tax Relief

Some people give because they don't want the money to go to the government. The tax benefits of philanthropy date back to 1917 when they were codified into the tax code, a mere four years after the income tax was first instituted. At that time, there were very few charitable tax-exempt institutions in the country. Uncle Sam clearly had a foresighted policy of wanting to encourage giving in return for tax relief.

Today there are numerous ways to give away assets and receive tax benefits. Each philanthropic option varies in its tax ramifications based on the types of assets you contribute, the amount of control you retain, administrative expenses, and your desire to remain anonymous.

In all cases, you can receive a deduction of the amount of the gift from Adjusted Gross Income (AGI) on your tax return, up to certain limits. So, for example, if you report AGI of $100,000 and you make a donation valued at $10,000, it reduces your taxable income to $90,000. There are limits on the size of the deduction, as a percentage of AGI, that you can take in any one year. But you can roll forward any unused amounts.

Maximizing the Tax Benefits of Giving

From the tax man's perspective (and by definition), making a donation means that you are offering a gift. You are not receiving goods or services in exchange for the gift. If you do receive something of substance in exchange, it's not a gift. It's a business transaction. That's why if you go to a charity dinner, a portion of your contribution goes to paying the cost of the dinner and is not tax deductible. To receive tax benefits, you must make a donation.

When offering a gift, it is almost always more advantageous from a tax perspective to donate appreciated securities (held longer than one year) than to donate cash to qualifying philanthropic causes because if you give cash, you only get a tax deduction on the after-tax value of your gift. However, if you give appreciated securities, you get an income tax deduction based on the gross market value of the gift. Here is an illustration of how this works: If you give appreciated stock with an initial cost of $1 and a current market value of $10, you get a $10 tax deduction and you don't pay a tax of $1.35 (assuming a 15% long-term capital gains tax rate) on the accrued profit of $9.

By giving the stock away, you never have to pay tax. In effect, by donating the stock, you control which worthwhile cause your portion of profits goes to, and the government waives its claim to the $1.35 in taxes and redirects it to the same worthwhile causes. If you plan to make charitable gifts, it's just one more reason why owning a diversified portfolio with an equity bias makes sense. Whenever a stock does really well, you can donate it instead of selling it and never pay tax!

There are some restrictions that the government imposes on annual giving for the purpose of receiving tax benefits:

- Total charitable donations cannot exceed more than 50% of your AGI.
- Cash donations to public charities cannot exceed more than 50% of your AGI.
- Donations of long-term capital gain property to public charities cannot exceed 30% of your AGI.
- Cash donations to a private foundation cannot exceed 30% of your AGI.
- Donations of long-term capital gain property to a private foundation cannot exceed 20% of your AGI.

If you make donations of goods and services to non-profits in lieu of, or in addition to, financial assets, make sure you have good documentation because the IRS is cracking down on abuse in this area. In a March 30, 2005, letter to the Chairman of the Senate Finance Committee, the IRS Commissioner cited as highly suspect taxpayers' donations of conservation easements for the purposes of preserving certain land and buildings for future generations. (Many people have been donating façade easements on their historic homes in exchange for tax deductions.) In a number of these cases, the façade was already subject to restriction under local zoning ordinances, so the taxpayer was, in fact, taking a deduction for giving up a right that didn't exist.

The IRS is also concerned about valuations of non-cash contributions to non-profits. For example, several years ago, the IRS developed tighter guidelines for the valuation of donated automobiles. Overvaluing donations, or not completely giving up use of donated assets, can pose real problems if you are audited.

MAKING BEQUESTS

If you make charitable donations as a bequest, it reduces the size of your estate by the value of the bequest. If you are subject to the estate tax, this gives you an opportunity to reduce the value of your estate and reduce or eliminate your tax liability. Because estate tax rates have traditionally been high for wealthy people, there is considerable value for individuals to include philanthropy as part of their estate plan.

People who have a financial goal of maintaining purchasing power don't want to run out of money. To protect themselves, they defer a portion of their philanthropy until death to give themselves more of a financial cushion.

But other people have plenty of cushion and should consider making donations now to reduce their taxable income and their taxes. If they give to an endowment, the donated assets have more time to grow tax-free. A non-profit recipient can use the gift, or the income from the gift, to do good works right now, rather than having to wait a month, a year, or a decade until the decedent's estate bequeaths it. And you, the beneficiary, get to enjoy the value that you've created in the form of increased social capital or simply the joy of helping others. Your leadership and your expression of passion can influence other people to rally around the cause and make greater contributions themselves.

OTHER OPTIONS

There are at least two charitable structures that integrate philanthropic goals with estate and tax planning. These structures, called charitable lead trusts (CLTs) and charitable remainder trusts (CRTs), are more complicated and require detailed legal and tax advice. In each case, you fund an investment vehicle that makes annual distributions for a period of years or until a specific event, like your death or the death of a spouse, occurs.

With a CLT, the cash flows must be directed to tax-exempt charitable organizations, but at the specified time the remaining principal is distributed to your children or grandchildren. With a CRT, the reverse occurs. The cash flows go to a person and then the remainder, at a predetermined time or upon a pre-determined event occurring, must go to designated charities.

The CLT is used as a way to transfer assets from one generation to another while limiting the gift and estate tax bite an alternative to life insurance plans. This is achieved since future trust appreciation going to your family escapes estate tax and the current value of the assets transferred are discounted using IRS present value formulas in determining the current reportable gift to your family since they will receive the gift in the future. The CLT can often result in less income taxes being paid to the IRS. This results from the fact that trusts can deduct charitable giving against taxable income without the percentage of gross income limitations that individuals are subject to, as discussed earlier in this chapter. The value of the assets in the CLT that will eventually be distributed to your family free of estate tax can be estimated based on some assumptions about the financial growth of the assets.

The CRT is a way to secure your financial well being or that of a loved one, usually until death, and reduce your income tax bite. This is achieved since you receive a current charitable deduction for your future gift to charity (discounted by present value formulas), and you are entitled to an annual annuity payment. The CRT also can reduce or delay capital gains taxes when appreciated assets are contributed to it and sold. The CRT does not pay income taxes and the annuitant only pays taxes on the amount received each year, which can be taxed at capital gains rates. This allows diversification of a large stock holding without current taxation on the full gain. Many high-flying stocks have been contributed to, and then sold by, CRTs with their annuitants enjoying many years of payments secured by a diversified CRT portfolio. The potential attractiveness of either of these vehicles is based on a number of factors. If you think such techniques may be of interest, I strongly encourage you to discuss them with your advisors.

In addition to thinking about the tax and societal benefits that will accrue from such trusts, also consider how you and your family will oversee the effective management of these trusts over a period that could span decades.

The CLT and CRT can integrate wealth management and philanthropic strategies. For example, in 2004, Harvard University got an innovative private letter ruling from the IRS allowing individuals to invest the assets of their CLTs or CRTs alongside those of the university's endowment. There is a catch, though. As part of the arrangement, Harvard must be the trustee and sole charitable beneficiary of the assets. On the other hand, Harvard's endowment has one of the best track records of any endowment in the country. If its track record continues, this arrangement can be very beneficial both to the university and to those individuals who care to partake. Harvard is so excited about this offering that they will even help you to set up a qualifying trust.

Harvard has another program for people who want to make a partial donation to the university. Harvard will still act as trustee but the assets are invested in a series of Vanguard tax-efficient (think index) funds. If past is prologue, these assets won't perform as well as Harvard's endowment. But if you have a CRT, there's an interesting tax dimension. Given the way Harvard manages its endowment, the tax rate on distributions to a taxable individual like you would be about double the tax rate on distributions from the Vanguard program. So you may not get the same asset growth in the latter program. But, all other things being equal, your spendable income, at least for some years, would be considerably higher.

I have no doubt that by the time this book is on the shelves, other organizations will have applied for similar IRS rulings.

Final Thoughts on Why People Give

If I had to categorize my great-grandfather's motivation for philanthropy, I would say it was a combination of all the reasons I've cited—depending on the specific situation. E.A. Stuart regularly used the term "living a useful life." It was an important lens through which he measured his own life achievements. He also believed passionately in perpetuating the strengths and values of American culture by empowering individual citizens through his philanthropic work and in everyday business. He always thought very long term, as evidenced by his explicit reference to "unborn generations of my descendants," as people that he hoped would benefit from this land of opportunity. His foundation's structure reinforced this perspective and, as such, he established it as a perpetual trust.

How to Be Philanthropic

A Wealth Strategist has four principal structural options for allocating funds to philanthropic causes. Ranked from simplest to most complex, they include the following:

1. Direct donations
2. Support organizations
3. Donor-advised funds
4. Private foundations

Direct Donations

You can make direct tax-deductible contributions to qualifying institutions under paragraph 501(c)(3) of the tax code. You can learn about whether a non-profit organization is a qualifying institution, and about filings that every non-profit must make to the IRS, at www.guidestar.com. When satisfied that the organization qualifies, you can make a tax-deductible donation and, if desired, can stipulate how you want your contribution used. Know that after you make the donation you lose control over its use; however, all reputable charities take donor intent very seriously. Most would not stay in business very long if they didn't. Practically speaking, most direct gifts are made for current use, and donations can be made anonymously.

Support Organizations

Some operating charitable institutions have endowments whose sole purpose is to provide financial support to that institution. The most well-known endowments are those of educational organizations, but they exist also in larger cultural institutions, religious organizations, and even non-profit media outlets like National Public Radio. Most of the grants to support organizations are made to an endowment. Sometimes the donor specifies some specific purpose for the cash flow from the endowed gift; other times it is left up to the institution. Donations can be anonymous.

Donor-Advised Funds

Community foundations pioneered the concept of letting people give money to a foundation and then indicate to which (type of) organization their contributions should be directed. Fidelity, Vanguard, and others picked up on the concept and developed donor-advised programs, giving the donor some flexibility for how funds should be invested and where their "fund" should be donated. If you are donating appreciated securities, you can expect that Fidelity or Vanguard will sell the securities immediately while, if requested, some community foundations may retain the security in a segregated account. In either case, you will get a tax deduction at the time you donate to the program and at the same rate as if you made a direct donation. Also, you can defer making grants for a number of years so assets can accumulate tax free. Grants can be anonymous.

Private Foundations

Foundations are the most flexible, but also the most complicated, way of doing planned giving. Although a foundation's governance structure is separate from your own assets, if you establish a foundation you can sit on the board and designate the characteristics of other board members and the procedure for selecting them. This makes private foundations the best way to control assets after they have been donated, either because you want them to hold on to appreciated stock you donated or because you want to direct the donations that the foundation makes. Also, the tax benefits are almost as good as the alternatives.

Private foundations are required to distribute at least 5% of their assets each year, either in the form of grants or in qualified expenses. Because of this restriction, they can't compound their tax-free growth at the same rate as donor-advised funds or support organizations that choose to distribute less. Also, they must file an annual report (Form 990) with the IRS and pay a modest excise tax. This filing becomes public information.

If you are considering making a donation of less than $250,000, it is probably not practical to set up your own foundation because the administrative costs and substantial reporting requirements will outweigh the benefits. If you are committed to this alternative, you should review a service offered by Foundation Source that lowers the cost and complexity of setting up a foundation at www.foundationsource.com. A foundation cannot make anonymous gifts.

Thoughts about Giving Options

I feel compelled to comment on two issues within the giving field: donor control of their gifts and the desire of donors to remain anonymous.

Amount of Control You Retain

I find a particular trend disturbing in the field of giving. Today, more and more donors are demanding to support specific programs rather than giving general operating support. Their argument is that supporting programs creates a greater level of accountability within the non-profit, and this is true up to a point. But it can have adverse consequences. Program-based fundraising puts a larger administrative burden on organizations because non-profits must make solicitations in many different forms and prove their success using many different formats subject to the idiosyncrasies of individual donors. The larger administrative costs that result can reduce fundraising efficiency, taking dollars away from where they are needed most.

Also, because of the popularity of program-based fundraising, it becomes difficult for many non-profits to raise money to support general administration, executive salaries, and basic infrastructure. Finally, program-based fundraising sometimes encourages organizations to engage in financial "shell games," wherein non-profit executives move money around on the organization's balance sheet, both to satisfy the whims of individual donors and to meet the overall operating goals of the organization. This behavior actually undermines accountability and diverts the focus of the organization away from its primary mission.

For these reasons, I am a big believer in providing general operating support to well-run organizations with clear missions despite the trend to the contrary!

Desire to Remain Anonymous

Some people desire to be anonymous when it comes to philanthropy, but I advise people to be on the record with their generosity. I encourage "on-the-record giving" because the donor's leadership encourages others to give to a cause as well. So, before you tick the "Anonymous" box, think carefully about whether you are maximizing the benefit to the organization(s) you are supporting.

Occasionally, there are reasons why you might want to be an anonymous donor. Sometimes, people assume that if you are a major named donor, you have disproportionate influence on the organization. This often isn't the case, but the appearance of influence can still be awkward for you or for other family members involved in the organization.

Innovations in Effective Philanthropy

With so many institutions engaged in philanthropy and so many dollars at work, it is no surprise that there is a lot of innovation in philanthropy today. Organizations like the Council on Foundations and academic institutions like the Harvard Business School are studying best practices and searching for new ways to make philanthropy even better. The most creative ideas are taking place in the areas of venture investing, advances in accountability, public-private partnerships, life-cycle debates, and governance.

Venture Investing

The $30 billion that U.S.-based foundations give away each year sounds like a lot of money, but when you compare this figure to, say, the $60 billion annual budget for public primary and secondary education just in the state of California, it pales by comparison. One of the ways that philanthropists try to leverage their relatively small dollars is by applying some of the principles of venture capital to the world of philanthropy.

They look for new ideas that appear to be effective and, if proven effective, can be scaled up. They conduct research to gather as much information as possible about the idea, to discern whether components of it have been tried elsewhere, and to determine what aspects of the idea still need to be crystallized. They then look to fill out the team of committed and talented people to manage a pilot project. If it is successful, they roll out the concept.

Sometimes, a need is recognized but no solution is yet evident. A philanthropist may pay for a group of experts to come together to "hatch" a solution. Then, there is more research, a pilot, and expansion as appropriate.

This kind of philanthropy is very exciting, hard work, and is only occasionally successful. But if it is successful, it can have a big impact. For example, the NPR Foundation was started as a venture capital operation, and its success is self-evident. The Stuart Foundation has helped to hatch a number of successful organizations in the fields of education and child welfare. The beauty of this type of investing is that you can begin your initiative with a fairly small amount of money. The creative and risk-seeking aspects of venture investing are beyond the skill of many established charities to implement. However, it's my firm belief that venture investing as a component of corporate and institutional philanthropy will grow in importance in the years to come.

Advances in Accountability

Historically, public service organizations have struggled with accountability. Their goals are often intangible, long-term, subject to personal taste (What is good art?), and hard to measure. Well, accountability is coming to philanthropy. Today, more than ever before, grant-making organizations are demanding specific performance commitments in return for the money they offer organizations. These commitments may be measured in myriad ways: hours spent, people served, secondary infection rates (for hospitals), nutrition per meal served, user satisfaction, teacher accreditation rates, and the list goes on.

Some grant makers, especially corporations, are demanding accountability to them as well as to grantees. Increasingly, they expect tangible and intangible public relations benefits that border on advertising. In some circles, it is called "altruistic product placement," whereby corporations want the world to see that they donate money to worthwhile causes and concurrently measure the impact that the "advertising" has on customer buying behavior.

The spotlight of accountability (even on investment performance) is shining on non-profit, charitable, and philanthropic boards of directors. Increasingly, membership on such boards is bringing with it specific performance criteria and fiduciary responsibilities: to participate regularly at board meetings, to give a minimum designated amount of money to remain on a board or to raise that money from other people, to recruit other qualified board members, and to provide specific business expertise. National Public Radio and many organizations today have begun to do annual evaluations of board members to justify their presence on the board and to evaluate people's contributions to board activities. Increasingly, if non-profit board members are not fulfilling fundraising responsibilities or other aspects of their non-profit board "job descriptions," they are being asked to step aside.

Public/Private Partnerships

Another trend in philanthropy is the formation of public/private partnerships. In such cases, private foundations or operating charities partner with government organizations to deliver services more effectively than if each operated independently.

This theory capitalizes on the innovation of the private sector and couples it with the infrastructure and money in the public sector to serve specific communities more effectively and efficiently. These partnerships take many forms, and each one is established to address a specific set of issues. Some partnerships have finite lives and are project-oriented while others continue successfully for many years.

In Chicago, the Ounce of Prevention organization has effectively partnered with government service organizations for a number of years to bring social services to newborns, infants, and toddlers who are at risk. In California, the Stuart Foundation partners with a number of county-level organizations to improve social services for children in foster care and to help more of them find permanent, safe homes.

Large philanthropic institutions that work extensively overseas—such as the Gates Foundation, AmeriCares, and the J. Paul Getty Trust—work directly with governments and quasi-governmental organizations to do research and deliver services around the world. These organizations exchange research and share resources to solve problems that neither could do alone.

Lifecycle Debates: Perpetual or Limited Life?

A debate has been taking place in recent years over whether private foundations should be required to have limited lives. As mentioned earlier, private foundations must distribute at least 5% of their assets each year, but this figure includes both grants and most administrative expenses. Foundations that have permanent lives incur substantial annual administrative costs, typically between .5% and 1.5% to maintain the perpetuity, so society may effectively benefit from only 3.5% to 4.5% of a foundation's assets each year. Yet the government gives donors a substantial and immediate tax benefit for their contributions to the foundation. There is discussion in government and in the private sector regarding whether there is imbalance in this equation.

Another debate taking place is over obsolescence and donor intent. Most people who establish foundations or endowments create language in the governing documents that gives future trustees the flexibility to change the focus of the organization if the original focus eventually ceases to be relevant. This creates ample opportunity for future trustees to apply funds in ways that the donor did not intend or may find objectionable. On the other hand, donors who write overly restrictive language into an organization's governing documents risk the possibility that their organization may eventually achieve its original stated goals and will eliminate its reason to exist. While some donors might wish for this scenario, I think that most foundation founders don't envision the day that the foundation they establish will cease to be relevant to the needs of society.

Given the changing nature of social and community needs, it's healthy to have an ongoing debate about the role and function of foundations in the philanthropic world today. One great philanthropist and a founder of Sears Roebuck, Julius Rosenwald, stipulated that his foundation must distribute all of its assets within 50 years of his death. Other philanthropists, like Joan Kroc, made their philanthropic commitments late in life to specific operating charitable organizations. Today, younger entrepreneurs, many of whom have made large donations to causes in the last two decades, have done so not as part of creating foundations, but as part of embarking on second careers in philanthropy. Many have made a life shift—from a focus on *success* in the traditional professional and financial sense—to a focus on *significance* in their life pursuits. Instead of creating and running foundations, they are rolling up their sleeves and using their business skills to manage or start operating non-profits or to become fundraisers, teachers, volunteers, and mentors.

Governance

Foundations are formed and financed privately. But after they are brought into being, theoretically they exist for public benefit. In effect, in exchange for the tax benefits of endowing a foundation and its tax-exempt status when it is established, the government insists that foundations support qualifying non-profit activities and do so responsibly.

The Sarbanes-Oxley Law, passed by Congress in 2002 to bring more discipline to corporate governance, has had repercussions far beyond the boardrooms of America's business leaders. Leaders in the foundation world are assuming that their turn will be next. Some states, like California, have already responded to Sarbanes-Oxley by legislating additional governance requirements for foundations and their boards. Inevitably, these changes will add cost, complexity, and the potential for liability to foundation directors and managers. Fortunately, today's direct donations, support organizations, and donor-advised funds offer attractive and simple alternatives to foundations for individuals and families that want to engage in planned philanthropy.

Foundations have a unique and privileged position in American governance, but it is one that is susceptible to both the perception and the reality of abuse. Foundations do not have customers, they don't need to raise money, and they don't have shareholders. Many foundations have no independent board members. The market mechanisms and checks and balances that constrain most other organizations in our economy do not exist for foundations. The only checks they have on complete autonomy are the ethics of the people that run and oversee them, the requirement that they disclose key (financial) information publicly, and their duty to file the Form 990 each year with the IRS.

From a policy standpoint, it's important that families continue to receive non-financial incentives to keep managing the half a trillion dollars that currently resides in America's foundations. We need to keep families engaged in foundation management and prevent the burden of regulation from becoming overly cumbersome.

At the same time, prudent levels of governance should be legislated to minimize abuse of foundations' special status. In coming years, policymakers will have to wrestle with ways to make governance more transparent without disrupting the pride that families derive from the good work that foundations do.

Philanthropy and Family

As you may have noticed, family is central to my makeup. I look at life through the lens of my family and am always searching for links that circle back to strengthening the family. Philanthropy, for me, is in part about seeking connections to family. When there was no longer a Carnation business to tie our family together, philanthropic pursuits and public service became primary areas of focus binding members of my family together.

Another family that has used philanthropy to bind its members together and to perpetuate the values of the family company is the Lehman family. The Lehmans are one of three families that built a company called Fel-Pro into one of this country's leading auto parts companies. Before the company was sold to General Signal in February 1998 for $720 million,[5] it was ranked as one of the best companies in the country to work for. This happened because one of the bedrock beliefs of the company's leadership was that a workforce that is respected, listened to, and supported by top management far exceeds in productivity any costs incurred by creating a more humane and supportive workplace. Auto parts manufacturing has always been a tough, competitive business, and Fel-Pro's human resources (HR) strategy was both a commercial success and a point of pride.

After the sale of Fel-Pro, the Lehman family decided to set up a charitable organization (not a foundation) to promote best practices in human resources for small- and mid-sized companies. They called the new organization Winning Workplaces. The organization today has a Web site, www.winningworkplaces.org, and a series of "Tool Kits" that it sells at modest prices that explain best practices in numerous areas of HR. To assure proper recognition of outstanding practitioners in the field, the family partnered with Fortune Small Business Magazine to establish awards for best practices in Human Resources. At an awards dinner only a few short years after the organization was founded, the family had over 300 paying guests in attendance along with four generations of the Lehman family. (Maybe good HR policies are correlated with longevity!)

Winning Workplaces has a board that consists of three family members from two generations as well as eight outside experts. Although the family has financed most of the start-up costs to date, it is now reaching out to others to share the burden.

Winning Workplaces has given the Lehman family a new, shared mission to replace the void left by the sale of Fel-Pro. This family is building on its collective business experience to provide a valuable service to smaller businesses in America, where most of the country's job creation actually takes place. Neither the new-found family wealth nor the focus on philanthropy has prevented individual family members from pursuing their unique and diverse passions: building a successful drag racing team, becoming a thoracic surgeon, entering politics, raising a family, and running the family's investment office. This is a family I admire very much for all they've accomplished.

In summary, foundations can be a way to reinforce family identity and values through public service, provide a forum for family members to explore common interests and to work together, and, as exemplified by the Lehman family's work, galvanize the family like a family business does.

Philanthropy and Children

Many of our religious institutions and schools teach us at a very early age to engage in what Judaism calls *tsedaka*. Each week, my own kids put a portion of their allowance into their *tsedaka* boxes, and when the boxes are full, they think carefully about how they want to give the money away. When I was growing up, I did something similar during the month of Lent and leading up to Christmas. Many religions encourage tithing and other forms of philanthropy and community outreach.

Today, my kids must complete public service requirements in school. There are innumerable reasons for families that believe in philanthropy to encourage and support the practice of goodwill and giving from a very young age.

Family Foundations

When deciding whether to set up a foundation within your family, you need to ask these vital questions:

- Does the foundation have a mission?
- Do you have assets that need to be managed in a particular way?
- Do you have the scale to amortize the costs appropriately?
- Are you going to make charitable grants to people and organizations that are not registered 501(c)(3) organizations?
- Do you want the foundation to have a specific and independent identity that will enhance your mission?

If the answer to all of these questions is "yes," a foundation is probably the right way to go. Keep in mind that foundations are expensive to administer, must maintain corporate records, file Form 990s on an annual basis, manage their assets, and do basic due diligence on grantees. For larger family foundations, there is the need to have permanent staff to evaluate grant proposals and a public relations program that includes maintaining a Web site. These administrative costs can easily exceed 1% of a foundation's assets every year, or one-fifth of their required distribution. They are also modestly less tax efficient than other philanthropic structures.

In multigenerational families, foundations are often established with a bequest. This technique is used to shrink the size of one's taxable estate in order to avoid or lessen the impact of estate taxes. Carefully crafting donor intent and having extensive discussion about governance with the next generation will make the difference between the foundation flourishing and being considered a burden by the next generation. If you are considering this option, I urge you to establish a foundation today at a reduced size and work through the issues of governance and focus with your family. This will give you all of the experience and confidence to fully fund the foundation with a bequest. You can also encourage your spouse or children to add more assets in the future.

Direct Service

There are many advantages to rolling up your sleeves and getting involved in direct service to non-profit organizations. I guarantee that it will make you a better philanthropist because you will understand the organizations you support and their constituencies even better. You will also build a network that can be useful in many ways. Mostly, it is gratifying because it is an opportunity to give of yourself to organizations and to make a positive impact on individual lives.

You feel that impact the most when you are working on the front lines of the organization. But without giving up that front-line exposure, you can broaden your impact if you also provide managerial leadership or committed board-level service. Again, there are many advantages to serving on the boards of non-profit organizations. You can use your business skills to help organizations function more effectively. You will become more familiar with governance issues that are peculiar to non-profit organizations. In some cases, you will learn about, and contribute to, how organizations invest their financial assets. You will see organizations that you believe in from the inside, and you will get into a rich flow of information that will help you and the organization make more informed decisions. Plus, it is fun.

Conclusion

My great-grandfather believed strongly that being wealthy carried with it a responsibility to live a useful life—in part as a show of respect for his ancestors and also as an example for his children. As James Marshall, author of his biography, noted: "My great-grandfather's [E.A. Stuart's] great wealth was truly in what he gave, and not what he retained, for his personal estate at the time of his death was very much less that what he had given and set aside for others during his lifetime."[6]

I have tried to embrace this philosophy in writing this book and in striving to be an active philanthropist, responsible family member, and entrepreneurial steward of my family's assets. Incorporating philanthropic values into an integrated wealth management strategy remains a lifetime goal. I hope that you share this perspective and that this book will lead you to fulfilling that dream for yourself and your family.

Chapter 10: Issues to Discuss with Your Family

1. Do you have a philanthropic mission? Why or why not? What is it?

2. Do you think that any one reason for being philanthropic is more valuable or legitimate than others? If so, why?

3. How do you feel about anonymous gift giving? Do you think that it dulls the effect of the gift?

4. Have you purposefully used philanthropy to maximum tax advantage? If not, why not?

5. What is the right structure(s) for your philanthropic activity? Are you using appreciated securities to make donations?

6. Do CRTs and CLTs hold appeal?

7. What gives you confidence that the organizations to whom you donate use the money well? Have you ever asked an organization to provide data that enhances your trust in their stewardship? Have you considered getting involved as a volunteer or board member?

8. If philanthropy and community service are important to you, what have you done to educate, encourage, and support your spouse, children, or grandchildren in these areas?

Endnotes

1 *The Merriam-Webster Dictionary*, 1998 Edition, p. 391.

2 The Foundation Center, *Foundation Yearbook*, 2004.

3 Elbridge A. Stuart, "Statement." The Elbridge Stuart Foundation, November 30, 1937, pp. 5 and 7.

4 Ibid, p. 7.

5 PriceWaterhouseCoopers, *Global Automotive Deal Survey*, 1998.

6 James Marshall, *Elbridge A. Stuart, Founder of Carnation Company*. Western Printing and Lithograph Company, 1949, p. 199.

11

PUTTING IT ALL TOGETHER: MULTIGENERATIONAL PLANNING AND WEALTH TRANSFER

"I must study politics and war that my sons may have liberty to study mathematics and philosophy. My sons ought to study mathematics and philosophy, geography, natural history, naval architecture, navigation, commerce, and agriculture in order to give their children a right to study painting, poetry, music, architecture, statuary, tapestry, and porcelain."

—John Adams, 2nd President of the United States

Good estate planning means constructing a valuable financial, family, and social legacy. And it's the successful outcome of implementing the Strategic Wealth Management Framework.

Several of my relatives have had a profound impact on my desire to build a valued legacy. My great-grandfather, E.A. Stuart, integrated his love of family into his company, the trusts he established, and his philanthropy. My Aunt Ethel taught me that wealth had nothing to do with how much money you have and everything to do with "how" you leave a lasting legacy. My mother's effort to encourage open communication about the difficult issues of estate planning has been one of her hallmarks in our family.

In our family, estate planning is not a private affair, and it never really has been. Even as a child, I remember getting an envelope under the Christmas tree from my grandparents that had a Carnation stock certificate in it. I didn't really understand what was going on at the time, and the envelope, when presented, quickly found its way into my mother's purse. But over time, I began to understand and appreciate my grandparents' generosity.

Now that we are adults and have families of our own, my siblings and I have been included in our parents' estate planning. Good communication is making my parents' plans more effective, but it also provides great learning for us as we plan our own affairs and prepare our children to be stewards of our wealth.

The Estate Planning Roadmap

My estate planning roadmap focuses on three fundamental points: ensuring that core needs of each generation are met, reinforcing family harmony, and empowering subsequent generations. The roadmap consists of six sequential steps, with each step building on the previous one to assemble a complete plan. Each step is defined by a goal with accompanying techniques you can use to accomplish that goal. More importantly, the roadmap reinforces the culture and values needed to sustain family wealth across generations. The six steps are:

1. Anticipate and communicate about your eventual demise.

2. Focus on defense; let your heirs worry about offense.

3. Deal with family houses and other "legacy assets."

4. Perpetuate the family's economic engine.

5. Prepare estate plans to create income streams.

6. Accomplish the must-dos.

This roadmap is remarkably simple and flexible, as any good estate planning process should be. You want to avoid, at all cost, estate plans that involve rigid legal structures, administrative overload, inadequately defensible positions if confronted by the IRS, and whopping legal bills. A few families of means opt for great estate complexity because the tax savings appear substantial and they have the infrastructure to manage the complexity. Even then, however, I recommend strongly that they take into account that they will be dealing with multiple generations, expanding family size, a changing and unpredictable future, and wide-ranging aptitudes for managing this kind of complexity. Such complexity can undermine family harmony and cost a lot of time, money, and Rolaids to resolve.

Whether your estate plans are simple or complex, following these six steps should go a long way to making them more productive. When interviewing prospective trust and estate lawyers to advise you on the details of your plans, make sure they are experienced in this type of work and have impeccable technical skills. Don't cut corners in this most important aspect of your wealth management plan.

Step #1: Anticipate and Communicate about Your Eventual Demise

Your first responsibility when it comes to multigenerational planning is to make sure your own house is in order. You want to do this for your own peace of mind, but you also want to do it for your children. It may seem obvious, but making sure that you are well taken care of in your later years relieves your children of a huge potential burden. Being wealthy puts you in a much better position than most people to give this gift to yourself and your children.

Putting your own house in order means:

Financial security. Make sure that you and your spouse (if you are married) have enough financial resources to last your lifetimes. Your Financial Administrator should be able to help you model how much wealth, and in what form, you will need to be financially secure. By regularly reviewing your financial position throughout retirement and by budgeting carefully, you can make appropriate midcourse corrections.

Research. Investigate services, such as those provided by non-profit organizations like Mather Lifeways, that provide a range of senior living alternatives, offer research on aging, and work with families to resolve issues of aging. Information on health like the Harvard Health Newsletter or the Mayo Clinic Health Newsletter can provide valuable suggestions for maintaining and improving the ways you take care of yourself as well as cutting-edge research on medical breakthroughs that could affect you.

Effective communication. Communicate periodically with your children about your wishes for your estate, your health management, and your loved ones. They need to know your desires because there may come a point where you won't be able to fulfill them without help from others. Topics include:

- Articulating if you want to stay in your "family house," move into the "doorman phase of life" (i.e., an apartment), investigate independent senior living communities, acquire in-house nursing care, or move into a quality nursing home.

- Discussing end-of-life issues and death. Americans do not like to talk about their own death. There is something in our culture that has stigmatized it. I don't know why it is the case, but I have lived in other cultures, namely Britain and France, where there is not the same stigma. They view death as a natural part of life. Talking about it only makes it easier to deal with its eventual onset. If you start the conversation early, it is not a conversation about an anticipated event, only an inevitability. The conversations don't have to be somber or morose. In fact, a good dose of humor is useful. Get rid of the stigma and try to enjoy the conversation. You won't regret it and neither will your children.
- Managing your health care if you cannot manage for yourself. The law relating to end-of-life health issues varies from state to state and regularly changes. The moral issues are both personal and societal. The more guidance you can give your children about how you want to deal with end-of-life issues, the more likely your wishes will be fulfilled and the less moral burden you place on them.
- Talking with your family about your estate plan, and about bequests you will make to friends or institutions, helps to establish expectations. It is easy, particularly in this mobile society in which we live, for adult children to be unaware of the bonds of friendship and companionship that their parents build. Someone you view as a dear companion may be viewed by your children as an opportunist or gold digger waiting for you to die so they can inherit your wealth. If you choose to differentiate among your children in your will, isn't it better to be able to explain to them why you are doing so rather than leaving the job to your estate's executor?

We have all read about contested wills, and we all know people who have endured emotional struggles about end-of-life issues. Good communication lifts these burdens from the next generation in the way that good asset management lifts the financial burden. These truly are valuable gifts.

Legal preparation. You will want to prepare Advance Directives and health care Powers Of Attorney to give someone—usually your spouse or children—authority to make medical decisions on your behalf, if you are unable. Advance Directives make clear an individual's wishes with regard to the use of life-prolonging procedures, such as use of ventilators and feeding tubes. The Terry Schiavo affair, so much in the news in 2005, only brings home the hard reality that making firm and concrete end-of-life plans can ease burdens of guilt and responsibility for one's family. In most states, an Advance Directive is all that is needed for a physician to act without fear of legal recriminations if patients are not capable of advocating for themselves. The absence of an Advance Directive leaves open the possibility that a terminally ill patient will be kept alive against his or her wishes as family members, physicians, lawyers, and sometimes politicians debate what to do.

A Power of Attorney provides a legal means for a person who becomes mentally or physically incapable of administering their own affairs to turn over decision-making responsibility to the person or people of their choice. A Power of Attorney is best used to address financial decisions, not medical decisions.

Therefore, it is important for you to have both a health care Power of Attorney *and* an Advance Directive in place and hope you never need to rely on either. If you have not already done so, I encourage you to discuss this issue with your lawyer and with your family. Don't wait until a crisis point to do this. Every adult should have these conversations with the people they trust and with competent legal counsel.

Backup. If you do not have a spouse or children, or your relationship with them is such that the actions cited so far are not appropriate, you will need someone else with whom to share your wishes and to act in a fiduciary capacity for both financial and health issues. Some wealth management firms and most trust and estate law firms provide services of this nature. Finding someone who is skilled and who you can trust, literally with both your life and your livelihood, is a very important decision. Make the decision sooner rather than later and take the time to develop the relationship, even if it costs some money.

Step #2: Focus on Defense; Let Your Heirs Worry about Offense

One of the first questions people ask about transferring wealth to their children is "How much should I give them?" No wealthy parent wants their heirs to become "trust fund babies" who do not lead productive or fulfilling lives. Asking "How much?" is the wrong question. Asking "How?" is the right question, as in:

- "How should I transfer wealth so that it empowers my children and creates new opportunities for them?"
- "How should I transfer wealth so they can learn to be effective stewards of their good fortune?"
- "How should I transfer wealth to protect those who cannot fend for themselves?"

Here is the short answer to these questions: Make your first priorities your children's and grandchildren's financial security in retirement, their education, and their health. If you can afford to help them out in these matters, they will have more freedom to take risks as entrepreneurial stewards or to pursue vitally important career paths that are less swayed by economic imperatives. They will have added incentive to pursue careers in religious life, medicine, the arts, or in teaching, like my brother and brother-in-law who are both outstanding primary school teachers.

Making these transfers of wealth requires no legal documents, no complex disclosures on your tax returns, and no incursion of estate or transfer tax. Here's how you do it:

Funding Your Heirs' Retirement

Annually, you and your spouse are each allowed to give away up to $11,000 (a total of $22,000) to as many individuals as you wish without incurring tax. This is called the Annual Exclusion gift. If you and your spouse have three children and you together give each of them $22,000 per year for thirty years, you can give away $1.98 million! It's also possible that the Annual Exclusion amount will rise in future years, making the gift potential even greater.

Taking this example a step further, if your kids marry and have a total of seven grandchildren between them, you can add Annual Exclusion gifts to all your relations over another 20 years, with the total dollars given away reaching $7.7 million!

These are pretty generous gifts if you can afford them because those children, spouses, and grandchildren, all told, are receiving $286,000 per year from you!

Let's look at this from the recipient's perspective to fully understand the power behind these simple gifts. At birth, a lucky baby receives $11,000 from each of his or her parents and two of four grandparents for a total of $44,000. The child receives similar gifts for each of the next 20 years. Starting at age 20 and continuing until age 50, this person continues to receive $22,000 from his parents, but nothing from grandparents because they are presumed to have died in this example. If the assets are invested in an equity index fund and it generates an 8% after-tax annual return over that 50-year period (about the long-term average at current tax rates), this lucky person will have accumulated $25.5 million just from Annual Exclusion gifts! Even if the recipient's parents do not make gifts in some years, the blend of regular gifts, prudent management, and compounding are still enormously powerful…if the gifts are invested and not spent.

If you are concerned about your children's financial discipline, you can make the gifts into a simple trust and stipulate in the trust that the assets cannot be distributed until your child reaches a certain age. If your children have good discipline, let them manage the assets directly. If you're not certain, do a little of both.

Now, let me add another wrinkle to further increase the power of Annual Exclusion gifts. At age 20, the fortunate beneficiary in this example earns enough salary that he or she qualifies to sock away $11,000 per year, pre-tax, into a tax-deferred retirement account.

Many young people, of course, can't afford (or choose not) to save for retirement aggressively in their early years. But this forward-thinking person *does* put the $11,000 from his salary into the retirement plan. He does so because his enlightened parents give him $11,000 in the form of an Annual Exclusion gift. Now his taxable income is reduced $11,000 by the retirement plan contribution, and he saves $11,000 each year courtesy of his parents' gift. And his retirement assets can grow on a tax-deferred basis for the next 50 years.

But it gets even better. Because his taxable income is reduced by $11,000, he does not incur a federal income tax liability on this amount, which could total $3,000 or more. He can spend this "saved" amount or put it in an Individual Retirement Account. The latter would further lower his taxable income and increase the dollars that are compounding tax-deferred.

By receiving Annual Exclusion gifts, this person can benefit in two big ways: spending more of his salary than he could before *and* putting away lots of money for retirement early in his career and watching it compound over the decades. Eventually, because of his good discipline, he may need to save less for retirement later in life and can use the extra money to give away to *his* children in the same manner that his parents did to him. And so the cycle continues: perpetual transfer of substantial wealth, no gift taxes, deferred income taxes, no big legal fees, and a simple investment strategy. It can work if your children are business tycoons, dancers, artists, or academics.

Funding Your Heirs' Education

Do you want to do even more, like pay for your children's and/or your grandchildren's education? Here's how:

By making payments directly to the relevant educational institutions, these payments do not count as gifts and are exempt from gift tax. Again, these are expenses your heirs do not have to incur, and this results in the student graduating debt-free. To exit the educational system with no debts is a real gift.

Many people have established so-called "529 plans" to help fund their children's and grandchildren's educations. Here's something to know, however: Contributions to a 529 plan count against Annual Exclusion gifts. What's more, even though 529s have certain tax benefits, they also have administrative costs. If you choose a 529 plan, make sure that the benefits outweigh the costs. For example, with the same money that you would invest in a 529 plan, you could give it directly to your child instead and invest it in an equity index fund at lower cost, with greater flexibility and almost the same tax efficiency. Finally, you can still pay your child's or grandchild's tuition directly and give them an Annual Exclusion gift.

Funding Your Heirs' Health Care

Do you want to do even more, like pay for your children's and/or your grandchildren's health care costs? Here's how:

Again, by making payments directly to medical service providers (hospitals and the like), these payments don't count as gifts and are exempt from gift tax. A benefit of this approach is that you can help your kids save money on their health insurance by having them raise their deductibles—thereby lowering their insurance premiums—while you take responsibility for making up the difference in covered costs should major medical bills arise.

I know what you're thinking. What happens if these lucky recipients of your generosity get used to you paying private school tuition, or medical bills, and they spend the money that would otherwise be earmarked for these purposes on different things?

If you are concerned about this issue, I recommend that you require them to save a portion of the money that would otherwise go toward these expenses. Put it in writing and have them sign a pledge. It will confirm the seriousness and significance of what you are doing and also give them experience with entering into a contract. Your generosity requires certain behavior on their part and should not be left unattended.

Funding Your Heirs' First Home Purchase

You may want to help your children buy their first house. Houses are great investments, and a bigger house means a larger investment and more potential appreciation. A bigger house can also mean a bigger mortgage deduction if your children borrow the money to finance the purchase. The mortgage deduction is a great perk. Other than accruing taxes on unrealized gains, it is about the best tax benefit around.

My one reservation here is that houses can be money pits. You would be doing your child a disservice if you helped them buy a house that they can't afford to maintain properly. Make sure that your son or daughter has budgeted all the costs of home ownership and can afford them before going ahead. If you don't, instead of giving them a gift, you have saddled them with an albatross.

By now, you have noticed that all the recommendations in Step 2 involve delayed gratification. Many of the benefits are deferred decades into the future or they simply reduce or eliminate debt that would otherwise be owed. They also require that the beneficiaries of your generosity generate their own earned income to meet their living expenses. They must budget carefully and invest prudently. Admittedly, they do get some current benefit because they don't have to save for retirement, repay loans, or to pay private school tuition. But these are all secondary benefits that are predicated on their own ability to earn a living.

Step #3: Deal with Family Houses and Other "Legacy Assets"

Though real estate is not often thought of as a "negative cash flow" item on the family balance sheet, it can be. Primary homes, secondary/vacation homes, and a few other assets—like an art collection or a special boat—can be integral to a family's traditions and can also be costly to maintain. People want to keep them in the family, but they are expensive luxuries. As families grow across generations, family members will have varying degrees of interest in these family assets and differing desires or abilities to manage them.

Children sometimes want to hold onto the family homestead in which they were raised. My wife and I ran across this a few years ago when we bought a house from a couple that wanted to downsize and move into the "doorman phase" of their lives. One of this couple's grown sons liked visiting and staying in the room in which he grew up, and he put pressure (unsuccessfully) on his parents to hold onto the house. Eventually, practicality won out over sentimentality.

Likewise, many adult children want to hold onto family vacation homes because of the happy memories they have of those homes from their days as kids. With the rapid rise in values of highly coveted vacation properties around the world in recent years, it may tempt a family (or family member) to consider selling a long-time vacation property to make a healthy profit. Yet sentimentality often keeps the home in the family and with that comes a whole host of financial and logistical challenges. How do you split time spent at the house among two or more adult children and their families? How do you share expenses and handle issues such as maintenance and taxes? I'm not saying that it's impossible to figure all of this out in a multigenerational scenario, just that it takes a lot of communication and teamwork to make it happen.

Sentimentality aside, there are various legal techniques you can employ to execute intergenerational transfers of real estate, and these can be highly tailored to your individual circumstances. One of the most common is a Qualified Personal Residence Trust. A "QPRT" ("Cue-purt"), as it's commonly called, lets you make a gift at current value some years into the future. Several features of the QPRT have the effect of lowering the value of the home for gift tax purposes. There are also some risks with the strategy, most notably that the donor has to be alive on the date the trust terminates. If you pre-decease the term of the QPRT, the house reverts to your estate and is subject to estate tax at its value at the time of your death. For a more detailed evaluation of QPRTs and related strategies, you should seek good legal advice to help you explore your options.

Looking beyond issues of sentimentality for a moment, I have two recommendations to make if you want to transfer your family vacation home to your children. First, before your kids inherit or buy the house from you, get them to prepare a written operating agreement that spells out how they will handle the expenses, operations, scheduling, and potential sale of the house. Is it something that just your children should own, or should spouses become owners too? How can they come to a fair agreement if some kids like to use the house but others don't? We've come to terms with all these issues, and so can you.

Second, try to shift their mentality from one of ownership to one of stewardship. A trust or limited liability partnership can be a helpful tool, especially if you can fund the entity not only with the house itself but also with an "endowment" to fund the house's operating expenses. By adding an "endowment," it takes the financial pressure off of your children, especially those who are not big wage earners, to cover the operating costs of the house. You should also restrict how interests in the entity can be transferred. Then there is no economic pressure on people to fund expenses they can't afford or would prefer to allocate elsewhere.

Your children can then think of the property as a luxury to share rather than an asset to manage. There is no requirement to use the house and no economic burden. Even with all this planning, it may come to pass that the house is no longer practical or pleasurable to retain. Then it's time to convert the luxury to cash. At that point, a majority, superma-jority, or all of the children (or grandchildren) can agree to sell the house. They may choose to buy another one that better suits them. Or they can distribute all the proceeds from the house sale and the endow-ment and liquidate the trust or partnership.

Step #4: Perpetuate the Family's Economic Engine

Successful businesses, unlike houses, usually have existing or anticipat-ed positive cash flow. Through astute estate planning, you can either transfer a family business from one generation to the next or provide financial support to your child or grandchild who wants to start or buy a business (or other income-producing asset), thereby maintaining the family's wealth-building capabilities across generations.

Under most circumstances, I am not an advocate of significant leverage when managing family wealth. But when it comes to promoting entre-preneurial stewardship through estate planning, my view is the oppo-site with regard to one particular kind of leverage—intergenerational family lending. In fact, I think it is one of the best estate planning tech-niques around. And it really gets to the heart of strategic wealth man-agement. Let's look at two examples so you can see what I mean.

Transferring the Family Business

First, let's take the case of a family business that is to be transferred from one generation to the next. For simplicity's sake, assume that both ownership and management control are being passed simultaneously. In this case, the technique is really nothing more than an intergenerational leveraged buyout, known in some circles as a "freeze" because it freezes the value of the company for one generation and allocates any additional value to the next one. The idea is to get an appropriate value for the company. Let's call it $1 million, based on annual pretax profits of $100,000. The parents agree to sell the business to their adult children (the "kids") for this amount, but they provide seller financing for 90% of the amount. There are specific IRS regulations that stipulate the rate of interest that intra-family loans must use to avoid being subject to gift tax, but the rates are quite attractive to the borrower, especially in a low interest rate environment. Using today's rates, the company profits in this example could more than pay the interest and still leave money to reinvest in the business.

The kids, having accumulated a number of Annual Exclusion gifts over the years, have savings in excess of $100,000 to purchase the equity. So now the parents have transferred the family business to the next generation without incurring any estate tax. Even if the company were worth $5 million, $50 million, or more, the same technique would deliver comparable results.

Now let's look at what happens going forward. The kids own the business and are now running it. They are under pressure to make the interest payments and eventually pay off the loan to their parents. They have real economic incentives to perform. Let's assume that the company was well positioned at the time of sale, the kids are good managers, and economic conditions are favorable. In the early years, things are tight because after payments on the loan and the business's capital requirements there is no extra cash. But in ten years, the kids have paid off the loan, the company has grown to be worth $10 million, and it's generating a million dollars a year of profit. This is clearly a good outcome. The entrepreneurial skills of the kids have paid off handsomely, and the parents get their money out of the business, plus interest too, to do with as they please.

But what happens if the business hits a roadblock? Then the debt covenants give the parents several options. If the kids are managing well but the company is experiencing a cyclical downturn, the parents may choose to accrue any interest and principal payments that are due and ride out the storm. If the kids are not managing well, the parents can regain control over the company and manage it back to health. If the company is just a dud, the parents have a problem, especially if the sale proceeds from the company are a substantial portion of their net worth. But this is a problem they would have had anyway. The moral of the last outcome is "Don't sell the duds to relatives!"

Family Funding of Business Ventures

Another type of intergenerational lending occurs when an entrepreneur finds a company to start or buy and approaches his parents for financial support. The parents have at least three options. They can lend the money directly to the project (on a non-recourse basis), much as was done in the previous example. They can provide financial guarantees to a third-party lender that lower the cost of borrowing for their kid. Finally, they can make a personal loan to their kid to buy the company's equity and secure the loan with the stock (and only the stock). The option you choose depends on the specific circumstances.

I like using intra-family loans and leveraged buyouts for several reasons.

- The technique is relatively simple to structure, and it remains flexible in the face of unforeseen future circumstances. Even if there are multiple siblings involved, you can split operational and ownership interests equally or unequally, depending on how many family members are involved in the business. If the parent(s) dies while still holding the note on the business, one can often document a strong case as to why the paper is worth significantly less than 100 cents on the dollar, making it possible to transfer the asset out of the decedent's estate more efficiently.
- The risk of the deal is separated from its potential upside benefits. I assume that if parents are trying to transfer wealth to their kids in this manner, they don't need more money. Yet they still capture cash value for the company as the loan is paid off. I also hope they have

diversified their assets, because they are taking most of the risk when structuring a freeze or intergenerational loan. At least in a worst-case scenario, if their loan is a write-off, it creates a good tax deduction, and they are more likely to be able to use it than the kids. The kid(s) gets most of the economic benefit if the business is a success, yet faces a significant disincentive with a loss of equity if it fails. With the right economic incentives in place, the parents can step back and let the next generation prove themselves.

• The structure encourages entrepreneurial instincts and it rewards success in the next generation. The next generation has a leveraged opportunity to generate a substantial return with limited risk. Empowerment encourages success and success translates into wealth creation. Does this create incentives to be entrepreneurial? You bet!

Still, there is cause to be cautious. First, hire a good lawyer to set up the appropriate structure. There are a lot of rules about making loans to related parties, and you want to make sure you follow them. Second, by using this structure you are artificially lowering the downside risk for your children (and you are taking disproportionate risk relative to your potential reward). Without the downside risk your children may become overly eager to take more risk than they should.

If you want to fund the next generation's business ventures, I encourage you to establish an advisory board or other independent mechanism to assess the viability of new business propositions that are brought to you by your children. Going through a rigorous vetting process will benefit all parties involved. Maybe you should consider allowing members of the advisory board to invest in a portion of the equity (with real money) as compensation for their expertise. This would go a long way toward aligning everyone's interests.

Step #5: Prepare Estate Plans to Create Income Streams

In Step #2, I talked about making gifts to fund your children's retirement. In that case, you created an income stream that they could tap into 20, 30, or 40 years in the future. But, if you have the financial scale, you may want to create income streams for your children and grand-children that start sooner than that. You can do so using retirement plans, irrevocable trusts, family companies, family partnerships, or other means. Sometimes the income stream gets transferred on the death of the benefactor. Other times it kicks in when the beneficiary reaches a certain age or milestone. Some benefactors create these income streams to protect the financial security of someone who cannot fend for him or herself. Others want simply to do something generous for people they care about. They give an individual a wine collection, an annual trip, a monthly evening out for dinner, or the money to buy new furniture. The assets have to get quite large before the income stream threatens to become demotivating. And, if the family has a financial goal of maintaining real per capita wealth across generations, they cannot afford to distribute a lot, and will have to work hard to keep the economic engine firing on all cylinders.

Retirement Plans

Everyone who has a 401k, IRA, or other retirement plan should designate beneficiaries and responsible stewards of the assets in case of death. It's possible, but not necessary, for the beneficiary and the steward to be the same person. If you use retirement plans as vehicles to pass wealth from one generation to the next, make sure that you get good legal advice on how to properly structure such transfers. You should also analyze whether the cost and tax structure of a retirement plan are the most economic ways to pass assets. (In most cases, if you have an estate that will be subject to the estate tax, you are better off drawing more heavily on a retirement plan during your lifetime so you can transfer other assets to your descendents rather than the other way around.)

Let me give you an example from my own life. Three years ago, my Uncle John passed away. He had a modest estate, no wife or children, and he was kind enough to bequeath to me part of his IRA. The $40,000 was a lot of money to him, he was very proud that he enriched my life with it, and I am very grateful for his generosity. Each year, I am required by law to withdraw roughly $2,000. For a year or so, I contemplated how to honor this money as a gift and to reflect on his memory.

After a while, I hit on an answer. Because I enjoy good wine, I've decided that each year after getting my distribution, I will buy two or three cases of wine and over the next decade build the John B. Lucas collection. His collection is segregated from my other wine, but I've opened one or two bottles so far for very special occasions. Using his bequest in this way allows me to think of him during my annual pilgrimage to the wine store, when I uncork the bottle, when I enjoy the bouquet and flavor of the wine, and even when I go past his collection to get a more commonplace bottle of what the British call "plonk."

I will treasure Uncle John's gift to me for a lifetime, and many years from now I plan to pass to my kids as many bottles as possible from the John B. Lucas collection, assuming they have similar tastes.

Irrevocable Trusts

A more effective way than retirement plans to pass assets to future generations is through Irrevocable Trusts. An Irrevocable Trust is a vehicle to hold your assets and manage and distribute them in specified ways. Although it may be self-evident, the terms of an Irrevocable Trust cannot be changed after it is established. One or several trustees must be designated to manage the affairs of the trust, but neither you nor your spouse nor any other current beneficiary of the trust should be trustee. This helps to protect the assets within the trust from creditor claims, including bankruptcy, lawsuits, divorce, and liens.

The trustee of the Irrevocable Trust is responsible for managing the trust according to the law and the terms of the trust document. Finding a responsible corporate trustee usually involves finding someone who combines traits of professionalism with the ability to say "No" if and when beneficiaries want to change the terms of the trust in ways the grantor did not intend. That said, it is equally important for there to be a separate individual who can review the performance of a trustee, and if necessary, remove it.

Sidebar 11.1: When Structural Rigidity in Wealth Management Planning is Good

Most rules have their exceptions, and mine do too. In the trust world, an element of rigidity is good. I highly recommend that any Irrevocable Trust creator make five critical (and unchangeable) decisions when designing a trust and that the individual communicate his or her intentions with regard to these issues as clearly as possible. Doing so can eliminate family friction later on and ensure that a trust creator's intentions and wishes are clearly followed.

1. *Make the rate of trust distributions consistent with your long-term financial goals.* For example, if you want the real asset value of the trusts to remain the same, distributing more than 2.0% to 2.5% in annual after-tax distributions will make the primary goal difficult to achieve. When your lawyer drafts the trust, you may want to include specific language to give trustees flexibility to distribute more or less than the designated amount. For example, the income beneficiary may have special needs due to a physical or mental handicap that require a larger payout. In contrast, the income beneficiary might be a spendthrift who, given the chance, spends money in ways that are self-destructive or otherwise inappropriate. There is precise legal terminology to deal with these issues that is well tested in the courts and is enforceable by a trustee.

2. *Stipulate the age at which distributions begin.* Distributions can be staged so that as your children get older, the size of the distribution grows.

3. *Adopt a uni-trust approach to calculate distributions.* For many decades, common trust language talked about distributing the income from a trust. However, in the past five years, more and more states have legislated trusts (uni-trusts) that distribute a certain percentage of assets rather than the income. The beauty of a uni-trust format is that it

continues

allows the trust assets to be invested for total return, and it aligns more closely the interests of income and remainder beneficiaries. Income beneficiaries receive regular distributions as long as the trust is in force. Remainder beneficiaries receive the remaining trust assets upon termination. Both benefit if the assets grow in value and both suffer if they decline in value.

4. *Stipulate the method of allocating assets within the family.* Typically the choice will be *per stirpes* or *per capita. Per stirpes* means that assets are distributed equally to the children of each person; *per capita* means that assets are distributed equally to the people in each generation. If a trust creator has two children and one of those children has four children and the other has one child the allocations are as follows. Under a *per stirpes* arrangement, in the third generation, four children each have a 12.5% interest in the trust and the fifth has a 50% interest. Under a *per capita* arrangement all five children have 20%. Under either scenario, the second generation shares the trust interests 50/50%. Finally:

5. *Stipulate the split of assets to be allocated between family and philanthropy.*

Beyond these selected decisions, the fewer decisions you can inscribe in stone and the more latitude you can offer a trustee, the better.

Some Irrevocable Trusts have attractive generation-skipping attributes that reduce or eliminate estate taxes. These trusts can save you and your family millions of dollars in taxes over the long run, as well as create income flows for the benefit of family members.

Family Companies and Family Partnerships

Family companies and family partnerships are additional structures people use to transfer wealth and to create income streams for beneficiaries. In many cases, family companies and partnerships are designed to limit the liability of some or all participants. Unlike Irrevocable Trusts, oversight and economic interests do not need to be separated in family companies or partnerships and usually aren't.

Let me explain. One of the benefits of family companies and partnerships is that management control, economic benefit, and oversight responsibility are changeable and can be easily tailored to specific circumstances. That makes it easier to delegate operating control to a management team, reward them with (tax efficient) capital appreciation if they create wealth, and give family members the power to reassert control if they need to or choose to, simply by achieving the necessary votes to exercise their power. Another benefit of these structures is that the governing documents can be modified to suit changing circumstances.

Economic interests can also be bought and sold as well as gifted, subject to governing documents. The careful structuring of governing documents will affect the value of economic interests for gift tax purposes. As a general rule, the less liquid an asset is and the less control an owner has, the less the asset is worth. The IRS periodically challenges use of these techniques in court, but well-structured and well-documented strategies have proven resilient to these challenges. These benefits are difficult, if not impossible, to achieve in a trust structure.

Just like trusts, companies and partnerships can be designed to distribute income to partners or shareholders. Companies and partnerships can also distribute salaries and ownership interests. Although they are operationally more flexible than trusts, they do not have the generation-skipping tax characteristics of trusts. In addition, the responsibility of those that oversee companies and partnerships do not rise to the standard of trust fiduciary. The person or people who control a company can pay themselves salaries at whatever level they like regardless of whether the decision erodes the value of minority shareholder interests. In other words, there is not the same obligation to be equally fair to all shareholders or partners. These entities are great, but confidence in the skill and integrity of management is a very important component in making them work well. So is having good oversight that will hold the managers accountable on a regular basis!

Many of the structures that wealth advisors promote are complex variations of the entities I've just described. In every case, you should compare the costs, risks, and benefits of these more complex structures against the simple ones I have described. In most cases, I think you'll find that simple is better.

One thing to evaluate very carefully when considering complex estate structures is how flexible they are. After they are put in place, complex estate plans can be hard or impossible to change. Do a number of different scenario analyses, even improbable ones, to see how well the strategy works. Ask yourself these questions:

- What if tax rates change?
- What if the strategy is exposed on the front page of your local newspaper or *The Wall Street Journal*?
- What if the value of the investment declines precipitously?
- Do I have the ongoing administrative capabilities in place to execute the strategy?
- What if there is a death or a divorce in the family?
- What if more children arrive on the scene, either naturally or by adoption?
- What if the investment returns wildly exceed your expectations?
- What if my children who are managing the business aren't competent, get distracted, or suffer ill health?
- How much change can strategies withstand and still hold up? The more inflexible they are, the greater the risk and the more caution, analysis, and experience you should have in estate planning before you charge ahead.

It will be worth the money to hire someone who is very practical, not only about estate law, but who also understands family dynamics and can advise you on how to administer an estate for many decades—regardless of the structures you set up.

Step #6: Accomplish the Must-Dos

Throughout this book, I have provided options for accomplishing various goals. Now, at the very end, I am breaking with that tradition and stating in the most declarative voice I can—do these things or you will undermine everything else that you've accomplished!

Must-Do #1: Write a Will!!

A will enables you:

- To state clearly your intentions for disposition of your property in ways not included in a trust.
- To address specific personal matters.
- To designate your preferred legal guardian for your minor children if both parents die unexpectedly.
- To make direct outright gifts of money or property (jewelry, furniture, housewares, art, and so on) to specific individuals or institutions.
- To describe your wishes for a funeral.

Without a will:

- The IRS could inherit half of your assets, and lawyers, accountants, and opportunists could inherit the other half.
- Beneficiaries of your estate can go on spending sprees, if they are unencumbered by any restrictions or guidelines in the will.
- Your estate will end up in probate. Probate is a court-supervised procedure for the distribution of a decedent's estate. It's an invasive, public process that bares the financial assets of the decedent for all to see and invites anyone who may have a claim against the estate to participate. It can even take place in the decedent's residence! All sorts of unexpected issues can arise that add costs and time to the estate settlement process, even if the issues are later deemed frivolous. Probate cannot be closed until all public claims are heard and rulings are made on each of them. And, few distributions can be made to rightful heirs until probate closes.

Don't put off estate planning just because you are busy, are young, don't like paying lawyers, or have some other excuse to procrastinate!

Must-Do #2: Set Up a Revocable Trust

A Revocable Trust keeps most of your assets, and especially your financial assets, out of probate. (Make sure that you actually transfer your assets into the trust once you set it up.) The Revocable Trust operates like a set of explicit written instructions clearly stating how you want the trust assets distributed upon your death.

While creditors can still make a claim on your estate, they have to convince a judge to freeze the estate assets while their claim is argued. While the grantor (you) usually acts as trustee during his/her lifetime, the trust documents will name a trustee (often a spouse) who is responsible for the management of the trust after the grantor's death. You should review your Revocable Trust every five years or so to make sure it is still operating as expected. If, for whatever reason, you wish to dissolve the trust or switch assets in or out of the trust, such actions are easy and inexpensive to undertake. It is a highly flexible structure.

Must-Do #3: Set Up a Marital Trust

If you have a spouse, a Marital Trust allows a spouse access to your assets after your death for specified purposes without actually giving him or her your estate. This helps to protect their financial security while allowing you to control the eventual distribution of the assets. It also allows you to use fully your estate tax exemption while still making it possible for your spouse to draw on the assets if needed. Be aware that the mechanics of setting up such trusts will differ by individual state and the rules governing this are continually changing. For example, in 2004, Massachusetts legalized same-sex marriages. You'll have to investigate the rules for establishing a Marital Trust in the state where you reside.

Must-Do #4: Consider Giving Assets to Your Spouse

If you are married and one spouse controls most of your combined assets, you should consider redistributing the assets between you. You are allowed to transfer an infinite amount of assets to your spouse without adverse tax consequences. But each person is only allowed to transfer a specified amount of assets (above the Annual Exclusion gift) free of estate tax to others. This is called the Estate Tax Exemption, and in 2005, it was $1.5 million. This right is not transferable. So if you and your spouse want to take full advantage of the Estate Tax Exemption, you need to make sure that each of your estates can take maximum use of it.

Must-Do #5: Consider Irrevocable Trusts

As part of your estate plan, consider setting up Irrevocable Trusts for your children so that if you (and your spouse) die, they will be provided for. In establishing the trusts, you will have to designate a trustee to be a responsible party. (You and your spouse should not be trustees.) Depending on your family dynamics and the complexity of the trusts, you may choose another family member, a close friend, or a corporate trustee. Especially if the assets in trust are, or will be, more than a few hundred thousand dollars, I encourage you to use a corporate trustee for reasons I explained in Sidebar 7.3, "The Case for Corporate Trustees."

If you die unexpectedly, you can structure your estate to fully fund the trusts and provide financial security for your children. Some people who buy life insurance designate these Irrevocable Trusts as the beneficiaries of the policy. With a responsible trustee, you have the oversight in place to manage the assets and to control spending. This can be particularly important if your children are minors or young adults. You can design Irrevocable Trusts to give control of the assets to your children as they reach a certain age or other milestone. Or you can establish the trusts as Generation Skipping Trusts that remain in trust for several generations and avoid several layers of estate tax.

Sidebar 11.2: The Murky State of Estate Tax Laws

When Congress passed the Tax Reform Act of 2001, it created havoc for estate planners. Over the next several years, the Estate Tax Exemption will bounce all over the place. It is slated to grow from $1,500,000 in 2005 to $3,500,000 in 2009. Then, in 2010, the estate tax is repealed. Then, in 2011, it reverts back to $1,000,000 per person, the level where it stood before the Act was put in place. Top marginal estate tax rates will fall from 47% in 2005 to 45% in 2009, then disappear for a year and then revert to 55%. This wild volatility creates a nightmare planning scenario.

---

continues

In 1976, Congress also passed into law a "Lifetime Exemption" provision to close a loophole in the gift tax that had allowed people to give away assets during their lifetime without taxing them at Estate Tax rates. This exemption currently allows people to make gifts above the Annual Exclusion amount of $1,000,000 over their lifetime. This is an aggregate amount *per donor*, not an amount per beneficiary. The Lifetime Exemption also forms part of the Estate Tax Exemption, so if you use a portion of your Lifetime Exemption, it reduces your Estate Tax Exemption by the same amount.

That is why, more than ever, you should put a premium on maintaining flexibility in your estate plans. Sometime over the next five years, Congress will re-address the estate tax and, hopefully, clean up this mess. Many in the Republican Party want to eliminate the estate tax that was most recently instituted in 1917. In fact, if the Republicans are successful, it will be repealed for the fourth time since the estate tax was first instituted in 1789. But there are many powerful forces, including Bill Gates, Sr. and Warren Buffett, who are lobbying against repeal of the estate tax. I happen to agree with these two that estate tax reform is needed but that eliminating the estate tax will not be beneficial to our American culture. Our country is strong because it rewards people who create wealth. Legislation that reinforces a permanent aristocracy of ultra-wealthy people is not consistent with the Land of Opportunity.

Conclusion

Estate planning should focus on three fundamental issues. The first is *insurance*: insurance that you can live the rest of your life feeling financially secure and well cared for and insurance that your heirs (and theirs) have good educations, adequate healthcare, and long-term financial security.

The second is *family*. Working through how estate planning will affect the harmony and functionality of your family will prevent or minimize friction that, left unchecked, often can undermine well-intended financial plans.

The third is *empowerment*. How can you transfer your wealth so it motivates and empowers your heirs rather than sapping their will to aspire and succeed?

If you succeed at these three fundamental issues, whatever you pay in estate tax is secondary. You will have created a great legacy because you will have nurtured and mentored people you love who are now prepared to accept the mantle of wealth with all its responsibilities and privileges. They may invest your wealth in ways that create even more wealth. Or, because they have financial stability, they may feel empowered to do other things, great and small, that are not motivated by money, but that are central to living a rich, useful, and productive life. Like my great-grandfather E.A. Stuart, my grandparents, and parents, this strikes me as the ultimate goal of strategic wealth management.

Chapter 11: Issues to Discuss with Your Family

1. Are you teaching the youngest members of your family about wealth management? If not, what do you think is preventing you from do so?

2. If you have held off talking to your family about your death, are you convinced now that it's important to do so? If not, what additional information do you think would be helpful?

3. Do you have confidence that there is someone who will carry out your wishes in case of impairment or death? If so, does this person understand your wishes? Have you committed your wishes to paper?

4. Do you think that funding your heirs' education, retirement, and so forth has the potential to "spoil" them? How can you support them while still encouraging them to work hard and be successful in their own right?

5. How do you encourage your children and grandchildren to save for retirement early in their careers when the power of compounding has the greatest opportunity to work its magic?

6. Have you set up a system of managing family assets—like a vacation home—so everyone clearly understands their rights, benefits, and obligations? Have you generated consensus around these issues? If you are the primary person responsible for managing these family assets today, how will you transfer these responsibilities over time, and to whom?

7. If you want to leave assets to your heirs, how much is enough? Too much? Why might you not want to leave most (or any) of your wealth to your family?

8. Is an irrevocable trust a concept that you find easily understandable? If not, are you convinced of its merits enough to seek out additional professional assistance to learn more about it?

9. What if there isn't a Wealth Strategist in the next generation or if no consensus can be reached on who it should be? What are the costs of fragmentation and the benefits of forging a consensus?

10. Do you have a will and a revocable trust that you have properly funded? Have you considered transferring assets from one spouse to another for estate planning purposes?

AFTERWORD

I wrote this book to help you and your family achieve your wealth management goals—whether for a single lifetime or for multiple generations. The Strategic Wealth Management Framework and the Eight Principles of Strategic Wealth Management that I've discussed throughout this book are the core tools that your family's Wealth Strategist can use to manage the intricacies of investments, taxes, philanthropy, entrepreneurial stewardship, estate planning, and, most importantly, values. If you integrate these tools effectively, you will secure your own financial future, and you will provide invaluable support to those individuals and institutions you care about the most.

That said, each reader of this book comes from a different history and has different aspirations. Every family is unique, and wealth management is a multifaceted subject. Given such an opportunity for rich interactions, this book's themes will resonate in different ways to different readers.

Authors are forced to write in a linear fashion, restricted to the two dimensions of the page. But real life is more complicated. After you become familiar with this book's content, you may not want to follow my linear path. Instead, I encourage you to follow your own path as you use this resource. You may want to spend more time on some sections of the book and less on others to address your own circumstances and areas of inquiry. I also hope you will share the book with family members and that it will stimulate productive conversations and become a reference tool that you all come back to periodically for fresh ideas and to remind you of core issues.

Even though we each have our individual priorities, goals, and concerns, most Wealth Strategists and their families grapple with similar wealth management issues. In that sense, we're a community, and we can learn a great deal from each other. But the members of this dispersed community don't have many ways to communicate directly with each other about their experiences and insights. I hope that this book will stimulate a discussion. I welcome the opportunity to hear what's on your mind regarding the issues and strategies I've raised in this book, and wealth management in general. Please feel free to contact me at:

Wealth Strategist Network, LLC
slucas@wealthstrategistnetwork.com
www.wealthstrategistnetwork.com

I wish you good fortune!

Sincerely,
Stuart Lucas

Appendix

LEARNING THE LANGUAGE OF WEALTH MANAGEMENT

Now that you're wealthy—or soon to be—it's important to learn the language of wealth management.

Throughout this book, I introduce you to hundreds of wealth management terms. Some of these words have common meanings in our language with which you are already familiar. But when applied in a wealth management context, these same words assume a whole new meaning—with tremendous implication for wealth building and wealth preservation. This can be very confusing. You need to know the "wealth management meaning" of these words to communicate on the same plane with your advisors and show your friends and colleagues that you are a Wealth Strategist who's in the know.

Thus, with tongue in cheek, I offer a sampler of those words here—each with its conventional meaning and its *new* meaning to you as a wealthy person.

Active Management:

- **Conventional definition (CD):** A boss that walks around a lot.
- **Wealth management definition(WMD):** Aggressively investing your funds.

Administrative Servicing Fee:

- **CD:** A mysterious charge on your hotel bill.
- **WMD:** A mysterious charge on your financial statement.

Advance Directive

- **CD:** An order given by the battalion commander prior to combat.
- **WMD:** A document that specifies how you wish to have your affairs managed if you're incapable of handling them yourself; i.e., health care and burial plans.

Aggregate Performance

- **CD:** Evaluating the Rockettes' kick line on Broadway.
- **WMD:** Evaluating how much kick you're getting out of your entire investment portfolio.

Alpha

- **CD:** The lead dog in the pack.
- **WMD:** The "value added" that your investment manager generates.

Angel (Investor)

- **CD:** A messenger from heaven.
- **WMD:** Someone who cash-starved entrepreneurs view as a messenger from heaven.

Bear (Market)

- **CD:** A large animal you might see in the woods.
- **WMD:** Downturn in the stock market. (Any similarity to a ferocious, meat-eating animal is purely coincidental.)

Bench

- **CD:** Something you sit on in the park.
- **WMD:** A group of financial managers you might hire.

Blind Offshore Trust

- **CD:** The hope of rescue that an inexperienced sailboat captain clings to when becalmed in an early morning fog.
- **WMD:** Funds held discreetly in a foreign country.

Bond

- **CD:** The outcome of spending quality time with someone.
- **WMD:** A type of investment issued by a corporation or a government entity.

Boutique

- **CD:** An elite dress shop.
- **WMD:** A small financial services firm that caters to niche markets.

Bull

- **CD:** A large animal that should not go into a china shop.
- **WMD:** 1) A positive trend in the market; 2) The nature of some investment advice.

Buyout

- **CD:** Going on a shopping spree.
- **WMD:** Going on a BIG shopping spree, and borrowing money to do so.

Calling

- **CD:** 1) Dialing someone on the telephone; 2) Your career passion.
- **WMD:** Having your loan brought to maturity prematurely. Can be disruptive to your career.

Commission

- **CD:** Sending a ship into battle.
- **WMD:** A fee paid to a financial services provider.

Conservation

- **CD:** Making sure that the environment is left unblemished.
- **WMD:** Carefully managing your money.

Deflation

- **CD:** Letting the air out of a balloon.
- **WMD:** 1) Persistent decrease in consumer prices; 2) What happens to your ego after your great investment idea goes sour.

Deposit Campaign

- **CD:** Cashing in a lot of used soda bottles.
- **WMD:** An aggressive initiative to attract funds into your local bank.

Discretionary

- **CD:** Trying to be modest.
- **WMD:** Available to spend as you see fit.

Equity

- **CD:** Trying to be fair.
- **WMD:** The fair value of assets minus liabilities; though in the last few years—as exhibited by Enron, MCI, Healthsouth, Adelphia, and others—"fair" has not been a requirement.

Estate

- **CD:** A mansion surrounded by a large plot of land.
- **WMD:** All of one's possessions at death, including one's estate [above].

Exit Strategy

- **CD:** Figuring out how to leave a bad relationship or a burning theater.
- **WMD:** A predetermined course of action for selling securities, some of which may be on the verge of flaming out.

Exposure

- **CD:** Wearing very little clothing.
- **WMD:** Risk.

Family Office

- **CD:** A desk in your house where you try to pay the bills while your kids instant message ("IM") their friends.
- **WMD:** An infrastructure for managing your family's assets, scheduling the private jet, and impressing your friends.

Financial Supermarket

- **CD:** A big bank.
- **WMD:** A big bank.

Floating (as in floating an IPO)

- **CD:** Gliding on air.
- **WMD:** Offering a new investment opportunity to the public. Most of these eventually sink (in value).

Foundation

- **CD:** Cement poured into the ground to support your house.
- **WMD:** Support for a better society.

Gifting

- **CD:** Wrapping packages at holiday time.
- **WMD:** Transferring your money to another person; wrapped or unwrapped, it makes no difference.

Gross Exposure

- **CD:** Showing unattractive skin mass.
- **WMD:** Total risk.

Growth

- **CD:** What your teenager experiences every minute.
- **WMD:** Companies in which one invests that are priced based on the hope that they will increase in size. (Note: Companies are less predictable than teenagers!)

Hidden Compensation

- **CD:** Knowingly paying your employees under the table.
- **WMD:** Fees you unknowingly pay an advisor.

Illiquid

- **CD:** Something solid.
- **WMD:** Assets that cannot easily be converted to cash.

Index

- **CD:** A way to categorize/organize things.
- **WMD:** Participating tax-efficiently in the growth of a broad financial market; i.e., the S&P 500 or the Wilshire 5000.

Inflation

- **CD:** Blowing up a balloon.
- **WMD:** 1) Upward trend in consumer prices; 2) What happens to investment results at cocktail parties.

Institutional

- **CD:** A place that lacks color or feeling.
- **WMD:** Professionally managed investments.

Interest

- **CD:** Something you express in a loved ones' activities.
- **WMD:** Amount earned as a lender or charged as a borrower for a loan.

Investment Vehicles

- **CD:** Cars driven by bankers.
- **WMD:** A device for buying, selling, and owning securities.

Leakages

- **CD:** Unpleasant household plumbing problems.
- **WMD:** Forces that erode your assets (i.e., inflation, spending, taxes, and fees).

Liquid

- **CD:** Not solid.
- **WMD:** An asset that is easily convertible to cash.

Load

- **CD:** Something that a trucker conveys from place to place.
- **WMD:** The reward you give an advisor for convincing you to buy an investment.

Margin

- **CD:** Space that you leave on either side of a typed page.
- **WMD:** The difference between the amount of money you invest and the amount that you actually own. Buying on margin is a fancy way of saying "borrowing in hope of making more money in the financial markets."

Marital Trust

- **CD:** Knowing that your spouse is faithful.
- **WMD:** A structure for giving use of your money to a faithful spouse.

Open Architecture

- **CD:** A room with no walls and high ceiling.
- **WMD:** Ability to construct a wide-ranging portfolio of investments.

Penalties

- **CD:** With athletes and kids, time-out for infractions.
- **WMD:** A fee for withdrawing funds earlier than planned.

Pots

- **CD:** What you cook things in.
- **WMD:** Discrete funds into which you place your money.

Power of Attorney

- **CD:** Why Perry Mason won every case.
- **WMD:** Legal designation allowing you to act on behalf of another person.

Prenuptial Agreement

- **CD:** Napkin colors for the wedding.
- **WMD:** What you sign if you're worried you can't agree on napkin colors.

Principal

- **CD:** Someone that runs a school.
- **WMD:** The actual face amount of a security.

Priority Claim

- **CD:** Thinking that you are the next to be served at the deli.
- **WMD:** Having legal authority to secure funds prior to anyone else.

Public Markets

- **CD:** Open-air selling of fresh fruits and vegetables.
- **WMD:** Investment arenas in which anyone can purchase without restriction.

Rebalance

- **CD:** Rotating your own tires.
- **WMD:** Adjusting the percentages of funds devoted to various types of investments.

Retainer

- **CD:** What a middle school kid wears to straighten his or her teeth.
- **WMD:** An amount of money you pay for professional services.

Scale

- **CD:** A machine that calculates weight.
- **WMD:** The weight of money.

Silent Partners

- **CD:** 1) A 14-year-old boy having his first slow dance; 2) A spouse who is really mad at you.
- **WMD:** Investors who do not participate in the operations of a company/investment.

Simple Trust

- **CD:** What children expect from their friends.
- **WMD:** A financial construct that describes how a discrete amount of funds is to be managed.

Small Cap

- **CD:** A tiny bottle top.
- **WMD:** A company with a market value of less than $1 billion.

Social Capital

- **CD:** Ft. Lauderdale, Florida; Aspen, Colorado; or Palm Springs, California.
- **WMD:** Admiration and envy from others because you have a home in Ft. Lauderdale, Aspen, or Palm Springs.

Spread

- **CD:** A sumptuous picnic.
- **WMD:** How a broker makes money.

Stepped-Up Basis

- **CD:** Walking a lot faster.
- **WMD:** Establishing a revised cost of an asset for tax purposes.

Stock

- **CD:** A key ingredient in chicken soup.
- **WMD:** An ownership share in a company.

Trade

- **CD:** Swapping an Al Kaline for a Carl Yazstremski baseball card.
- **WMD:** Swapping IBM for Microsoft.

Trust Lawyers

- **CD:** Oxymoron.
- **WMD:** Lawyers who organize all your worldly assets.

Unearned Income

- **CD:** Winnings from the lottery.
- **WMD:** Income from sources other than wages/salaries.

Will

- **CD:** Shakespeare's first name; also, grit and determination.
- **WMD:** Something King Lear should have put more thought into.

Writer

- **CD:** Someone who convinces a publisher he's got something worthwhile to say.
- **WMD:** Creator of a high-risk derivative security.

INDEX

Page numbers followed by *n* indicate endnotes.

CHECK OUT...

Your Credit Score

How to Fix, Improve, and Protect the 3-Digit Number that Shapes Your Financial Future

Liz Pulliam Weston

ISBN: 0-13-148603-9

$17.95

©2005 Pearson Education, Inc.

Here's a sneak peek of Chapter 1...

1

WHY YOUR CREDIT SCORE MATTERS

In recent years, a simple three-digit number has become critical to your financial life.

This number, known as a credit score, is designed to predict the possibility that you won't pay your bills. Credit scores are handy for lenders, but they can have enormous repercussions for your wallet, your future, and your peace of mind.

How Your Credit Score Affects You

If your credit score is high enough, you'll qualify for a lender's best rates and terms. Your mailbox will be stuffed with low-rate offers from credit card issuers, and mortgage lenders will fight for your business. You'll get great deals on auto financing if you need a car, home loans if you want to buy or improve a house, and small business loans if you decide to start a new venture.

If your score is low or nonexistent, however, you'll enter a no-man's-land where mainstream credit is all but impossible to come by. If you find someone to lend you money, you'll pay high rates and fat fees for the privilege. A bad or even mediocre credit score easily can cost you tens of thousands and even hundreds of thousands of dollars in your lifetime.

You don't even have to have tons of credit problems to pay a price. Sometimes all it takes is a single missed payment to knock more than 100 points off your credit score and put you in a lender's high-risk category.

That would be scary enough if we were just talking about loans. But landlords and insurance companies also use credit scores to evaluate applicants. A good score can win you cheaper premiums and better apartments; a bad score can make insurance more expensive and a place to live hard to find.

Yet too many people know far too little about credit scores and how they work. Here's just a sample of the kinds of emails and letters I get every day from people puzzling over their credit:[1]

> *"I just closed all of my credit card accounts trying to improve my credit. Now I hear that closing accounts can actually hurt my score. How can I recover from this? Should I try to reopen accounts so that I can have a higher amount of available credit?" Hallie in Shreveport, LA*

> *"How do you get credit if you don't have it? I keep getting turned down, and the reason is always 'insufficient credit history.' How can I get a decent credit score if I don't have credit?" Manuel in San Diego, CA*

> *"I am a 25-year-old male who made a few bad credit decisions while in college, as many of us do. I need to improve my credit drastically so I do not continue to get my eyes poked out on interest. What can I do to boost my credit score fast?" Stephen in Dallas, TX*

> *"I joined a credit counseling program because I was in way over my head. But my wife and I plan on buying a house within the next three years, and she has expressed concern that my participation in this debt management program could hurt my credit score. What should I do to help my overall chances with the mortgage process and get the best rate possible?" Paul in Lodi, NJ*

> *"I'm 33 and have never had a single late payment or credit issue in my life. Yet, my credit score isn't as high as I thought it would be. What does it take to get a perfect score?" Brian in South Bend, IN*

---

1 As with other real-life anecdotes in this book, the writers' anonymity has been protected and their messages might have been edited for clarity.

What these readers sense, and what credit experts know, is that ignorance about your credit score can cost you. Sometimes people with great scores get offered lousy loan deals but don't realize they can qualify for better terms. More often, people with bad or mediocre credit get all the loans they want, but they don't realize the high price they're paying.

What It Costs Long Term to Have a Poor or Mediocre Credit Score

If you need an example of exactly how much a credit score can matter, let's examine how these numbers affect two friends, Emily and Karen.

Both women got their first credit card in college and carried an $8,000 balance on average over the years. (Carrying a balance isn't smart financially, but unfortunately, it's an ingrained habit with many credit card users.)

Emily and Karen also bought new cars after graduation, financing their purchases with $20,000 auto loans. Every seven years, they replaced their existing cars with new ones until they bought their last vehicles at age 70.

Each bought her first home with $350,000 mortgages at age 30, and then moved up to a larger house with $450,000 mortgages after turning 40.

Neither has ever suffered the embarrassment of being rejected for a loan or turned down for a credit card.

But here the similarities end.

Emily was always careful to pay her bills on time, all the time, and typically paid more than the minimum balance owed. Lenders responded to her responsible use of credit by offering her more credit cards at good rates and terms. They also tended to increase her credit limits regularly. That allowed Emily to spread her credit card balance across several cards. All these factors helped give Emily an excellent credit score. Whenever a lender tried to raise her interest rate, she would politely threaten to transfer her balance to another card. As a result, Emily's average interest rate on her cards was 9.9 percent.

Karen, by contrast, didn't always pay on time, frequently paid only the minimum due, and tended to max out the cards that she had. That made lenders reluctant to increase her credit limits or offer her new cards. Although the two women owed the same amount on average, Karen tended to carry larger balances on fewer cards. All these factors hurt Karen's credit—not enough to prevent her from getting loans, but enough for lenders to charge her more. Karen had much less negotiating power when it came to interest rates. Her average interest rate on her credit cards was 19.9 percent.

Credit Cards

	Emily	Karen
Credit score	750	650
Interest rate	9.90%	19.90%
Annual interest costs	$792	$1,592
Lifetime interest paid	$39,600	$79,600
Karen's penalty		$40,000

Emily's careful credit use paid off with her first car loan. She got the best available rate, and she continued to do so every time she bought a new car until her last purchase at age 70. Thanks to her lower credit score, Karen's rate was three percentage points higher.

Auto Loans

	Emily	Karen
Credit score	750	650
Interest rate	5.00%	8.00%
Monthly payment	$377	$406
Interest cost per loan	$2,646	$4,332
Lifetime interest paid	$21,166	$34,653
Karen's penalty		$13,487

The differences continued when the women bought their houses. During the 10 years that the women owned their first homes, Emily paid $68,000 less in interest.

Mortgage 1 ($350,000)

	Emily	Karen
Credit score	750	650
Interest rate	5.50%	7.375%
Monthly payment	$1,987	$2,417
Total interest paid (10 years)	$174,760	$243,020
Karen's penalty		$68,261

Karen's interest penalty only grew when the two women moved up to larger houses. Over the 30-year life of their mortgages, Karen paid nearly $200,000 more in interest.

Ideas. Action. Impact.
Wharton School Publishing

Bernard Baumohl
THE SECRETS OF ECONOMIC INDICATORS
Hidden Clues to Future Economic Trends and Investment Opportunities

Randall Billingsley
UNDERSTANDING ARBITRAGE
An Intuitive Approach to Investment Analysis

Sayan Chatterjee
FAILSAFE STRATEGIES
Profit and Grow from Risks That Others Avoid

Tony Davila, Marc Epstein, and Robert Shelton
MAKING INNOVATION WORK
How to Manage It, Measure It, and Profit from It

Sunil Gupta, Donald R. Lehmann
MANAGING CUSTOMERS AS INVESTMENTS
The Strategic Value of Customers in the Long Run

Stuart L. Hart
CAPITALISM AT THE CROSSROADS
The Unlimited Business Opportunities in Solving the World's Most Difficult Problems

Lawrence G. Hrebiniak
MAKING STRATEGY WORK
Leading Effective Execution and Change

Jon M. Huntsman
WINNERS NEVER CHEAT
Everyday Values We Learned as Children (But May Have Forgotten)

Eamonn Kelly
POWERFUL TIMES
Rising to the Challenge of Our Uncertain World

Doug Lennick, Fred Kiel
MORAL INTELLIGENCE
Enhancing Business Performance and Leadership Success

Vijay Mahajan, Kamini Banga
THE 86 PERCENT SOLUTION
How to Succeed in the Biggest Market Opportunity of the Next 50 Years

Alfred A. Marcus
BIG WINNERS AND BIG LOSERS
The 4 Secrets of Long-Term Business Success and Failure

Robert Mittelstaedt
WILL YOUR NEXT MISTAKE BE FATAL?
Avoiding the Chain of Mistakes That Can Destroy Your Organization

Peter Navarro
THE WELL-TIMED STRATEGY
Managing the Business Cycle for Competitive Advantage

Kenichi Ohmae
THE NEXT GLOBAL STAGE
Challenges and Opportunities in Our Borderless World

Mukul Pandya, Robbie Shell, Susan Warner, Sandeep Junnarkar, Jeffrey Brown
NIGHTLY BUSINESS REPORT PRESENTS LASTING LEADERSHIP
What You Can Learn from the Top 25 Business People of Our Times

C. K. Prahalad
THE FORTUNE AT THE BOTTOM OF THE PYRAMID
Eradicating Poverty Through Profits

Michael A. Roberto
WHY GREAT LEADERS DON'T TAKE YES FOR AN ANSWER
Managing for Conflict and Consensus

Arthur Rubinfeld, Collins Hemingway
BUILT FOR GROWTH
Expanding Your Business Around the Corner or Across the Globe

Scott A. Shane
FINDING FERTILE GROUND
Identifying Extraordinary Opportunities for New Ventures

Oded Shenkar
THE CHINESE CENTURY
The Rising Chinese Economy and Its Impact on the Global Economy, the Balance of Power, and Your Job

David Sirota, Louis A. Mischkind, and Michael Irwin Meltzer
THE ENTHUSIASTIC EMPLOYEE
How Companies Profit by Giving Workers What They Want

Thomas T. Stallkamp
SCORE!
A Better Way to Do Busine$$: Moving from Conflict to Collaboration

Glen Urban
DON'T JUST RELATE — ADVOCATE!
A Blueprint for Profit in the Era of Customer Power

Craig M. Vogel, Jonathan Cagan, and Peter Boatwright
THE DESIGN OF THINGS TO COME
How Ordinary People Create Extraordinary Products

Yoram (Jerry) Wind, Colin Crook, with Robert Gunther
THE POWER OF IMPOSSIBLE THINKING
Transform the Business of Your Life and the Life of Your Business

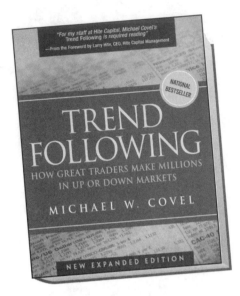

Trend Following
How Great Traders Make Millions in Up or Down Markets, New Expanded Edition

BY MICHAEL W. COVEL

"For my staff, Michael's *Trend Following* is required reading."
—From the Foreword by Larry Hite, CEO,
Hite Capital Management

For over 30 years, one trading strategy has consistently delivered extraordinary profits in bull and bear markets alike: *Trend Following*. Just ask the billionaire traders who rely on it...traders like John W. Henry, whose profits bought the Boston Red Sox! In *Trend Following, New Expanded Edition,* you'll meet them. More importantly, you'll discover how to use *Trend Following* in your own portfolio: how to limit risk, employ market discipline, and—when the moment is right—swing for the home run! Want proof it works? This New Expanded Edition includes 100+ pages of easy-to-understand performance charts. Want even more proof? You'll find comprehensive information on backtesting *Trend Following* for yourself.

ISBN 0131345508, © 2006, 448 pp., $29.99

Deal with Your Debt
The Right Way to Manage Your Bills and Pay Off What You Owe

BY LIZ PULLIAM WESTON

Most people will carry debt for most of their adult lives. That's just reality...yet the majority of books on debt focus mainly on how to pay it all off, and live forever without it. Too often, following that advice leads only to failure. People either give up or pay off the wrong kinds of debt. They strand themselves with too little flexibility to survive a financial crisis—and land in bankruptcy court. They neglect saving for retirement, homes, or college, and end up poorer than they might have been. For most people, it's more realistic—and smarter—to control and manage debt effectively, rather than eliminating it completely. *Deal with Your Debt* shows how. Award-winning personal finance columnist Liz Weston explains the rules and explores the myths surrounding debt. You'll discover the crucial role debt can play in your portfolio, identifying debts that actually contribute to your wealth and flexibility, and managing those better—as you avoid or eliminate "toxic" debts. Weston presents effective strategies for evaluating, monitoring, and paying every form of debt, from credit cards and mortgages to student and auto loans. She offers practical guidelines for how much debt you should take on, and early warning signs that tell you you're getting in too deep. You'll find realistic (and often surprising) guidance on everything from home equity loans and 401K borrowing to small business loans. Follow these strategies, and debt can work for you—instead of the other way around!

ISBN 0131856758, © 2006, 240 pp., $17.99

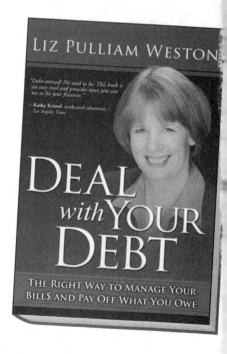